THE LANCASTER STORY

This paperback edition first published in 2025

First published in Great Britain in 2024 by
Michael O'Mara Books Limited
9 Lion Yard
Tremadoc Road
London SW4 7NQ

EU representative:
Authorised Rep Compliance Ltd
Ground Floor
71 Baggot Street Lower
Dublin D02 P593
Ireland

A CIP catalogue record for this book is available from the British Library.

This product is made of material from well-managed, FSC®-certified forests and other controlled sources. The manufacturing processes conform to the environmental regulations of the country of origin.

For further information see www.mombooks.com/about/sustainability-climate-focus

Report any safety issues to product.safety@mombooks.com and see www.mombooks.com/contact/product-safety

ISBN: 978-1-78929-748-5 in paperback print format
ISBN: 978-1-78929-650-1 in ebook format

1 2 3 4 5 6 7 8 9 10

Cover design by Ana Bjezancevic
Designed and typeset by Claire Cater
Cover picture credits: Cover illustration from the painting 'Bomber Force' by Nicolas Trudgian, www.nicolastrudgian.com
Printed and bound by CPI Group (UK) Ltd, Croydon, CR0 4YY

www.mombooks.com

FSC www.fsc.org
MIX
Paper | Supporting responsible forestry
FSC® C013604

THE LANCASTER STORY

TRUE TALES OF BRITAIN'S LEGENDARY BOMBER

SARAH-LOUISE MILLER

Michael O'Mara Books Limited

For Brian and Susan Thompson

To take upon our journeying,
She opened wide her arms to share,
With us the perils of the air,
Her steadfast spirit, loyal, true,
Was with us always as we flew,
She never faltered, even though
She might be wounded, weak and slow,
We raise our glasses, drink a toast,
Remembering a very host
Of things that time cannot transcend,
A gallant mistress, servant, friend,
We loved her to the very end.[1]

CONTENTS

FOREWORD
BY SEB DAVEY

EVERY TIME WE BOARD OUR BEAUTIFUL LANCASTER, it is impossible to ignore the significance of what those who went before us achieved, and endured, approximately eighty years ago. As a nod to the importance of what we are about to do, on embarkation as a crew, we all tap a small brass plaque mounted just aft of the entrance door. It is engraved with the Bomber Command crest and four simple words that sum up the whole *raison d'être* of the Battle of Britain Memorial Flight: 'To Remember The Many'.

I feel exceptionally fortunate to have been a Royal Air Force BBMF Lancaster pilot for over ten years. During this period of my RAF service I have, of course, enjoyed the privilege of flying one of the rarest aircraft in the world and showing her off at airshows and flypasts throughout the UK and, on occasion, in northern Europe. But this only really scratches the surface of what it means to carry out this voluntary flying duty, which, for all of BBMF's bomber aircrew, is in addition to their primary front-line role in the modern RAF.

In this book, Sarah-Louise Miller has successfully captured, from first-hand accounts, what it was to be one of 'The Many' of Bomber Command, not only from the perspective of the aircrew but from that of all the support personnel without whom the 125,000 *volunteer* aircrew of the time would not have been able to carry out their most terrifying and dangerous of duties. To a man, those who experienced operating these aircraft under invariably heavy fire are humble, almost to a fault. They endured conditions and peril that are unimaginable to modern-day military aircrew, let alone to people going about their day-to-day lives in the countries they fought so hard to protect – and yet, their most common response to recognition of what they did is 'we didn't do anything special'.

Sarah has also delivered a fabulous account of the aircraft itself, the mighty Lancaster Bomber. The Lancaster was a showcase of British engineering expertise of the time. Arguably the most capable of all the heavy bombers, the brilliant Avro airframe design was mated with the thunderous power of the Rolls-Royce Merlin engine, four of them, to create an aircraft that was dearly loved by the crews that flew her. They felt they had been provided with a cutting-edge, state-of-the-art machine that would protect them from what lay ahead.

As you read this book, I ask that you to do as I have done when thinking about the account that is being presented to you. Imagine how you would have felt doing what these exceptionally brave men did. There are few of them still present to give their account, but the legacy of what they did is all around us, presented in the freedoms that we enjoy and, sometimes, take for granted today.

The most common sentiment expressed by those that I have been lucky enough to converse with and, in many cases, call friends, is that they want to be remembered. They want their less lucky friends who did not return to be remembered. The next time you see a Lancaster in the air or on the ground, I implore you to grant their wish and join us in figuratively tapping that plaque: 'To Remember The Many'.

Flight Lieutenant Sebastian Davey
BBMF Lancaster Captain

INTRODUCTION

'I CAN REMEMBER VERY WELL THE FIRST aeroplane I ever saw,' says Sidney 'Stevie' Stevens.

> We all turned out one day from school in Torrington, looked up at the sky, caught sight of an aeroplane. It was only a biplane, but we were very excited. There was a small patch of cloud and the plane went right through it. We were all saying to each other, 'It will come down now, it's hit that cloud!' I never dreamed then that I would one day be flying one myself, nor that when I did, it would be an aircraft as wonderful as the Lancaster.[1]

Millions of people around the world have, as Stevie did so many years ago, fallen in love with the magic of flight, flocking to air shows for the chance to see aircraft out of the ordinary. The Avro Lancaster – of which there are only two flying examples left in the world – is high on the list of coveted sightings. There isn't much that will cause 15,000 people to all fall silent at once. The hubbub suddenly subsides, ice creams are left un-licked and the pages of programmes flutter in the breeze. It's instinctive; the sound of the Merlin engines causes all eyes to look to the horizon. She rolls into view – the mighty Lanc, leviathan of the Royal Air Force in the Second World War, flanked on either side by a Spitfire and a Hurricane. The three of them rumble and glide through the sky together like old friends. We watch in awe.

This aircraft is more than just an aircraft – she *means* something to us. The Battle of Britain Air Show at Imperial War Museum Duxford has a packed flying programme, but this is the moment we've all been waiting for. 'When the Lancaster is appearing at an air show', IWM Air Show event manager Philip Hood tells me, 'it's going to be a popular one.' One Sunday in 2014, two Lancasters appeared in the sky together at Duxford and 24,000 visitors turned out to watch. It was the first time that Duxford had had to close their car parks to stop more people trying to access the site, causing the museum to implement a traffic management system and a move to advance ticket sales only for air shows. In testament to the Lanc's pulling power, the only other air show that sold out at Duxford was the 2018 Battle of Britain Air Show in celebration of RAF100, which featured a special formation of the Lancaster, the Tornado and the F35. Some 25,000 tickets were sold for each of the two days.

In 2023, I was one of the 33,000 people who turned out to watch the 'museum without walls' that is the Battle of Britain Memorial Flight. Based out of RAF Coningsby, the BBMF treats us to a beautiful display of British aviation heritage, with the Avro Lancaster right at the centre. These historic aircraft, lovingly and painstakingly preserved and flown by regular RAF aircrew, serve both to commemorate the past and to promote the modern-day RAF, inspiring future generations to take to the air. The BBMF reflects – as do we all at the sight of the Lanc – on the work and sacrifices of the thousands of men and women who, in the air and on the ground, toiled toward freedom on our behalf. It is these men and women, in particular those who are part of the story of the Avro Lancaster, that this book is about.

Today, air shows are among the UK's most-attended outdoor events, with several million spectators turning out each year. IWM Duxford is a significant venue in this field, priding itself on drawing 'potent links' between the past and present in aviation and possessing a 'distinct magic' in its air shows.[2] The United Kingdom has a long history of flying displays, dating back to October 1909, when intrigued observers assembled to watch the strange new flying machines take to the sky. From then on, public fascination with aviation grew.

It was clear to many, however, that the invention of the aeroplane was about more than exciting days out – it also carried military possibilities. The combining of aviation with war was not a new idea in the early twentieth century. Aerial warfare began in ancient times with the use of kites in China, and eventually hot air balloon would be used by various different countries for military purposes, like reconnaissance and observation. The aeroplane, however, could be controlled much more exactly, which meant reconnaissance and surveillance could be carried out according to more specific requirements. The aeroplane possessed the power to change the very nature of warfare, and it was clear that it carried the potential to turn the sky into a battlefield. While fighting against the Ottoman Empire in November 1911, Italian lieutenant Giulio Gavotti wrote to his father: 'Today I have decided to try to throw bombs from the aeroplane. It is the first time that we will try this.'[3] Gavotti took off in his Taube monoplane with four small bombs, weighing around 1.5kg each – three in a leather case near his seat and one in the front pocket of his jacket. Once he was over his target, he used one hand to steer the aircraft and the other to ready the bomb and throw it out onto the enemy below. In doing so, he carried out one of the first bombing raids from an aircraft in history.

Gavotti may not have achieved spectacular success with his one-man raid, but it made a crucial point – it was possible to wage war from the air. In 1912, the British military established the Royal Flying Corps (RFC), containing a military wing, a naval wing and a training centre. In July 1914, the RFC split to become two separate services, with the Royal Naval Air Service (RNAS) serving the Royal Navy and the RFC serving the British Army. Just a few months later, both would be called upon to fight in the First World War, and over the course of the conflict these men in their flying machines would come to constitute the greatest air force the world had ever seen. The dawn of the aviation age would change the way that war was waged – forever. To be able to see what the enemy was doing from above afforded certain intelligence advantages. The capabilities, and sometimes the intentions, of military forces could be deduced from aerial reconnaissance over enemy territory and the fighting front. At the beginning of the First World War, aircraft would be used to this end.

It was not long, however, before aviation would assume a more sinister purpose. At the start of the war the German armed forces possessed several Zeppelins – lighter-than-air craft filled with hydrogen and which, unlike balloons, kept their shape due to their steel framework. These could float silently at around 85mph, carrying up to 2 tons of bombs.[4] It was decided to use these against coastal towns and cities in Britain, and the first raid was carried out on Great Yarmouth and King's Lynn in January 1915. By May 1917, a new aerial threat had arrived over Britain in the form of the powerful German Gotha bombers. On 25 May, a mass air raid was carried out over south-east England and almost 100 people were killed, with nearly 200 more wounded. The huge twin-engined Gothas would soon be joined by four-engined 'Giant' bombers on multiple raids over Britain, with a total of 836 people killed and 1,982 wounded across a twelve-month campaign.[5]

The Entente powers also carried out bombing from above. To begin with, RFC pilots would throw small explosives from their aircraft by hand, and in 1914 the RNAS carried out bombing raids against Zeppelin bases in Germany. Perceived as a grave threat, Zeppelins were feared in Britain for their capacity for silent attacks, and their bases made good targets because they housed large amounts of extremely flammable hydrogen.

On 21 November 1914, the first strategic air raid in history took place when three RNAS Avro 504s were tasked with attacking the Zeppelin sheds at Friedrichshafen on Lake Constance.[6] This would mean a round-trip of around 250 miles – a very long flight for the aircraft of the day. It was the maiden flight for all three aircraft, and the first bombing each of the three pilots had ever carried out. On the morning of 21 November, the pilots set off from Belfort airfield in eastern France, in the direction of Friedrichshafen. They reached their target around midday, and released their bombs on the Zeppelin sheds.

Although no Zeppelins were destroyed and one of the 504s was shot down, the raid was significant. At a time when a boost in morale was badly needed, the Avro 504s and their pilots demonstrated to the world that strategic air raids were possible. After a particularly bad Gotha raid in July 1917, British Prime Minister David Lloyd George instructed Jan Christian Smuts to produce a report addressing the organization of the war in the air – in particular, the feasibility of creating a single air force. The two existing air forces in Britain – one under the navy and the other under the army – were struggling to communicate and co-ordinate. Smuts had achieved fame as a Boer commander in the South African War (1899–1902), and at the conclusion of the conflict he worked with the British toward the repairing of the Boer–British relationship. Smuts was pro-British but also an outsider, which placed him in a useful position to comment objectively and negotiate between the two services. Smuts had experience brokering talks, which he had managed to do between the republicans and unionists in Ireland, and he was a believer in the potential military uses of airpower. The resulting report would have far-reaching consequences for British airpower. Smuts concluded that a new, independent air force should be established as soon as possible, and that this service should be unified rather than have separate land and sea components. Of this single air service, he said, 'there is absolutely no limit to the scale of its future independent war use'.[7]

Smuts also acknowledged inevitable changes in the way war would be waged due to the inclusion of airpower in military tactics and strategy. 'The day may not be far off,' he wrote, 'when aerial operations with their devastation of enemy lands and destruction of industrial and populous centres on a vast scale may become the principal operations of war, to which the older forms of military and naval operations may become secondary and subordinate.'[8] A new, independent, unified service was needed to take the fight to the enemy in an offensive capacity. On 1 April 1918, the RAF was formed as a separate service, the first truly independent air force in the world. Under its own ministry and with a Secretary of State for Air, the RAF was 'the most powerful air force in the world', with more than 290,000 personnel and nearly 23,000 aircraft. It would fight over the Western Front for the remainder of the First World War. At the start of the conflict, aircraft had supplemented military operations. By the end of it, they had become an integral and vital element of modern warfare.

The way that war was waged had changed forever, and in the second of the two total wars in the twentieth century, aircraft and aviation would play an even bigger role. War is a catalyst for technological development and innovation, and various aircraft were born in the Second World War that affected the way in which it was fought and played out. There is, of course, the Spitfire, and its sister, the Hurricane – famous fighters that have stolen the hearts of many for decades. This book, however, is about the Avro Lancaster – the main heavy bomber used by Bomber Command in the second half of the conflict. It is the story of an aircraft: an impressive feat of aeronautical engineering, capable and versatile, loved – and feared – by many. And it is also the story of people. The people who designed the Lancaster, who built her, who looked after and flew her, who kept the stations she flew out of running and cared for her crews. It is the story of many whose lives were affected on a daily basis by her existence and presence on the ground and in the sky – those who lived and died, endured, suffered and survived the war in which she fought. This is the Lancaster story.

CHAPTER ONE

INCEPTION OF A LEGEND

The Birth Of Bomber Command

IN THE YEARS BETWEEN THE WARS, the memory of the bombs that had fallen on Britain's cities lingered in the minds of many, and the threat of further attacks from above was an ever-growing concern. The first Chief of the Air Staff, Sir Hugh Trenchard, was a firm believer that the only effective defence against bombing raids was for Britain to build up a bomber force of its own – offence, he believed, was the best form of defence. If Britain could threaten its enemies with the kind of destruction that a bomber force could bring, they might be deterred from attacking in the first place.

To this end, Bomber Command was created in 1936. The RAF would contain four commands, each with a specific function – Bomber, Fighter, Coastal and Training. Bomber Command comprised the RAF's light and heavy bomber squadrons. In addition, a succession of rearmament programmes were approved for the RAF as the nation edged closer to another major conflict. The speed at which war was approaching, however, meant that Fighter Command, responsible for the aerial defence of Britain, assumed greater importance, and when the Second World War broke out in September 1939 Bomber Command was in no fit state to launch an effective bombing offensive. With twenty-three operational bomber squadrons and 280 aircraft, the size and strength of the force did not match the huge role that it had been designed to play. Still, it was capable of striking back at Nazi Germany, and early raids were carried out in daylight against military targets such as ships and airfields. In August 1940, Bomber Command began to bomb Berlin, but these raids were largely fruitless and exposed serious weaknesses in Bomber Command's methods and abilities. Flying in daylight, for instance, left bomber aircraft vulnerable to attack from enemy fighters, and there were significant problems with navigation and target identification.

Following the invasion of France in 1940, the RAF began a night-bombing campaign over Germany, tasked with targeting German industry. There continued to be problems with target identification, however, as Bomber Command crews struggled to make out specific factories, manufacturing works, gasworks and refineries in the dark of night, flying much further distances than their Luftwaffe counterparts had to. Bombs fell far from their targets, failing to do any major damage to Germany's ability to fight. Though it was growing in size and strength, the command continued to struggle with navigation into 1941. In the waters to the west of Britain, German submarines (U-boats) relentlessly prowled, waiting to pick off Allied ships. As an island, Britain was dependent on vital supplies of food, fuel and war materials from its colonies and from North America, and these supplies were transported in merchant ships across the Atlantic. U-boats wrought havoc, stalking the ships and sending them to the bottom of the ocean, placing Britain in serious danger. The fall of France in June 1940 provided the U-boats with bases on the Atlantic coast, and more and more U-boats were being produced. The 'Battle of the Atlantic' – the longest continuous battle of the Second World War – placed greater importance on Britain's ability to hit back at Germany.

If the RAF was going to achieve its strategic aims, things needed to change. It needed more aircraft – as many as it could get its hands on. It wasn't just numbers that were important, however: it also needed a new *type* of bomber. In the early years of the war, the RAF relied on twin-engined bombers such as the Bristol Blenheim and the Vickers Wellington. These aircraft, though impressive in their own way, were simply not capable of achieving the strategic aims of the RAF. In addition to carrying out raids that would act as a deterrent against future attacks, Bomber Command needed to inflict enough damage to the enemy's war-fighting capabilities that it would no longer be able to fight. What was needed was an aircraft with a longer range, so that it could travel further into enemy territory and back – and an increased capacity to carry bombs. To increase range and payload capacity, the size of the aircraft itself would have to be increased.

The need for such an aircraft had been anticipated before the Second World War, which was fortunate, as aircraft design and production would take years to result in an effective product. The Air Ministry issued 'specifications', so aircraft manufacturers could design and present proposals to produce a suitable aircraft, and one or more would be selected and ordered. In 1935, specification B.12/36 sought a four-engined bomber. The eventual result was the Short Stirling, the first of the RAF's four-engined heavy bombers. The Stirling carried a crew of seven, and could hold 14,000lb of bombs. There were various problems and drawbacks with the aircraft, however – not least that it could not reach the kind of 'service ceiling' (or maximum operating altitude) needed to be able to achieve high levels of effectiveness in bomber operations, which made it susceptible to enemy fighters and flak.

There was still hope, however. Another specification was issued in September 1936: P.13/36 sought a twin-engined bomber. 'It should be an aircraft', the specification stated, 'that can exploit the alternatives between long range and very heavy bomb load which are made possible by catapult launching in a heavily loaded condition.'[1] The aircraft needed to be able to carry a maximum bomb load of 8,000lb. There were to be power-operated gun turrets in the nose and tail, and the aircraft needed to possess the best possible bomb aiming and navigational facilities. The specification was issued, and aircraft designers got to work.

Success from Failure

As a youngster, Roy Chadwick spent a lot of time making gliders and elastic-driven model planes. 'For a long time these models wouldn't fly,' he recalled, 'and friends used to sympathise with my mother about her strange offspring.'[2] Roy's mother helped him with the models, and after a series of tests carried out at night for fear of ridicule, he had models that would fly. Roy had taken a keen interest in aviation and in 1911, at the age of eighteen, he got to know pioneer aviator Edwin Alliott Verdon Roe and Reginald John Parrott, an engineer who worked with the Roe family. Alliott hired Roy as his personal assistant at his business – A. V. Roe and Company. 'This was the Avro team of those days,' Roy said in a BBC broadcast in 1942. Alliott was the 'leading spirit' and 'inventive genius'. Humphrey, Alliott's brother, handled the financial side of things, while Parrott dealt with construction and Roy was the drawing office staff – the draughtsman.

Initially working in the cellar of an old mill in Manchester, this small team designed and built experimental aircraft, including the Avro 504 biplane, which was supplied to the Royal Flying Corps during the First World War. During this first major conflict of the twentieth century, the A. V. Roe team accumulated a knowledge and understanding of aircraft that was deemed invaluable by the admiralty and the War Office, who wanted large quantities of aircraft to turn into war machines. The team was joined in 1914 by Roy Dobson, who would work closely with Roy Chadwick. Suddenly Chadwick was supervising 100 draughtsmen who possessed little to no knowledge of aeroplanes, tasked with teaching them all he knew. Chadwick's talent is clear in the fact that many of these men stayed with the company for years and a number went on to be of importance in the aircraft industry.

In 1915, the team designed a large twin-engined biplane with a gun station and 'internal stowage for bombs'. The War Office authorized the building of an experimental prototype, which would be developed throughout the war but not put into production. The idea of a purpose-built bomber, however, was firmly lodged in Chadwick's mind. After the First World War, he designed and built light, modern aeroplanes, including the Avro 'Baby' and 'Ava', as well as the Avro 549 'Aldershot', a large single-engine bomber.

By 1935, the 'Avro' brand was under the ownership of Hawker Siddeley Aircraft Limited and Roy Chadwick was the chief designer, working closely with Roy Dobson, the new managing director. In terms of design features, it was control, flying characteristics and methods of construction that interested Chadwick. 'I strive to obtain the best possible all-around performance from each new type,' he stated. With Chadwick's leadership, Avro contributed several aircraft in the Second World War, including the Anson and the Manchester.

Designed in response to the Air Ministry's P.13/36 specification for a long-range bomber and submitted as a tender in January 1937, the Avro Type 679 Manchester was an all-metal, mid-winged, monoplane twin-engined bomber, with twenty-four-cylinder Rolls-Royce Vulture engines. Chadwick's design was 'graceful but rugged' and featured a bomb bay in the fuselage that could hold 10 tons of bombs – the fuel and oil tanks having been placed in the wings to create the space.[3] Prototypes were built and tested, and by the end of January 1940, the Air Ministry had placed an order to Avro for 1,200 Manchesters.[4] The Manchester, however, was exhibiting serious problems. It was unable to reach an altitude that would keep it above enemy anti-aircraft fire, and the engines would habitually and suddenly fail, leaving it to fly on a single engine – which it simply could not do.

In April 1943, pilot Sidney 'Stevie' Stevens was training at No. 1654 Conversion Unit at RAF Wigsley in Nottinghamshire, where he flew a Manchester. He was unimpressed by the aircraft: 'The engines were heavy and very liable to oil up, and the aircraft used to dip into the ground when you were taxying. You had to use both engines to turn it around with the drag. It was hard work and difficult to taxi.'[5] More Manchesters were lost to engine failure than to enemy fire. The problems, it was concluded, stemmed from the Rolls-Royce Vulture engines, which were unreliable and heavy. These engines – one of the few failures of Rolls-Royce – were cancelled, and the Manchester would be withdrawn from operations in mid-1942 and retired from service in 1943.

The RAF's need for a bomber with improved capabilities persisted. Roy Chadwick, who according to his daughter 'always had several machines on his drawing board at a time', saw the answer.[6] He was convinced that the airframe itself would still work. He made some modifications to the design, and in 1940 work began on turning the twin-engined Manchester into a four-engined bomber. The aircraft was given a new wing section, increasing the wingspan to 102ft in order to accommodate four engines. When Chadwick and Dobson presented the designs to the Air Ministry, it was decided that rather than trying to improve the troublesome Vulture, the Merlin engine would be used and production of the new bomber should proceed. An order for two prototypes was placed and the new aircraft was designated the 'Manchester III'. The Manchester's centre section would remain the same, but modifications had to be made to the engine mountings and the nacelle panels to accommodate the new engines.[7]

After completing engine runs in December 1940, the first prototype, BT308, was cleared for its maiden flight in January 1941. Though it was known as the 'Manchester III', the name 'Lancaster' was annotated on the aircraft's Air Ministry design certificate. Test pilot Harry 'Sam' Brown and his deputy, Bill Thorn, took to the sky in the first Lancaster on 9 January, and it showed immediate promise. For its second test flight on 21 February, BT308 had larger twin fins fitted and the central fin removed. The modifications made such an improvement that during this flight Brown was able to fly with two engines shut down, using the larger rudders to continue to fly straight. A second prototype, DG595, was constructed, and this aircraft was much more representative of the production standard aircraft that would follow. This version boasted four improved Rolls-Royce Merlin XX engines, a new undercarriage, an increased span tail plane with larger twin tail fins and improved fuel capacity from 1,700 to 2,154 gallons.[8]

The aircraft's maiden flight took place on 13 May 1941, and test pilot Sam Brown reported to Roy Chadwick that 'it was an absolute delight to fly'.[9] During this flight the aircraft's real potential was tested, and the test pilots put it through its paces by taking it into a 360mph dive. For a bomber, this was a remarkable feat. The design was officially named the 'Type 683 Avro Lancaster'. The first production Lancaster, L7527, flew from Woodford on 31 October 1941. The Avro Lancaster I was powered by four Rolls-Royce Merlin XX V12 engines, providing 1,280 horsepower each. Unlike the Manchester, the Lancaster only needed one pilot, with the flight engineer assuming responsibility for the mechanical running of the aircraft and stepping in to assist or replace the pilot when needed. It was designed to be crewed by seven men: the pilot and the flight engineer, a navigator, a bomb aimer (doubling as the front gunner), a wireless operator, a mid-upper gunner and a rear gunner. Early production Lancasters sported two-gun, power-operated turrets in the nose, mid-upper and ventral positions, with a four-gun turret in the tail.

By November 1942, operational Lancasters were functional up to 63,000lb, and by May 1944 this had increased again to 65,000lb (with an overload weight allowance of 72,000lb in January 1945).[10] The design of the Lancaster was so effective that it required little alteration or development during its operational existence. The Manchester may have been a failure, but it was the origin of the best, most important and most numerous of the British heavy bombers of the Second World War.

Building the Beast

Now that the RAF had a new, very effective bomber, it needed to get as many into operational service as possible, as quickly as possible, to replace its existing bombers. The previous aircraft had done their job and would now be replaced with their far superior successor. With a second world war clearly looming in early 1939, the Air Ministry had approached Avro to request that they expand their manufacturing capabilities in readiness for the emergency production of large numbers of aircraft. It was now imperative that they use this to produce as many Lancasters as the factory could churn out.

The Lancaster was designed to be relatively simple to build and did not require huge amounts of especially skilled labour, and thousands of people would be involved in what would become a streamlined, efficient manufacturing process. Many of the Lancaster's parts were the same as those on the Manchester, so conveniently the same tools, skills and facilities could be used to manufacture the new bomber. At the Avro facility in Chadderton, Greater Manchester, men and women worked as tracers in the Drawing Office, producing high-quality drawings that could be reproduced and sent to every Lancaster production facility in the country. Large-scale production was planned, and factories belonging to Avro, Austin, Metropolitan-Vickers and Armstrong Whitworth were asked to make themselves ready to build the new bombers. It cost an average of £58,974 to build a Lancaster (more than £2,300,000 today), and at the peak of production twenty-seven Lancasters were completed each week.[11] More than 10,500 drawings were required. A Lancaster consisted of 55,000 separate parts (even with the engines and turrets counted as single items and excluding nuts, bolts and rivets), and an estimated 500,000 different manufacturing processes and operations were involved in making those parts and putting them all together.[12]

The huge fuselage was divided into five sections. The first section was the nose, which housed the front gun turret and the bomb aimer's position. The front centre section housed the pilot, navigator and radio operator stations, and the centre section contained a rest compartment. The rear centre section housed the mid-upper gun turret, and finally the rear section had the tail unit and the rear gun turret. Each section was built separately, and the five were then bolted together to form the framework of the fuselage. Sheets of a light aluminium alloy were then riveted to the metal skeleton. The central sections of the Lancaster were held together by two main spars which crossed the main fuselage. The front, or 'main' spar, was situated just behind where the radio operator sat, and the rear spar crossed the fuselage a little further back. These spars had to be climbed over by the crew inside the aircraft. The huge, 33ft long bomb bay's doors in the belly of the aircraft had a hydraulic jack attachment at each end, and this bay could hold a variety of bombs. The Lancaster was an extremely versatile aircraft – it could carry different loads for different mission requirements and could be modified to carry specialist weapons for specific operations.

Building the Lancaster in separate sections meant that the different pieces could be manufactured anywhere and then easily transported to the assembly site – which was much easier than transporting entire aircraft from their site of manufacture to an airfield for flight tests. The interior of the aircraft was spartan, with exposed metal edges, cramped conditions and very few touches of comfort. The nose turret was fitted with two Browning .303 in. machine guns, each holding 1,000 rounds of ammunition. The gunner could rotate through 190° using two handles, which also contained the firing mechanism. The mid-upper turret also had two Browning .303 in. machine guns, each holding 1,000 rounds. The gunner gained access to the turret via a stowable step and sat in a hammock-style seat which clipped into position. This turret was capable of rotating a full 360°, and a fail-safe mechanism prevented him from shooting the tail of his own aircraft. The rear turret in the tail of the aircraft was fitted with four Browning .303s. Ammunition was fed into these from stainless steel tracks, running along either side of the fuselage, that connected to two ammunition boxes attached to the floor. The tracks could supply

2,500 rounds for each of the four guns, keeping the tail gunner capable of firing at enemy chasers for longer. Early Lancasters had a ventral gun turret, but as it was not initially used very much the decision was made to remove it. This would later prove disastrous, as the ventral turret would have helped to protect the Lancaster's underbelly from enemy fighters firing from below.

Then there was the painting. The aircraft needed to be difficult for the enemy to spot during night bombing raids, even when using searchlights, so they were painted matt black underneath. The rest of the aircraft was painted in dark green and brown camouflage. The final touches were the RAF roundel, and the numbers and letters that identified the individual aircraft. Lancasters were identified within a squadron with a letter, which was extended with a word: C-Charlie, for instance. These identifier words led crews to come up with nicknames for their aircraft. Lancaster crews were usually assigned to a specific aircraft, and painted 'nose art' on it that was personal to them. In this way, there was a powerful bond between the men and the machine that carried them to their target and brought them home again.

In the Factories

In preparation for the war, aircraft factories would need thousands of workers to make the many different components of various different kinds of aircraft. Those workers would come from all over the country to keep the factories operating twenty-four hours a day, seven days a week. One of the first factories built was Avro Yeadon, located alongside Yeadon Aerodrome in Yorkshire. This was a 'shadow factory', one of a number of factories in Britain used for wartime aircraft production and hidden from the enemy as an obvious target for the Luftwaffe.

Shadow factories were often built 'in the shadow of' existing factories, like motor transport production facilities, where equipment and skills could be transferred. Yeadon was designed so that a large part of it was underground, but the flat roof was also elaborately camouflaged with grass. It was also given fake buildings, walls and bodies of water to make it look like a field. Experts from the film industry worked to hide buildings in this way, keeping them out of sight of prowling enemy bombers, and in the case of the Yeadon factory going as far as to move fake animals around on the roof so it looked like real livestock were roaming. Throughout the war the factory produced 608 Lancasters, as well as thousands of other aircraft of various types.[13]

At the height of its wartime operation, more than 17,500 people worked at Avro Yeadon, arriving by bus and lodging in the local area. One of them was seventeen-year-old Audrey Callaghan, who was responsible for fetching items from the various stores when they were needed for construction. Conditions in aircraft factories could be very challenging to cope with. Another worker, Lillian Grundy, manufactured small screws at Avro's plant at Newton Heath. 'It was a twelve-hour shift,' she says. 'It was freezing cold in the winter and in the summer, it was mad hot.'[14] These were busy, loud places, with hazards that weren't always noticed until it was too late. After a year, Audrey was told by a doctor that she needed to leave her job, as the paint spraying in the section next to hers was slowly poisoning her.[15]

With so many men away fighting the war, many of the people working in aircraft factories were women, and their integration into the workforce was not always smooth. Before the war, Rhoda Turner had been working at the *Daily Express* printworks on Great Ancoats Street in Manchester, but once the conflict began, she found herself working in a factory making munitions for Royal Navy anti-aircraft guns. Rhoda was then transferred to Avro. Instead of making 'pom-pom' shells, she would now be working on the wingtips for the new Lancaster bombers. Having been specially selected for the work, Rhoda arrived at the Avro facility with a number of other women – to be greeted with wolf whistles and smiles from the men already working there, who thought the women were just visiting. This warm welcome turned icy, however, once it became clear why they were really there, and that they were there to stay. The foreman explained that the women were going to be building bomber components, and that the men would be required to teach them the craft. The male workforce, Rhoda remembered, were not happy and downed tools, only returning to work after much convincing. Rhoda and her colleagues learned to rivet and wire and spent the remainder of their war working hard on the wingtips with their newly acquired skills.

As more and more men were needed to fight overseas and the need for manpower worsened, some parts of the factories – an entire section of the Chadderton Machine Shop, for instance – were entirely staffed with women workers, who came to be involved at every stage of the Lancaster wing and fuselage major assembly process. Some women even donned white coats and armbands to assume the more senior role of inspector, checking that the work being done was as accurate as possible. Women loaded and unloaded pressed items in the heavy press department, assembled detailed components, helped their male colleagues with Lancaster fuel tank inspections and put together the main wing structures in large jigs. It was unusual for women to have had any formal education or experience in technical subjects or in maths or science; in keeping with accepted societal gender roles and expectations, they were educated in domestic subjects instead. The vital contribution the female workforce made to the wartime production of Lancasters was not something they were initially considered capable of, but defying social stereotypes and expectations they worked hard and proved themselves extremely capable and efficient in aviation factories and workshops around the country. They were fast learners and keen workers and dealt with hazards calmly, rather than succumbing to hysteria as had been expected.

The factories could be dangerous places, and not just because of the heavy machinery and potential accidents. Any sort of potential war industry would be targeted by the Luftwaffe, and the factories were bombing targets. Rhoda Turner's factory was bombed several times during the course of the war, as was the factory where Susan Jones worked. Susan was sixteen years old when she elected to work as a riveter at Avro's Chadderton site (which produced 3,032 Lancaster bombers in the Second World War). For the first year of her employment there, she worked twelve-hour shifts, seven days a week, without a whole day off. When she did manage to scrape the odd afternoon off, she attended dances with her friends. She was 'very proud' of her work, she said in 2017.[16]

Some women were thanked for their critically important work in unusual ways. One woman working on installing the wiring in Lancaster centre sections impressed the workshop foreman so much that she was rewarded with a visit to a Lancaster base in Lincolnshire. She was allowed to sit in the tail turret and fire the Browning machine guns during calibration work. She enjoyed it so much that she wouldn't stop, and the mechanics had to tell her they had run out of bullets to get her out.

On the Move

Once all the sections of the aircraft were finished, they would be transported by road to an assembly site in the vicinity of an airfield. The Avro factory in Chadderton built up to seven bombers a day during the war, and the individual sections had to be transported from there to Woodford Aerodrome in Stockport, where they would be assembled. Woodford was Avro's main assembly plant and completed the assembly of 4,101 Lancaster bombers.

Once assembled and ready to go into service, the aircraft needed to be moved to the airfields from which they could fly. One method of doing so was to have ferry pilots of the Air Transport Auxiliary (ATA) fly them. The ATA was a civilian service founded in 1939, tasked with the delivery of aircraft from factories to the squadrons of the RAF and the Royal Navy, as well as the delivery of supplies. Beginning with twenty-three pilots, the ATA was staffed by men who could fly but who were exempt from wartime service for reasons of age or health. In December 1939, however, accomplished female pilot Pauline Gower successfully convinced the RAF and the ATA that women could fly too, and she was appointed leader of the new women's section of the ATA. 'Some people believe women pilots to be a race apart, and born "fully fledged". Women are not born with wings, neither are men for that matter,' Pauline said. 'Wings are won by hard work.'[17]

The ATA built a reputation for being able to 'take anything to anywhere'.[18] During the war, 1,250 men and women from twenty-five different countries flew without radios or instruments, in all kinds of weather, to ferry a total of 309,000 aircraft of 147 different types.[19] Among them were Lancaster bombers. At first restricted to light, non-operational aircraft, by 1942 ATA women were flying twin-engine medium bombers, and in September 1942 woman pilot Lettice Curtis was selected to train on four-engine bombers. 'Situated as I was in an all-male Ferry pool, I was lucky to have had … a commanding officer who was prepared to put forward for the first time a woman,' Lettice says.[20] 'The main doubt, I was told afterwards, was whether women would have sufficient physical strength to cope.' Hailed as the best British female pilot of the Second World War, Lettice passed the tests to fly the four-engine Lancasters in February 1943, followed by colleague Joan Hughes.[21]

By the end of the war, eleven ATA women had passed the test to fly the Lancaster. Marion Wilberforce, for example, delivered Spitfires and Lancasters all over the country, many of which were then flown into zones of conflict all over the world throughout the rest of the war.[22] She made 114 deliveries in the second half of 1944 alone.[23] Lettice Curtis, meanwhile, was so skilled at flying Lancasters that a month after her first delivery – transporting Lancaster ED396 from RAF Llandow in south Wales to RAF Elsham Wolds in Lincolnshire – her superiors selected her to take part in the preparations for a very special Bomber Command raid, led by Wing Commander Guy Gibson.[24] She delivered Lancaster ED817/G from Farnborough to 617 Squadron at RAF Scampton in May 1943, just a few days before Operation Chastise – the Dambusters Raid. The 'G' in the aircraft's serial number meant that it was a specially modified Lancaster that would carry secret equipment, and as such would require constant supervision and guarding when not flying. Although in the end

ED817/G did not take part in the raid, it was part of the same batch of aircraft that would breach two of the dams.

Lancasters for Christmas

On Christmas Eve 1941, Women's Auxiliary Air Force (WAAF) R/T operator Pip Beck watched in astonishment as three large aircraft approached, her colleagues in Flying Control at RAF Waddington as transfixed as she was. The aeroplanes landed, and the first one rolled around the perimeter to the Watch Office and into Pip's view. 'I stared in astonishment at this formidable and beautiful aircraft,' she says, 'cockpit as high as the balcony on which I stood and great spread of wings with four enormous engines. Its lines were sleek and graceful, yet there was an awesome feeling of power about it.'[25] The Avro Lancaster had arrived. No. 5 Group's 44 (Rhodesia) Squadron had been chosen as the first squadron in Bomber Command to receive the Lancaster, having had a prototype – a converted Manchester – resident at Waddington since 9 September.

The three Lancasters which arrived on 24 December 1941, though, were the first three operational Lancasters to be delivered to the RAF, and 44 Squadron would be the first unit to bring the new bomber into service and fly operational missions with it. It was, as Pip put it, 'a magnificent Christmas present for the Squadron.'[26] The squadron was proud – the air and ground crews in particular – and Pip had attended a dance at the Assembly Rooms in Lincoln where the Lancasters' imminent arrival was celebrated. No. 44 Squadron had been operating Handley Page Hampden twin-engine bombers since February 1939, and both air and ground crews underwent conversion training to learn how to operate and maintain the new four-engined, heavier Lancasters. There were inevitable teething issues, including a few minor accidents – pilots running out of runway, for instance, and engines and wheels falling off. As former Lancaster pilot Jack Currie muses, everyone who flew the Lancaster soon discovered that when lightly loaded, it was 'an aeroplane that did not like to stall: it would float forever if the speed was just a little bit too high'.[27]

The second squadron to receive the Lancaster was 97 (Straits Settlements) Squadron, based at Woodhall Spa. Flying Officer Edward Ernest Rodley of 97 Squadron was flying a Lancaster shortly after the aircraft had arrived and lost a wingtip in flight, which was serious enough to warrant a visit from Roy Chadwick and some subsequent modifications to the wings. Both 44 and 97 Squadrons put the Lancaster through its paces in these early flights, learning its limits and marvelling at its capabilities. It was found that the aircraft could fly reasonably well on three engines if one was rendered unusable. Lancaster pilot Hugo Trotter remembers seeing fellow pilot Ron Holmes, of 101 Squadron, limp back to base on just two – he was awarded an immediate Distinguished Flying Cross.[28] ('Super chap,' Hugo says of him.) It was an aircraft that endeared itself to its crews. With the ability to cruise at altitudes in excess of 20,000ft, a bombload capacity of 22,000lb, a maximum speed of 275mph while fully loaded and a range exceeding 1,500 miles, the Lancaster was reliable, capable and unlike any other bomber they had flown.

Beginning with 44 and 97 Squadrons, the Lancaster was to be inducted into Bomber Command's main force to take part in routine bombing operations. One of the tasks assigned to 5 Group was minelaying. The admiralty made plans to drop mines into north-west European waters and recognized that certain sections of sea would be much more easily accessible by long-range aircraft. RAF aircraft from Coastal and Bomber Commands were thus used to carry out aerial minelaying, which accounted for a large majority of mines laid by the Allies in European waters, from the Norwegian fjords to the border between France and Spain.[29] The hope was to disrupt and destroy German shipping, and to force the use of enemy resources in minesweeping operations.

The areas chosen for the RAF to drop mines were called 'gardens', and each was given the name of a common flower or fruit as a codename. The mines to be dropped into them were referred to as 'vegetables', and the minelaying process became known in Bomber Command as 'gardening'. No. 5 Group took part in gardening operations, using their Hampdens to deliver one mine per aircraft. Things changed, however, on 3 March 1942, when the Lancaster entered operational service and four of 44 Squadron's Lancs were tasked with laying mines. The garden would be the mouth of the River Elbe in the North Sea, and the Lancasters took off from RAF Waddington for the bay of Heligoland Bight. Lancasters could carry four to six vegetables each – significantly more than the Hampden – and could take them further too. Around five hours later, they returned, the Lancaster's first operational mission complete.

A few days later, on the night of 10/11 March, two of 44 Squadron's Lancasters were loaded up with 5,000lb of incendiary bombs each, and participated beside Avro Manchesters, Short Stirlings, Vickers Wellingtons and Handley Page Hampdens in a raid on Essen. The Lancasters were a welcome addition to Bomber Command, quickly endearing themselves to their crews.

Change in the Wind

In addition to receiving a new and very promising aircraft, there were other significant changes in Bomber Command in early 1942. Difficulties with precision bombing and mounting losses early in the war led to conversations about the future of British strategic bombing and attempts to clarify exactly what role Bomber Command should play. In September 1940, Churchill had said in a memo to Cabinet: 'The navy can lose us the war but only the air force can win it … The Fighters are our salvation … but the Bombers alone provide the means of victory.'[30]

Initial attacks by Bomber Command had been infrequent and relatively light, targeting enemy ports and oil and communications targets. In 1940 it was decided that oil, particularly synthetic oil production, should be the main focus of the British bombing campaign. If Germany lacked oil, it would not be able to mobilize its machines of war, so refineries and synthetic oil plants were prioritized as targets. In 1941, however, the Air Ministry ordered that communications targets be foregrounded, tasking Bomber Command with using its full force against a number of rail centres to prevent supplies from entering and leaving the vital Ruhr industrial region. Though the Air Ministry was intent on pursuing precision bombing and believed that it would seriously damage Germany's ability to wage war, it soon became clear that Bomber Command's attempts to hit specific targets were not proving very successful.

In August 1941, losses were high and Nazi Germany seemed stronger than ever. A report was commissioned to investigate the accuracy of the RAF's bombing, and the resulting Butt Report was cause for alarm, confirming that these raids were, in fact, badly inaccurate. In the Ruhr region – the industrial heart of Germany, where Bomber Command was hoping to cause serious damage to Germany's ability to produce war materials – only one in three bombers was getting to within 5 miles of the target. There were those in Whitehall and in the military service departments who remained unconvinced of the utility and potential of strategic bombing and who called for the resources being given to Bomber Command to be distributed elsewhere – to the Royal Navy, for instance – instead.

But Bomber Command was Britain's sword – its best offensive weapon and one of its only means of taking the fight to the enemy. Prime Minister Winston Churchill could not sheath such a weapon at a time when it was critically needed. He and the Chief of the Air Staff (Air Chief Marshal Sir Charles Portal) held to their belief in the ability of airpower to hasten war's end. The Butt Report revealed, though, that if Bomber Command was going to be successful in damaging the German war economy, something would have to change.

Bombers were vulnerable flying in daylight, and many were picked off by German fighters and increasingly effective anti-aircraft defences. The switch was made to night bombing – but even though Bomber Command slowly grew in strength in 1941, heavy losses continued, denting morale. There needed to be more bombers – lots more – and the aircraft and their crews needed better technology to be able to locate their targets and drop their bombs more accurately.

In September 1941, the Air Ministry came up with a list of generalized areas in Germany that it deemed industrially and economically significant enough to become the targets of sustained, heavy bombing. If targets of economic and military facilities of strategic value could be hit, it was predicted, the German economy, as well as the morale of its workers, would be damaged enough to weaken Germany and make it vulnerable. The switch to area bombing did not mean the abandonment of precision bombing altogether – if strategically important targets could be accurately identified and bombed, they would be. On 14 February 1942, the Air Ministry issued Directive 22: 'You are authorised to employ your effort without restriction, until further notice, in accordance with the following directions. It has been decided that the primary object of your operations should now be focused on the morale of the enemy civil population and in particular, of the industrial workers.'[31]

The directive outlined how 'primary industrial areas' in German cities were to be attacked. Operations, it stated, should be of a 'harassing nature, the object being to maintain fear of attack over the city and to impose ARP (Air Raid Precautions) measures'. Essen was identified as the most important of the selected primary targets, which also included Cologne and Düsseldorf. In addition to 'primary industrial areas' like these, the directive also listed 'alternative industrial areas', such as Bremen, Frankfurt and Kiel. Berlin was to be continuously attacked. The intended damage would be physical, of course, knocking out factories, docks, fuel facilities and other targets that would reduce Germany's war-fighting capabilities.

It is notable, however, that the directive also stated that operations 'should now be focused on the morale of the enemy civil population'. Damaging the morale of the German people could, it was hoped, cause them to lose the will to continue the fight. Such a change in bombing policy inevitably invoked a moral dilemma. Enemy civilians would be killed – women and children, the elderly and the sick. But Britain was in a fight for its life, and it was felt that area bombing was necessary to defeat an enemy that seemed unstoppable and dangerously close to victory. Area bombing became the main form of attack by Bomber Command, which was allocated a vast number of resources to carry out its mission.

Arthur 'Bomber' Harris

With new aircraft and tactics, Bomber Command also acquired a new leader in February 1942, in the form of Air Chief Marshal Sir Arthur Harris. Very soon after Directive No. 22 was issued, Harris took up his position at the head of Bomber Command. The command itself had not created the new bombing policy – that task had fallen to Air Ministry planners – and despite the fact that he is often associated with it, Harris himself did not devise it or influence its development. He had, however, long been convinced that a bomber offensive would be needed and was fully committed to delivering one in accordance with the directives given to him.

His 'belief in the heavy bomber as the predominant weapon for the war' was, he stated in 1947, based on his past experiences.[32] Harris had learned to fly with the Royal Flying Corps, and during the First World War he had formed and commanded a detached flight – and later a squadron – in the first Home Defence squadron of night fighters, in which the first enemy Zeppelin had been shot down. He also commanded a flight in a fighter squadron in France, protecting artillery spotters. Unexpectedly granted a permanent commission as a Squadron Leader in the newly formed RAF, Harris was given command of No. 58 Squadron at Worthy Down – the first heavy bomber squadron to be reconstituted as such after the war. Harris then moved to the Air Ministry, where he remained until 1938, in a position to be able to understand exactly what Britain's military situation was in the approach to another world war.

Spending some time with No. 4 Bomber Group in 1938, he was

involved in cross-country flights and training for night bombing in Whitley aircraft. After a year as an air officer commanding RAF Palestine and Transjordan, Harris returned to Britain on the eve of war. 'I could see only one vista through the wood which seemed to end in the faintest gleam of daylight,' he later stated. 'That was the bomber offensive.'[33] Such an offensive, Harris maintained, was the only hope of defeating Germany. It was the means of destroying the enemy's war potential, of knocking them out of the fight. He did not consider damaging enemy morale to be a main priority of Bomber Command's operations, which were instead focused on destroying physical facilities and the enemy's machinery of war. Rather, civilian morale would inevitably be damaged as a by-product of these operations. At the start of the Second World War, Harris took over No. 5 Group, Bomber Command, based in Grantham.

In 1940, now Deputy Chief of the Air Staff, he stood on a rooftop in London with Charles Portal, Chief of the Air Staff, and watched one of the worst nights of the Blitz: 'I watched the old city in flames from the roof of the Air Ministry, with St Paul's standing out in the midst of an ocean of fire – an incredible sight. One could hear the German bombers arriving in a stream and the swish of the incendiaries falling into the fire below.' Harris commented to Portal: 'Well, they are sowing the wind.'[34] Harris was convinced that a bomber offensive 'of adequate weight and the right kind of bombs would, if continued for long enough, be something that no country in the world could endure'. When, in February 1942 he was appointed to lead Bomber Command, it would become his job to direct such an offensive. Bomber Command's new aircraft, the Lancaster bomber, would be critical in its execution.

Harris inherited a less-than-ideal situation. The war was not going well for the Allies. In the East, the Germans had recovered from their winter problems and were once again making progress. The Soviet Union was appealing to the Allies for help, and in the Pacific theatre the Japanese had been successful in sweeping across a vast area with their own version of Blitzkrieg. The Battle of the Atlantic raged on, constantly threatening to strangle Britain via her supply lanes.

Aware of how the wider war was going, Harris inherited a sorry state of affairs in Bomber Command itself. On the day he took over as Commander-in-Chief, he recalls, 'there were 378 aircraft serviceable with crews, and only sixty-nine of these were heavy bombers. About fifty aircraft in the force were not even medium bombers but the light bombers of No. 2 Group ... In effect, this meant that we had an average force of 250 medium and fifty heavy bombers, until such time as the command really began to expand.'[35] Harris knew that he was under pressure to deliver positive results – hopefully, a series of strategic blows against German industry and war capabilities – but before he could do that, Bomber Command needed to grow. He needed more bombers – but they needed to be the *right kind* of bombers. They needed to be four-engined, heavy bombers. Secretary of State for Air Sir Archibald Sinclair told the House of Commons on 4 March that the intention was to 'resume the bomber offensive against Germany on the largest possible scale at the earliest possible moment'.[36] Bombers were, he stated, the 'only force upon which we can call in this year, 1942, to strike deadly blows at the heart of Germany'. The Lancaster had the capacity to be Bomber Command's game-changer.

CHAPTER TWO

BOMBER COMMAND PEOPLE

Joining Bomber Command

YOUNG MEN WHO VOLUNTEERED FOR THE RAF did so for a variety of reasons. Many felt a strong sense of patriotism and duty and wanted to fight back against Nazi Germany and the destruction and suffering the Third Reich was wreaking. Al Lovett was fourteen when the war broke out. He remembers the bombing raid that drove him to join the RAF as soon as he could. The air raid sirens began blaring, and his family rushed to get inside their Anderson shelter. 'The aircraft came,' he says, 'and we heard a lot of bombs going off. Then they turned and came across, and dropped three bombs. One across the road from where we lived. My mother was screaming in fright. My father wasn't too keen – he'd been in the Medical Corps in World War One. They dropped more bombs. I got a bit annoyed after that.'[1] Al joined the Home Guard and carried out his duties as a firewatcher until he was old enough to register for service with the RAF – and as soon as he was eighteen, he did so.

Sidney 'Stevie' Stevens also saw his family endangered by German bombs. He had joined the Air Raid Precautions Service

(ARP) in 1938, and by 1940 he was working as a controller in the ARP Centre at Thornton Heath. One day, when he was just starting an eight-hour shift at Thornton Heath Control Centre, he received a message:

> A message came through during my shift to say that my own house had been bombed. There were so many bombs reported in the area that I stayed on duty until I was relieved at about 6 a.m., when my shift finished. I cycled back home over fire hoses and rubble. When I arrived at my road, sure enough, my house had received a direct hit and was just a ruin. Ironically, my mother had just come from Torrington, where she had been staying with her sister, because she thought things were getting quieter. She and my father and my uncle, who had popped in for a cup of tea, were all in a shelter, badly shaken. We had a large, sturdy farmhouse table and when they heard the bombs coming down, they had got themselves underneath it. The bruised face of my father, the white bomb dust in my mother's hair, and the broken leg of my uncle, who had not managed to squeeze all of his body under that table, etched themselves in my mind forever.[2]

When Stevie was on his way to the ARP Centre, the woman who lived next door asked him if he would like some tea. He stopped for a cup and a chat, and then continued on to work. 'The next I saw of this poor lady, she had been smashed into her own front door – it was like a cartoon from a comic with jam all over the place, but in reality, it was anything but funny. The bomb blast had turned her into smelly human paste.' Stevie lost everything in the raid:

> I came out of the house at the end of the raid when the sirens were sounding the All Clear. Everything for which I had worked and saved was pulverised except for

> a torn shirt, a pair of Boy Scouts shorts and a school prize dated 1935. They were my sole possessions, apart from the clothes I was wearing ... I knew straight away then I wanted to be a bomber pilot; not many people wanted to fly bombers, but I knew I did, and I was determined that I would.[3]

Some young men chose the RAF because they knew they'd be called up and wanted to be able to choose how they would serve in the war effort. At the coming of war, Harry Parkins was working as a warehousing clerk. One day, he was having lunch with his friend and colleague, John Smith, in the canteen: 'We were talking about the war and what was going to happen, both the same age, and I said, "We are going to get called up any minute now," so he said, "What do you want to go in for?"'[4] Harry and John decided that if they volunteered rather than waiting to be called up, they stood a better chance of being placed in the service of their choice. Harry was put off the army by his father, so John suggested the navy. 'I said, "Ooh I don't know, I can only swim across the canal" ... I never tried any further, so I said, "I know ... I think it is safer in the air than on the ground ... I reckon I'll volunteer for the RAF!"'

To be selected for aircrew, recruits had to complete an interview and pass a medical exam. After their lunch break, both Harry and John reported locally to volunteer for the RAF and underwent their medical examinations. They passed and were accepted into the service – but it was at this point that some hopeful potential airmen came unstuck. Peter Jenkinson was thirteen years old when he suffered a serious attack of pneumonia and pleurisy. In 1937, he joined the Bristol Aircraft Company as an apprentice engineer, and when the war broke out in 1939 he volunteered immediately for service in the RAF. Unfortunately, due to his childhood illness he was declared medically unfit after his examination, and was rejected. Peter continued to work as an aircraft engineer but was desperate to use his skills to help toward the war effort in the RAF and attempted twice more to join.[5] On a further fourth attempt, after a superhuman effort, he was successful.

Another hopeful, Benny Goodman, persisted when his eyesight seemed like it might be a barrier to becoming a pilot. In September 1939, Benny had sat next to the wireless as Prime Minister Neville Chamberlain announced that Britain was at war with Germany. His first instinct was to leave his university studies and join the military, and he telephoned his father to talk things over. 'There was no doubt in my mind I was going to join up,' Benny says.[6] He just needed to decide which service to join. He chose the RAF and decided that he wanted to become a pilot. His Jewish faith meant that should he be shot down and captured by the Nazis, Benny was in extra danger, but he was not deterred: 'I was almost nineteen and had no idea what war entailed, but with the ignorance and cheek of youth I presented myself at the RAF recruiting office and told the officer who interviewed me what I wanted to do. He didn't say a word, finished filling in the form he had in front of him and told me I would be hearing about my application very soon.' Shortly afterwards he underwent a general medical, and after passing was sent for a more extensive medical specific to potential RAF aircrew. 'Everything went well except when it came to the eye test. My eyesight had never been top class, so I went to the back of the queue and learnt the two or three lines each candidate was being asked to read. I passed!'

Once recruits had been accepted into the RAF, it was then a matter of waiting for their call-up papers. The RAF's process was to first train existing and experienced aircrew to the required standard, and the new recruits would follow them into battle later. 'Without you, time might be lost at a critical moment in filling up the training facilities left vacant by those who have joined the ranks of the first line combatants,' the restless young men were reassured.[7]

An International Effort

The RAF's work in the Second World War was a vast multinational effort, and men and women from sixty different countries joined Bomber Command – including Australia, New Zealand, Canada, India, the West Indies and Poland. People from around the world felt so strongly that they needed to take part in the fight against the Axis powers that they travelled great distances and settled far away from the safety of home to be able to do so. There was good integration of personnel from around the world into Bomber Command, and aircrews made up of men from different countries functioned extremely effectively. At the start of the war, a number of personnel from Canada, Australia and New Zealand were already serving with the RAF, and many others volunteered to join once the Second World War had broken out.

Arthur Bishop volunteered to join the Royal Canadian Air Force (RCAF) in October 1940, travelling 70 miles to Halifax in a bread lorry to get to the recruiting station.[8] From there, he was sent to Manning Depot in Toronto, where he learned how to march, how to handle a rifle and received his inoculations against various diseases. After that, he began a multistage training process. He was selected for pilot training and sent to an Elementary Flying Training School (EFTS) in London, Ontario, where he learned to fly with an instructor before 'going solo' – flying for the first time on his own. By spring 1941, Arthur was sent to an overseas posting unit in Halifax and boarded a ship that would sail in convoy to Belfast. He then crossed the Irish Sea by ferry to the Scottish port of Stranraer.

Upon arriving in Britain, personnel from overseas were exposed to the harsh realities of war. Arthur joined a group of Canadian sergeant pilots to board a packed train, which took him to London and then to Bournemouth. It was a depressing ride. 'Many passengers were crying,' he says, 'having lost a loved one in air raids or disasters at sea. To sergeant pilots from Canada, it was a shock treatment never forgotten.'[9] Arthur would go on to complete two full tours with Bomber Command – one on Stirlings and a second on Lancasters. Arthur took part in several major operations, including one raid on Duisburg in the Ruhr, where his aircraft was one of 700 four-engined bombers. His crew saw a lot of action – much of it harrowing in nature. On one occasion, another Allied bomber was hit by enemy flak just 500ft from Arthur's Lancaster and he watched as it disintegrated and a body fell past his wing. At the end of the war, Arthur says, 'it was hard to accept that so many of my friends were killed and I was spared'.[10]

Like Arthur, Colin Flockhart decided to join the Allied fight in the air and travelled a great distance to be able to do so. Another international volunteer, Colin was eighteen years old when he enlisted in the Royal Australian Air Force (RAAF) in 1942, completing his pilot training in stages in Australia and in Britain. After two years of training and moving around, and still only twenty years old, Colin found himself on the other side of the world to his home, flying operations in Lancasters with No. 619 Squadron.

As more and more people volunteered to join Bomber Command, it became necessary to look for places where training could take place out of range of the Luftwaffe. Rich with open spaces ideal for flying, in 1939 Canada agreed to provide facilities and training, inviting prospective aircrew from all over the Commonwealth. The Empire Air Training Scheme (EATS), also known as the British Commonwealth Air Training Plan (BCATP), was a joint military aircrew training programme created by the United Kingdom, Canada, Australia and New Zealand. The RCAF was relatively small in 1939, with only around 4,000 personnel and the facilities to train around 400 ground crew per year. It would be a huge undertaking to prepare to host EATS. Military flying instructors were joined by their civilian counterparts, and members of flying clubs helped too. Aircraft – including Lancasters – were built in Canadian factories, and farmer's fields were turned into air bases, runways and training schools. These schools were built to train aircrew in general flying, but also in their individual specialist trades. By the end of the war, there were EATS installations in every Canadian province, and US President Roosevelt called Canada 'the aerodrome of democracy'.

The Canadian people embraced their guests and did what they could to make them feel at home. By the end of the war, EATS had graduated 131,533 aircrew from all over the world, including 2,000 from France, 900 from Czechoslovakia, 680 from Norway, 450 from Poland, and around the same number of Belgians and Dutch. A similar programme was set up in South Africa, where the Joint Air Training Scheme trained 33,347 aircrew for the South African Air Force and other Allied air forces. Some Bomber Command personnel completed portions of their training in the United States, where the vast open skies were similarly safe from the Luftwaffe menace.

Some RAF units from the dominions were attached to the RAF under Article XV of the Empire Training Scheme. These were distinct dominion squadrons within the RAF's order of battle. These were known as Article XV Squadrons.[11] In October 1942, No. 6 Group Bomber Command was created. The Group would be manned entirely by Canadian airmen, and by VE day it would contain fourteen squadrons. No. 405 Squadron RCAF finished the war serving with the Pathfinder Force in No. 8 Group. In total, No. 6 Group flew 40,822 sorties during the war, dropping 126,122 tons of bombs. Not all personnel from Canada, Australia and New Zealand served in distinct, separate squadrons – some served in mainstream RAF squadrons, living, working and flying beside people from different countries. At one point, one in four aircrew personnel was from the Dominions. Of the 10,250 Canadians killed while serving with Bomber Command, 3,349 were killed overseas in Lancasters.[12] Around 10,000 Australians joined Bomber Command. They served in regular RAF squadrons, but in addition, eight Australian squadrons were formed: Nos 455, 458, 460, 462, 463, 464, 466 and 467 Squadrons.[13] Of the RAAF personnel serving in Bomber Command, 4,059 – more than one in three – were killed, constituting 20 per cent of all Australian combat losses in the Second World War.[14] New Zealand also made a significant contribution to Bomber Command's war. When war broke out in September 1939, the Royal New Zealand Air Force contained 756 full-time personnel and 404 territorials, and around 420 New Zealanders were serving with the RAF. A recruitment drive was launched to supply the Empire Air Training Scheme, and recruits travelled to Canada for training. They were then transported to Britain for operational service with the RAF. Around 10 per cent of the 7,002 Kiwi airmen to join via EATS served in one of the RAF's seven New Zealand Squadrons – Nos 75, 485, 486, 487, 488, 489 and 490. As many as 1,139 personnel of 75 (NZ) Squadron lost their lives during the war, in service in the RAF.

Also serving in the RAF in the Second World War, across all the commands and in every theatre of war, were thousands of aircrew who had managed to escape Poland. These men were fully committed to defeating the Luftwaffe, with the wider goal of defeating the evil that had taken over their homeland. At the start of the war, the Polish Air Force had managed, against the odds, to use their 300 aircraft to shoot down 126 of the Luftwaffe's 1,300 fighters and bombers. Most of the Polish airmen who remained after the battle escaped, joining the French Air Force until 1940, when France fell, and eventually making their way to Britain, which they called '*Wyspa Ostatniej Nadziei*' – 'The Island of Last Hope'.

Despite the fact the Polish fighters had survived two aerial campaigns and accumulated precious battle experience and knowledge of operational flying, the RAF was reluctant at first to let them fly in service. For one thing, there was a language barrier, and not being able to communicate in English was considered a major problem. As the need for trained pilots grew ever greater, however, the Polish airmen were included in the RAF's fight, and two Polish fighter units participated in the Battle of Britain. Nos 302 and 303 Squadrons fought impressively, and indeed 303 Squadron became the most successful Fighter Command unit in the entire battle.

In August 1940 the Polish Air Force was granted independent status, remaining under the command of the RAF, and over the course of the war it would contain fifteen squadrons, supported by 14,000 airmen and airwomen. English lessons and translated manuals and documents aided integration. The Polish contribution to the strengthening of the RAF's bomber force was crucial, with 300 Mazovian Bomber Squadron and 301 Pomeranian Bomber Squadron forming in July 1940.[15] These two squadrons were made up of men who had managed to get to England in late 1939 or early 1940. On 22 August, 304 Silesian Bomber Squadron was formed, and in September it was followed into existence by 305 Wielkopolska Bomber Squadron. Polish escapees from France and North Africa arrived to join the Polish squadrons and set about learning English and training to fly with Bomber Command.[16] By the time Arthur Harris assumed command in February 1942, the four Polish squadrons, containing up to seventy-six aircrews, represented around a quarter of the total force at his disposal.[17]

When the first of the 'Thousand-Bomber Raids' was launched on Cologne in 1942, 101 of the bombers involved were crewed by Polish airmen.[18] In March 1943, 301 Squadron was dissolved and some of its crews were seconded to 138 Special Duties Squadron at Tempsford, where they worked to transport people and supplies into and out of enemy-occupied Europe for the Special Operations Executive.[19] Polish squadrons in Bomber and Coastal Commands dropped 14,708 tons of bombs on targets in enemy-occupied territory and fought with exceptional skill, indestructible dedication and immense courage throughout the war.

In both the First and Second World Wars, Afro-Caribbean people volunteered to serve in the British military services – including in the Royal Air Force. These men and women served with dedication and courage – facing not only the dangers and difficulties of war but prejudice, discrimination and racism. When they arrived in Britain, many black volunteers found that very few British people had ever met a black person before. The RAF had no official 'colour bar' and in November 1940 recruited in British colonial territories without official prejudice. An Air Ministry Confidential Order confirmed this emphatically: 'All ranks should clearly understand that there is no colour bar in the Royal Air Force ... any instant of discrimination on grounds of colour by white officers or airmen or any attitude of hostility towards personnel of non-European descent should be immediately and severely checked.'[20]

Sadly, that did not always mean black personnel had an easy time enlisting, particularly in the African colonies where the colonial authorities made it difficult. According to the RAF Museum's 'Pilots of the Caribbean' exhibition, as well as the black British personnel who served, around 6,000 black Caribbean men volunteered for service with the RAF – 5,500 of them as ground staff and 450 as aircrew. In addition, around eighty women joined the WAAF – Sonia Thompson, for example, travelled to Britain from Jamaica and became a WAAF instrument repairer.[21] In February 1945, there were over 3,700 Jamaicans in the air force. In Africa, only sixty volunteers were accepted, but a further 5,200 joined the West African Air Corps, which supported RAF units based in Nigeria, Gold Coast (Ghana), Sierra Leone and Gambia.

Of the Afro-Caribbean aircrew who served, four fifths did so in Bomber Command. One of them was Flight Lieutenant William 'Billy' Strachan from Jamaica, who trained as a wireless operator and air gunner. Billy left Jamaica with little over £2 in his pocket and a suitcase containing a single change of clothes. He arrived in England in March 1940, and once he had qualified as a wireless operator/air gunner he completed a tour of thirty operations aboard Wellingtons. With no obligation to sign up for a second tour he decided to retrain as a pilot, and in 1942 he qualified. Pilot Officer Strachan served with 156 Squadron, of the Pathfinder Force, and Billy became famous for his risky but clever escapes from pursuing German fighters. 'The trick', he said, 'was to wait until the enemy was right on your tail and, at the last minute, cut the engine, sending your lumbering Lancaster into a plunging dive, letting the fighter overshoot harmlessly above.' Billy was eventually promoted to flying officer, and then to Flight Lieutenant.

Young black men selflessly and courageously fought beside their white colleagues in Bomber Command operations, and some lost their lives in service. To name just one, wireless operator/air gunner Sergeant Arthur Young was killed in July 1944, along with all six of his Lancaster crewmates, when their aircraft crashed. Despite the risks, people came from far and wide to join Bomber Command's aircrews, displaying courage beyond comprehension. Born in Trinidad, Philip Louis Ulric Cross watched what was happening in September 1939 and said, 'The world was drowning in fascism and America was not yet in the war, so I decided to do something about it and volunteered to fight in the RAF.' He travelled to Britain and trained as a navigator in the RAF, and was posted to 139 (Jamaica) Squadron at RAF Marham – the Squadron took its name from the fact that the bombers it flew were paid for by the people of Jamaica. A capable and courageous pilot, Philip was assigned to the Pathfinders as a navigator. With their important role of marking bombing targets accurately for the bomber force that would follow, the Pathfinders only selected the very best navigators, and Philip was exceptional in the role. By the end of the war, he had completed an incredible total of eighty operations. So well respected was he that in 1990 he was appointed High Commissioner for Trinidad and Tobago in London.

On the Ground

Vital to the smooth running of bomber operations were the aircraft ground crew. This group included engineers, scientists, weapons specialists and handlers, air traffic controllers, intelligence officers, cartographers and many people with wide and varying skills and abilities. Ground crew personnel were highly trained and specialised. Some of them came to their roles with existing knowledge and training. John David Murray, for example, had a degree in electrical engineering from Queen's University in Kingston, Ontario, when he joined the Royal Canadian Air Force in 1939. John was recruited because of his special engineering knowledge and skills. Lancaster navigators needed to be able to carry out calculations, at speed and consistently throughout each operation, and John was tasked with teaching them maths during their training.[22] Later in the war, he returned to civilian life and joined Victory Aircraft in Ontario, Canada, where Lancasters were assembled. John was the electrical engineer in charge of the electrical systems on the aircraft being produced.

Ground crew underwent rigorous training with the RAF, which was in-depth and specific to their area of expertise. Engine mechanics needed to accumulate vast amounts of knowledge and understanding of aircraft engines, for example. Lancaster ground crewman Kenneth Ball was an engineer who took a course on the operation of Lancaster bombsights – devices used by military aircraft to assist with dropping bombs as accurately as possible – which included studying the 'theory of bombing'.[23] Kenneth learned about things like bombing angles, sighting lines, the imaginary flight of perfect bombs and bombing trajectory and range, and his work involved a lot of mechanical drawings and complex data.

Once recruited as ground crew, the men and women of Bomber Command worked hard to possess the skills and knowledge that they needed to keep the Lancasters flying. The operational success of the aircrews depended on them. Before an aircrew could climb aboard their Lancaster ready for an operation, various things needed to happen on the airfield. For one thing, the aircraft had to be readied for the specific operation it would be taking part in. Each Lancaster had a dedicated team of ground crew assigned to it, made up of highly skilled individuals who worked efficiently and effectively as a team. They carried out a number of processes and procedures to ready the aircraft for operations. 'A Lancaster could go nowhere at all without fuel, the right amount of which had to be pumped into it from fuel tankers, or 'bowsers'. As with the Augsburg Raid, aircrew could sometimes tell roughly how far they would be travelling from the amount of fuel being pumped into their aircraft.

Then there were the bombs. Ground crew armourers handled the weapons, transporting the bombs from their storage locations at the airfield to the waiting aircraft, using trains of long, low trollies connected together like carriages on a train. One load of bombs for a single aircraft could cause serious damage if anything went wrong – the airfield, and everything and everyone on it, could be blown to pieces, so it was important to handle them with great care. Armourers also loaded the Lancasters' machine guns with ammunition, checking over the guns to make sure they were in good working order.

All the tasks carried out would be double-checked by the ground crew non-commissioned officer (NCO), to ensure everything was correct – after all, lives depended on it. Mechanics, electricians, instrument fitters, fabric workers, engine fitters, airframe fitters, radio mechanics and spark-plug testers checked over each individual Lancaster and saw to it that the aircraft were working as efficiently as possible. Ground staff engineers carried out final checks in the Lancaster cockpit, checking oil and coolant temperatures and oil pressure, making sure the bomb bay doors were closed, that the flaps were where they should be and that the brakes, hydraulics, navigation lights and instruments were all working efficiently. Once they knew they were flying that day or night, the aircrew would also conduct tests on their Lancaster. This usually included an engine run, to check that all four engines were working well. All this did not come without risks. Working as a ground crew engine maintainer, Kenneth Warburton found that spending so much time in close proximity to roaring Merlin engines took a permanent toll. Kenneth had loved music before the war, but a lack of ear protection while working on the noisy Merlins damaged his hearing so badly that he told his son he 'gave his hearing to the country'.[24]

If there were any issues at this point, the ground crew belonging to the Lancaster had some time to correct faults and make sure the bomber would be ready to take off on time. If an aircraft was found to have a fault that could not be fixed quickly enough, a spare bomber would be allocated – which was considered to be bad luck. The aircrews relied heavily on their ground crews to keep the Lancasters working as well as possible, and the ground crews looked after their aircraft lovingly and with the highest possible attention to detail. Once the final mechanical and electrical checks were complete, the aircraft could be cleared for operations, and signed over to the aircrew who would be flying it.

It took a number of people to keep a bomber station and its aircraft running efficiently. Men and women filled all sorts of roles, from cooks and clerks to storekeepers like Hugh Gascoyne and radar mechanics like John Johnson. Hugh was in charge of a store on RAF Methwold, keeping the station's personnel supplied with what they needed on a daily basis. Hugh had joined the RAF in 1934 at the age of eighteen, and spent several years overseas in Iraq, Egypt and Libya before returning to England in 1941. 'Lancaster bombers were at RAF Methwold during my time there and I would often count them out on raids wondering how many of those brave lads would return. One pilot who had a dog called Whisky sadly never returned, so I looked after his dog who became a great companion, sleeping in his own chair in my bunk area with plenty to eat and a ready supply from the sergeants' mess.'[25]

When John Johnson arrived at RAF Methwold, he had to get to know the layout of the site. 'After the usual booking-in rites, while sleeping for the first couple of nights in a small shed, I was assigned a bed in a Nissen hut about a mile from the radar station.' Most people on airfields used bicycles to get around, and John was issued one when he arrived. With more than thirty Lancasters using the airfield, plus spares, there was a pressing need for more ground crew. John worked on aircraft radar equipment, making sure it remained in good working order for operations. He was promoted: 'Still an "erk", I had now risen to the dizzy height of aircraftsman, first class.' An 'erk' was the RAF equivalent of the British Army's 'Tommy' – an airman below NCO status. 'It is the Erk', the Air Ministry proclaimed, 'who keeps the RAF in the air, maintains its bombers, fighters, transport and training aircraft.' The work of the ground crews did not, the Air Ministry recognized, look as 'spectacular' as the work of pilots, but the pilots, it assured, knew how much they depended on men like John, who did jobs 'without which the big job could not go on.'[26]

Ground crew could find themselves living and working on an air station with people from all over the world. John Johnson worked at RAF Methwold with fellow radar mechanic Thomas Durosimi Sigismund Johnson from Sierra Leone, and they were joined by another radar mechanic from Nigeria. John also made friends with Ken Rough, a Canadian radar mechanic. 'I have always admired Ken and his stance to the war in Europe. Early in the war he sold all that he had and volunteered to go to Britain and join in the fighting, truly believing that he might not be coming back.'[27] John and Ken shared their Nissen hut with a mixed bunch of trades, including both bomb and gun armourers.

Hugh Gascoyne remembers being lucky in that the food at RAF Methwold was particularly good, 'and much preferred to the food in the Western Desert – and of course no sand storms to worry about'.[28] The dining room area doubled as a dance hall, and Hugh remembers dances being frequent and well attended. Sometimes, when things were quiet on the station, ground crew used their time and skills toward personal projects. Radar officer Sam Fox was a tinsmith in civilian life. Soon-to-be married, Sam would use scraps of aluminium to make pots and pans for his bride as a surprise. Once the pots were completed, he'd store them in the bottom of the valve cupboard, which was usually locked. One day, the base commander carried out a surprise inspection and asked to see inside the cupboard. Sam duly opened it, and the commander spotted the pans. 'Whose are these?' he demanded to know. With what John Johnson describes as a 'stroke of genius', Sam answered, 'Yours sir!' and the pans became an unintentional gift to his superior officer rather than to his new wife.

Due to the 'manpower crisis' – the vacuum left in the pool of labour Bomber Command could draw from, created by the need for as many men as possible to serve in combat and overseas – women filled many roles on bomber stations alongside their male colleagues. On 28 June 1939, the Women's Auxiliary Air Force was established for duty with the RAF. Mobilized on 28 August 1939, the purpose of the WAAF was to substitute women into non-combatant RAF roles, so men could be released for front-line duties. At first women volunteered to join the WAAF, and after conscription was introduced for women in December 1941, even more joined.

By 1945, a quarter of a million women of forty-eight different nationalities had served in the WAAF, in over 110 different trades. They played an integral role in keeping the RAF functioning and fighting, and many worked on bomber stations. They supported Bomber Command as nurses and medical staff, and as domestic staff keeping the quarters and messes clean and supplied. They were also storekeepers and cooks, keeping everyone fed and watered – no small task on a bomber station, particularly with rationing in place throughout the war. WAAF parachute packers supplied airmen with their parachutes before every operation, having taken the utmost care to pack the parachutes as well as they could, in the knowledge that they might be the only thing standing between an airman and a horrible death. Ron Pain was immensely grateful to the WAAF after his parachute saved his life when he bailed out of his Lancaster. After the war, he went personally to thank the WAAF in the parachute section for supplying him with a parachute that 'worked perfectly'.[29]

Women also worked in roles that were, prior to the outbreak of war, reserved exclusively for men. WAAF signals officers maintained and tested the intercom systems in Lancasters on the ground between operations, and worked as mechanics and electricians looking after equipment around the station. Mary Clayton Gedhill was responsible for trolley accumulators and worked in a large hangar overlooking the main runway. This could be a dangerous place to work: 'One day a German aircraft followed our kites in early one morning and created just a little mayhem before being sent about his business! I don't think anyone was hurt.'[30] Trolley accumulators were used to start aircraft engines and to carry out various systems checks on the ground, and Mary had to take a six-month course to qualify as an electrician to work with them. Another member of the WAAF, Clare Kemp, worked in signals, initially in the Signals Office at RAF Methwold. 'My saddest moments', she says, 'were having to read off the board the missing aircraft after an operation. In this section the atmosphere was always tense throughout the night when we were on watch.'[31] Later, Clare worked in the radar section for 149 Squadron at Methwold:

> This time there were four WAAFs to a section of men mechanics, a number of them were Canadians. At first we WAAFs felt very inadequate and I felt sure that the lads felt lumbered at a very vital time. However, time was short and work excessive, so there we were. There were a few jokes and remarks at our expense, then we were soon accepted...

Clare and her colleagues maintained the radar systems on Lancasters. 'Strangely enough, the men would stop swearing immediately when my pal Freda and I appeared on the Lanc,' she says.

> And never once can I say that the men were anything but helpful to us. Freda was on the short side – not so easy when you are trying to pull yourself and the radar equipment into a Lanc. We fell in sometimes, laughing. I was popular in one respect since I always had warm hands (still have), even when the snow was about, and many times the electricians etc. would find that their hands were too cold to fix that awkward nut or screw, then I would come into my own when they enlisted my help. I can only hope that we airwomen played a small but useful part in what was going on.

Personnel working on bomber stations often became very close, experiencing the best and worst of times together. 'There are many memories of playing snowballs outside the radar section,' Clare says, 'and sad times when our lads came back shot up. Even sadder moments when after an op we poured tea for the crews, and with notebook in hand ready for fault-finding in the radar equipment we learned that some would never come back.'

Ground crew often lived and worked in challenging conditions and had to find ways to overcome daily challenges. The Nissen huts they slept in were often cold and draughty, and though they contained heat systems of sorts, fuel could be hard to come by. John Johnson explains:

> A pot-bellied stove sat in the middle of the Nissen hut, with a supply of coke for fuel. Coal was too valuable a commodity to be given to mere airmen. We each took turns to clean out the stove and sweep the Nissen hut floor. Making the fire meant finding newspaper and wood to get things started and they weren't easy to come by, so we needed to forage. One day one of the other 'trades' decided to give the fire lighting job a boost. After adding the paper, wood and coke in order, he poured a little gasoline onto the coke. Then he went looking for a match. Meanwhile the gasoline was turning to vapour. When he put a match to the paper via the small door at the bottom of the stove there was a bang, the lid of the stove shot up into the air, the ball of paper, untouched by the flames, shot out through the door at the bottom of the stove and made it to the Nissen hut front door ... and the fire was burning merrily!

Aircraft dispersal areas were on exposed airfields, where they were at the mercy of the weather, whatever time of year. It could get very cold and wet, with wind and snow in the winter. Pilot Doug Harvey remembers his ground crew:

> They worked in rubber boots, turtleneck sweaters and sleeveless leather jerkins. They would get cold and wet, clambering up the metal scaffolding, changing props or guns or aerials. The two hangars on the base were only used for major overhauls, all other work was done in the open, day or night, rain or shine. Ground crew were masters of improvisation, designing and making special tools that could make the work go faster.[32]

Ground crews sheltered as best they could, often not much warmer inside the hangars than they would be outside. It was important to keep the airfields hidden from prying Luftwaffe eyes, so it was common for them to be blacked out, meaning that ground crews might have to work in some degree of darkness. The work could be dangerous. John Johnson remembers a poster on the wall of his radar section warning of the dangers of the very high voltage of the equipment he was working with, with the caption: 'Remember, you're a long time dead'. John soon accumulated personal experience of why the poster was necessary:

> In order to check out a set it is arranged on the work bench fully connected and running but with the outer cases of each unit removed so that you could get to the innards for testing. Only in this way can you check the various voltages with an Avometer and waveforms with an oscilloscope. A good practice was to put one hand in your pocket and in that way you couldn't ground yourself on a piece of the equipment while poking at some high voltage with the other hand. On this particular occasion, a radar mechanic was checking the innards of an H2S set. In the next moment, he was flung across the room and his hand disappeared somewhere up under his armpit. He had hit a 10,000 volt contact. Luckily, the resultant current caused the voltage to drop very rapidly and all he got was a very nasty shock, both electrical and personal. But he could just as easily have been killed. All radar mechanics received shocks of one kind or another during their working career and after a while it seemed that, although we never got used to them, we built up a slight immunity.

John remembers dangerous incidents on his air station. Not long after he arrived at RAF Methwold, something happened to one of the bombs in the bomb dump that meant it was live and needed to be defused. This was an extremely dangerous job – if the bomb had detonated, it would have ignited all the others in the bomb dump. Ground crew personnel like Philip Lamb (one of the more than 5,500 black Caribbean volunteers mentioned earlier) put themselves up for the dangerous role of bomb disposal and were called upon when things like this happened. 'Two armourers worked on the bomb for two days,' John remembers, 'eventually rendering it safe. Meanwhile an area was marked off and it was necessary to detour around the neighbouring area of the perimeter track if you wanted to go to the other side of the airfield. Later it was announced that the two airmen in question had been awarded a "Mentioned in Dispatches" for their achievement.' On another occasion, John was underneath a Lancaster that was being loaded with bombs:

> The last bomb had been taken from the trolley and had been almost completely winched up into the bomb bay, the trolley having been taken away. I was walking under the Lancaster towards the Jennie [generator], when either the winch cable broke or the bomb clip disconnected, and the bomb dropped just behind me. Another foot or two and I would have been 'brained' ... or de-brained. The safety pin was secure and all that happened was a bent fin. Only shortly before this we had heard of a Lancaster, PD 325 of 514 Squadron at Waterbeach, that had gone up due to the premature explosion of one of the bombs. We learned that two radar mechanics had been seen pushing their generator away from the aircraft just before the incident. They just disappeared, no trace of them or the Jennie ever being found.

Planning an Operation

Bomber Command operations were never as simple as aircrews running out to their aircraft, climbing in and taking off. A lot of work had to happen before a bomber could get airborne safely, carrying who and what it needed to complete its daunting task. Some of the processes behind bomber operations took weeks – some took months. Others happened minutes before the aircraft took off. All were of vital importance.

Around a million men and women worked on the ground supporting and enabling Bomber Command, across four distinct stages to bombing operation. First, the action had to be carefully planned, in as much detail as possible. Then the aircrews had to be briefed and given the information they needed to carry out the operation to the best of their ability. Next, it was over to the aircrews to carry out the job, and finally, when – if – they returned, they needed to be debriefed so any valuable information they had on what was happening in enemy-occupied territory could be collected and used in future operations.

Many people were involved at every stage. In order to utilize the bomber force at maximum effectiveness and efficiency, planners needed timely and reliable information. The command's main report in 1945, 'The War in the Ether', stated that without the 'extraordinary range and accuracy' of intelligence with which it had been provided, 'no worthwhile' offensive effort could have been possible.[33] Operations staff worked together with intelligence personnel, collecting, analysing and sharing information that could help to determine when, where and how it would be most useful to deploy the bomber force. Various sources provided this crucially important information, including aerial reconnaissance photographs taken over enemy-occupied territory, intercepted enemy communications and information collected during the debriefing of aircrews after they had completed an operation. Notably, much of this intelligence work was carried out by the WAAF.

All this data was used to decide which targets would be hit, what types and loads of bombs should be used and how much fuel would be needed to carry out the operations. Intelligence also factored into route-planning, helping navigators to steer their crews away from known areas where enemy defences were particularly hazardous. The information might reveal, for example, where enemy anti-aircraft defences were particularly strong or weak, which could mean the difference between the success or failure of an operation – and between life and death for the aircrews involved.

Intelligence Officer Joan Baughan kept records of the most up-to-date information on enemy defences, including fighter aircraft, gun sites, balloons and searchlights, and made regular changes to a large map of north-west Europe, which showed the disposition of the Luftwaffe. Using information from enemy communications supplied by Bletchley Park, the home of British codebreaking during the Second World War, she paid particular attention to where the Luftwaffe concentrated its night fighters. WAAF at Bletchley Park and at Y Service interception stations around the country tapped into German land, air and sea communications to supply such information. Joan kept a book of information which was picked up and taken to Winston Churchill at the weekends. It contained numbers and types of RAF bomber aircraft sent on operations, routes taken to and from the targets, bomb loads, losses and information gleaned from crew debriefs. Sometimes the information Joan had to process came through her teleprinter in a 16ft-long list, nicknamed the 'toilet roll', and it was her job to read it all and reproduce it in a concise report for operational use. Joan enjoyed the work, saying: 'We were all so happy, wrapped up in the work that had to be done, as well as putting our heart and soul into it. We did not leave a single stone unturned in case it caused death and sorrow.'[34]

WAAF also worked as watchkeepers, ensuring the commanding officers on bomber stations were supplied with the most recent information collected on the station's own aircraft and crews prior to, during and after operations. Also working in intelligence, WAAF watchkeeper Audrey Smith spent her shifts receiving information over the scrambler phone in the station's operations room. She felt a 'tremendous thrill and pride to do the job'.[35] Information she collected would be used that day or night to brief the aircrews and underpinned the entire operation. Another WAAF member, Eileen Smith, worked at RAF East Kirkby, a Bomber Command station home to 57 and 630 Squadrons and their Lancaster bombers, in a building with no windows. She prepared the call signs for the aircrews – codenames used to identify them over the radio in place of their real names – and distributed them prior to an operation taking place. Grace Hall worked in the operations room at RAF Mildenhall, receiving the target information for the impending operation. Often she would know what the target for that day or night was before it was confirmed to anyone else on the station. This information came through on the scrambler phone from the RAF Group Controller to all stations in the group. Grace was surprised when she broadcast information over the loudspeaker on her station for the first time and 'received an immediate and interesting variety of telephone calls, including one offer of marriage from the senior flying control officer', who was not used to working with 'golden voiced' WAAFs.[36]

Edna Skeen – the 'Map Queen' of RAF Scampton – catalogued and organized thousands of maps covering most of the world. Able to find whatever she was asked for at a moment's notice, she supplied navigators and bomb aimers with maps and charts for operations and could be on duty for twenty-four hours at a time. She was given caffeine tablets to help her stay awake and only slept when the aircrews were out on operations. Map clerks pinned up the dreaded red string on the maps in the briefing rooms that showed the routes the crews would take that day or night.

Joan, Audrey, Eileen, Grace and Edna worked under conditions of extreme secrecy in atmospheres charged with pre-operation tension. The men and women involved in the collection and dissemination of intelligence in Bomber Command took their jobs very seriously and worked long, often tense hours, aware that the more information an aircrew was armed with, the more chance they had of surviving the operation ahead.

Men and women from all over the world joined Bomber Command, performing a wide variety of jobs and applying a range of skills and abilities to ensure that Allied bombers could take the fight to the enemy. Whatever their role, every single one of them was vital to the overall effort. They faced tough conditions and dealt with immense pressure, aware of how important their work was in the wider Allied fight – and knowing that the losses would be high. As Lancasters continued to be produced, they would become familiar to many of the air and ground crew personnel on bomber stations who would fly and care for them. The Lancs lining the airfields were sturdy symbols of hope that the offensive effort against Nazi Germany might succeed and that one day it might all be over. The aircraft meant a lot to everyone who worked with them, and the ground personnel looked after them as if they were living, breathing loved ones. More than to anyone else, though, the Lancasters were special to the courageous men who would fly them into battle, risking everything to do so.

CHAPTER THREE

AIRCREW

Becoming an Airman

DURING THE SECOND WORLD WAR, a total of 125,000 men – all of them volunteers – served in Bomber Command aircrews. The vast majority of them were in their late teens or early twenties, but some were older. Around 25 per cent of them were officers, and to begin with young civilian volunteers joined the RAF and were commanded by RAF officers who had belonged to the service before the outbreak of war. As the conflict went on, these young men became hardened professional airmen, displaying incredible courage, strength and character in the face of immense danger and difficulty. A typical tour for aircrew personnel was thirty operational flights. If they were lucky enough to survive their first tour, aircrew would take a six-month break, during which they worked as instructors training new airmen. They could then, if they chose to, volunteer for a second and final tour. It was vital that a Bomber Command aircrew could work effectively together as a team. Each member of the crew had their own individual, specialist role, but they all relied on one another to make it through their dangerous operations.

Having been accepted into the RAF, Bob Jay continued in his civilian life and waited patiently to be officially called up. Enlisted

'D.P.E.' – 'for the duration of the present emergency' – he was given the rank of Aircraftsman Second Class, and a few months later he was called up for basic training. Bob attended No. 3 Aircrew Receiving Centre at RAF Regent's Park in London. In the first few weeks of his RAF career, he received a regulation haircut, a thorough dental check (at which time he lost most of his top teeth), inoculations against diseases like diphtheria and typhoid, and his basic RAF kit, including 'service dress' uniform (or 'Best Blues'). Trainee aircrew had a white insert in their caps which identified them as not yet fully qualified. Bob marked all of his kit with his service number and learned how to keep it all spotlessly clean. He was also issued with a pair of identity discs, made of fire-resistant material and marked with his service number, name and religion. It was chillingly clear why he would need to wear them on operations – for identification, should the worst happen. Another volunteer, Roy Briggs, was deferred for three months before his call up, and when it came he was called to Lord's Cricket Ground in London, where an RAF reception centre had been set up. 'We went in the long room and had our injections,' Roy says. Then came the FFI ('free from infection') examination. 'W. G. Grace was up on the wall,' Roy chuckles. 'When we dropped our trousers, they told me they turned him around.'[1]

Once inducted into the RAF, the men underwent basic training – several weeks of rigorous fatigues, inspections, training drills, lectures and exams. Then, trainee airmen appeared before an RAF interview committee to determine which aircrew role they would be assigned. One of the committee looked at Harry Parkins' recruitment papers and said, 'It's got down here you can mend clocks, is that right?' Harry nodded. 'Well,' said the Group Captain, 'that sounds like a bit of engineering, so maybe a flight engineer will be OK for you.'[2] It was common when assigning roles to RAF and WAAF personnel to identify existing skill sets and aptitudes and match these with available roles.

After basic training, trainee aircrew were sent to Initial Training Wings (ITW). This stage of their training would prepare the airmen by inducting them into the discipline, physical fitness and frame of mind needed in the RAF, and provided knowledge of the service itself. The syllabus included things like aircraft recognition, aerial reconnaissance and learning about engines, instruments, meteorology, navigation, signals and the principles of flight. It also covered armaments, introducing the cadets to the use and safe handling of weapons. Aircrew were issued with war service uniforms and flying clothing, consisting of a helmet with oxygen and communication mask, goggles, a flying suit, a life jacket (known in the RAF as a 'Mae West') and a parachute harness.

Continually assessed throughout the course, the trainees had to pass examinations in order to be able to progress to the next stage of their training. They then proceeded to more specialised training at intermediate and advanced levels, according to their assigned role in the aircrew. The training was a mixture of theory (including mathematics and various aspects of mechanics and engineering) and flying, taking place both in the classroom and in the air. A typical Lancaster crew consisted of seven members: pilot, flight engineer, navigator, bomb aimer (who doubled as a front gunner), the wireless operator, the mid-upper gunner and the rear gunner.

Pilot

The role of the pilot was to fly the aircraft and give directions to the other crew members. Regardless of his rank or age, the pilot was the 'Skipper', the leader of the seven-man crew. Pilot recruits received a certain amount of ground instruction, covering topics such as navigation and the principles of flight and maths, before taking to the air. Posted first to an Initial Training Wing, and then to an Elementary Flying Training School, it was common to learn to fly the de Havilland Tiger Moth – a training aircraft that served to provide the majority of the RAF's pilots with their elementary instruction. Initially, trainee pilots flew with an instructor sat beside them, and once they were ready they would fly solo. Then it was on to bombers.

Pilot Hugo Trotter initially trained on Airspeed Oxfords and Vickers Wellingtons, improving his flying skills and learning about bombing. As a 'sprog' pilot, he flew as a 'second dickie' with an already qualified crew, watching them and learning from them before he'd have to fly alone with his own crew. 'The first few trips I did were on French marshalling yards. Dijon, Villiers etc., to stop ammunition and supplies going out to the German front,' he says.[3] Pilots also had to learn how to approach a landing strip, both with power from the engines, and without. Lancaster pilot Bryan Coventry listed elements of his early training as including things like familiarity with the layout of the cockpit, the effect of the controls, taxying, straight and level flying, stalling, climbing and gliding, taking off into wind and his first solo flight.

If they passed the elementary level, trainees moved on to advanced pilot training at Service Flying Training Schools, where they began to fly more powerful aircraft. The classroom study continued, and the pilots had to pass final exams. Bryan listed further training to include things like low flying, steep turns, forced landings, action in the event of fire, abandoning the aircraft – for which the pilot would need to give the order in real operations – restarting engines during flight, aerobatics and evasive manoeuvres, air navigation, night flying and formation flying.[4] It was important that pilots could carry out evasive manoeuvres in bombers, to escape enemy fire if necessary. Evasive action could be violent – rear gunner Don Miller remembered his pilot falling out of his seat once during a steep evasive dive.[5]

It could take between six months and two years for a pilot to be fully trained. Ultimately, the pilot of a Lancaster bore great responsibility for his crew and had to lead them competently and confidently in the face of great danger. Gunner Bob Howes said after the war that he put his survival mostly down to his pilot, Freddie Belasco, who had been a peacetime commercial pilot. Freddie was able to use his experience to deviate off-course when necessary, to keep his crew alive.

Flight Engineer

The flight engineer's responsibility was to ensure the smooth running of the aircraft, as well as covering for the pilot when necessary. He sat in the 'dicky' seat, which folded up, beside the pilot. The duties and responsibilities of the flight engineer included the operation of the controls at the engineer's station, which meant a lot of watching gauges and levels. He advised the pilot 'as to the functioning of the engines and the fuel, oil and coolant systems, both before and during flight' and ensured 'effective liaison between the captain of the aircraft and the maintenance staff by communicating to the latter such technical notes regarding the performance and maintenance of the aircraft in flight'.[6] The flight engineer was on standby at all times, not just to assist the pilot in 'being able to fly straight and level and on a course' but to act as a gunner when necessary and to carry out practicable emergency repairs during flight.

Flight engineers had to accumulate vast amounts of knowledge and understanding in a relatively short space of time. After passing basic RAF and initial aircrew training, Bob Jay attended No. 5 S.o.T.T. ('School of Technical Training') at RAF Locking. This was where he completed the first phase of his 'trade' training as a flight engineer – a ten-week course of preliminary training on airframes, engines, carburettors, electrics, instruments, hydraulics and propellers.[7] Once he passed this, he was allowed one week's leave, followed by a posting to No. 4 S.o.T.T. at RAF St Athan in south Wales. There, he completed the second and third phases of his training. The second phase was a seven-week intermediate course, and the third and final phase was a seven-week advanced course on a specific service-type aircraft, which included spending time at an aircraft factory.

Flight engineers studied things like fuel and oil systems, hydraulic, pneumatic and electrical systems, aeroplane controls (trimming tabs, undercarriage control, flaps control, bomb doors), engine controls and operating data (including data on the Merlin XX engines, flying limitations, position error corrections, recommended operating speeds etc.).[8] They also learned about emergencies they might need to deal with, such as engine failure during take-off or in flight, emergency operation of the flaps and undercarriage, bomb jettisoning, fuel jettisoning, crash and parachute exits, dinghy and ditching, hydraulic failures and oxygen systems. All flight engineers were issued with a book of notes on their aircraft – 'Flight Engineer's Notes' by A. V. Roe & Co. Ltd, for instance – which they were expected to supplement with information from other official publications, weekly orders and other approved sources.[9]

After passing his final week of training – a week filled with written and oral exams – Bob Jay attended his 'passing out' parade, where he was presented with his flight engineer's brevet and promoted to the rank of sergeant (the minimum rank for aircrew). This was accompanied by a pay rise. He would go on to fly Lancaster bombers on operations.

Navigator

At the age of eighteen, Peter Carpenter volunteered for the RAF at his local recruitment centre. After undergoing the usual extensive medical examination, he was accepted and assigned the position of navigator. The navigator in a Lancaster crew sat behind the pilot and the flight engineer, at a table where he could spread out his charts and maps. He used instruments to register the airspeed, which helped him to work out where the aircraft was, and kept notes on altitude, turning points and manoeuvres. The navigator was responsible for following a predetermined course to get to the target and another to get the aircraft back to its home base. Of course, it was not always possible to stick to the prescribed routes, and it was the navigator's job to plan alternative routes when necessary. The role was once said to be like 'taking a seven-hour maths exam while people tried to kill you'.[10]

Accuracy was of the utmost importance, and navigators had to work fast, non-stop throughout the flight. They were trained to use instruments and mathematics to direct their aircraft safely to the target and back, but they also learned to navigate using the stars. Peter remembers a sort of 'probationary period' as a navigator, during which his flight logs were analysed and plotted back. On his third trip, he was told after submitting his flight log: 'Excellent trip ... One more like this and you will be fully trained.' Eventually, he became 'trusted', and though his logs were checked they were not vetted to the same extent. Based at Elsham Wolds with 103 Squadron, Peter soon learned the importance of being able to work accurately *and* quickly. This, he says, when combined with good anticipation, was the key to success. 'Even now, and in my mind's eye, I see that great navigation sign – "Keep on track, keep on time, keep on living".'[11]

The navigator pored over his maps, which showed the location of take-off and of the target. He would write any additional information he needed onto the map – additional town or city names, for instance, as the maps sometimes only showed major ones – and he hand-drew the route to and from the target. Different coloured pencils and arrows showing the direction of travel differentiated between the route out and the route back. Secondary targets could be indicated by circling towns and cities. In addition to monitoring the progress of his aircraft on his carefully annotated maps, the navigator filled in charts at very regular intervals during the entire flight. At the top, the chart had information such as which squadron the aircraft was flying with, the aircraft number and letter, the names of the pilot and the navigator, the date of the sortie, the weather forecast (including temperatures and wind speed, at various altitudes), the expected times that the sun and moon would rise and set, the target, the estimated time of arrival over it and 'general observations' such as information on bombing, intelligence and enemy action.[12] Information would be constantly logged throughout the flight.

Different navigators had different ways of doing things. Peter says: 'On our operations, particularly early on, I used to like to take a look at the target. I always had the course out of the target ready and gave it to the pilot at "bomb doors open". I then repeated it after "bombs gone" and I think in common with most navs offered the course on an "as soon as it's possible" basis.' Navigator Charles 'Ches' Halford was commended by his crew as a 'first-class navigator' who was 'always calm and unflappable, partly because he had a reluctance to look out of the window of the aircraft when the situation was hectic'.[13] Just as with the pilot, the navigator played an important role in instilling confidence and calm in his crew. Peter, who was a navigator for a full tour of thirty sorties on a Lancaster, was commended for his 'successful and accurate work' in a variety of operations. His work was recognized in his recommendation for the Distinguished Flying Medal (DFM) as 'of especial value when attacking precision targets and his personal qualities of resource, determination and unfailing confidence have been an inspiration to his crew at all times'.[14] With his 'calm and quiet manner', his 'commendable courage and determination' and his 'skill as a navigator and strong devotion to duty', Peter was a 'source of inestimable confidence to his crew'.[15] In this way, Peter took his role extremely seriously: 'Generally in navigation terms I felt I coped OK and also felt I had the confidence of all crew members on our operations. Again, and like all of us, I felt heavily the need not to let the crew down.'

Bomb Aimer

The bomb aimer was responsible for guiding the aircraft on the 'bombing run'. His position was in the nose section of the Lancaster, where he would operate the bombsight. The bomb aimer also doubled as the forward gunner when necessary. Bomb aimers had an important job – it was on them to ensure that the bombs were dropped as accurately as possible, which was a huge responsibility. As the Lancaster made its final approach to the target, the bomb aimer guided the pilot and decided the exact moment that the bombs would be released. Al Lovett remembers undergoing extensive training to become a bomb aimer on Lancasters. After four weeks of studying mathematics and signals, he then attended an ITW for a twelve-week course, covering navigation, astronavigation, signals, mathematics, law and administration, weapons and gunnery, and most importantly theory of flight. Al passed his ITW exams and became a leading aircraftsman, ready to progress to the next stage of his training. Next stop was an EFTS at RAF Desford in Leicestershire. Al learned to fly in the Tiger Moth, and next he completed a Bombs and Components course.

There was one part of his training that Al found particularly memorable: 'One of the unusual experiences was when we had to enter a cylindrical tank and the air was extracted to simulate the pressure we would be expected to fly in at 25,000ft.'[16] Bomb aimers learned to fly so they understood how aircraft worked and flew – which would help them to instruct the pilot during the bombing run. They also learned about bombs and how they worked, and underwent extensive navigation training. Al's navigation training took place in Canada, where he learned to use new navigational and radar aids which were being introduced to help with accuracy. Through the clear Perspex in the nose of the Lancaster, the bomb aimer had a good view of the ground and would often be the first to see and be able to confirm exact location. He would use his view and his skills to direct the pilot when necessary, and it was vital that he be trained to a high standard to be able to do so.

Mid-Upper Gunner

The mid-upper gunner's role was to warn the pilot if enemy aircraft were sighted in the vicinity of the Lancaster and to return fire if they attacked. He would be confined to a hammock-style seat in his turret – a Perspex bubble – which could rotate through 360°, allowing him to shoot at enemy fighters in any direction. The turret contained two Browning .303 in. machine guns, each with 1,000 rounds of ammunition. The gunners had to learn how to assemble and disassemble these and practised relentlessly until they could do it automatically and without thinking. They were even trained to do the job blindfolded, to simulate the darkness of a night operation. Familiarity with their weapons systems would enable them to use them more effectively in chaotic emergency situations, so it needed to be second nature.

As with the rest of the crew, air gunners had to learn about flying and aircraft, but they also had to accumulate specialist knowledge of and experience with guns and ammunition. Like the other members of the Lancaster crew, the gunners were specialists in their fields. Air gunners were highly trained in air gunnery, including things like bullet trajectory and deflection. As well as extensive weapons training, they were also trained in aircraft recognition, to help them to distinguish enemy aircraft from friendly, and to give them specialist knowledge of enemy aircraft capabilities so they knew what they were up against and how best to fight it. Gunners also underwent turret training, which included learning how to maintain and operate the turrets they occupied. These were either electrical or hydraulic, powered by the aircraft's engines. During training, gunnery students used life-sized turrets on the ground to practise, and these were fitted with cine cameras which allowed them to see how accurate their shooting was. Training included live fire exercises on firing ranges, using both static and moving targets. The latter simulated air-to-air firing, in which both the shooter and the target would be moving. As well as completing classroom and ground training, air gunnery students also underwent aerial training. One aircraft deployed a target – in some cases a huge flag – in the air, and the students fired upon it from another. Again, cine cameras recorded their efforts to help them understand how they could improve.

Keith Sneddon enlisted in the RAAF in Melbourne, Australia, and training as an air gunner he practised circuits and landings, becoming familiar with Lancaster aircraft and going on cross-country practice flights. He also had to familiarize himself with the turret he'd spend long hours in and with the guns he would be using, and got some practice firing them over land and sea. After he qualified, Keith travelled to Adelaide and made the long journey to England, where he would serve as a mid-upper gunner.[17]

Like the other crew members, gunners needed to possess a high degree of skill, but they also needed endurance and courage. They were the protectors of the Lancaster and its crew, which was a big responsibility. Keith's DFM citation acknowledged his 'skill and fortitude in operations against the enemy' – qualities all gunners needed.[18] Mid-upper gunners and rear gunners were interchangeable and sometimes switched positions according to what was needed for an operation. Irish gunner Christopher Walsh and fellow gunner Ron Tootell spun a coin to decide which of the gun turrets they would occupy on their Lancaster. As a result, Chris became the mid-upper gunner and Ron took the rear turret.[19] *General Hints for Air Gunners*, a course at the No. 2 Bombing and Gunnery School in Canada, advised student air gunners to always search the sky before take-off and landing, when the aircraft would be at its most vulnerable. 'Always watch your own tail,' it advised the gunners, and 'never fire until fired upon.'[20]

It was important that the gunners understood their role, the course stated. Where the aim of an enemy fighter was to destroy, the aim of an RAF air gunner was to get safely to the target and back to base. All aircraft approaching them were to be considered enemy until identified otherwise, and if there was gun fire, the Lancaster should take evasive action – a series of quick and violent direction and altitude changes – while the enemy aircraft was located. Ammunition was to be conserved as far as possible. 'If your own guns fail or are damaged during an attack,' the gunners were told, 'use your ingenuity to outwit the attacker.' Teamwork was vital, and 'REMEMBER,' the guide said in capital letters, 'TO BE SURPRISED IS TO BE LOST'.

Rear Gunner

Like the mid-upper gunner, the rear gunner was responsible for continuously scanning the sky for enemy fighters and defending the Lancaster against attack. Nicknamed 'Tail-end Charlie', the rear gunner occupied the loneliest position in the aircraft, right at the back in the rear gun turret. Here, he was cut off from the rest of the crew – when entering the aircraft, everyone else turned right while the rear gunner turned left. He would climb into his turret and close the doors behind him. The turret rotated to allow the gunner a wider field of vision, and the doors had to be closed to prevent him from falling out. He was alone, enclosed in a capsule with his guns. An intercom system connected him to the rest of the crew, which was vital if he needed to warn them of the presence of enemy fighters. The crew could then remain in contact to co-ordinate their response – if an enemy fighter dropped out of range of one turret, it was important that another knew to be on the lookout, ready to take over.

Conditions on Lancasters were particularly difficult and dangerous for rear gunners. Sometimes the Perspex of the turret fogged up with condensation, and to be able to see clearly (which was vital when watching for enemy attackers) the gunner would push the Perspex out. This exposed him to the freezing cold air, for which his heated flying suit and thick gloves were not much of a match. Gunners needed to maintain good night vision at all times and had to get used to gazing into the darkness, straining to see potential threats. Experienced gunners knew not to look at fires or bright lights for long, as this would inhibit their vision. Rear gunners were at particular risk if anything went wrong because they were not already wearing their parachutes, which were too bulky to fit inside the turret. These were stored in the fuselage just behind the doors of the turret. To get out in an emergency, the gunner had to open the doors behind him and reach into the fuselage for his parachute. He then had to attach it to his harness and swivel his turret around to one side to bail out backwards. He had to do all of this at speed while a terrifying situation evolved around him, and the process required a cool head in the chaos.

Gunners were faced with the possibility of combat every time they took off and carried the heavy responsibility of defending their crew – their friends. Lancaster crews were tasked with a tremendously dangerous job, and it was important they were as confident as possible going in to an operation. Knowing that their aircraft was protected against enemy fire by mid-upper and rear gunners – however effective this protection was or was not – boosted their confidence.

Wireless Operator

Due to the highly technical nature of the work, the training for wireless operators was highly intensive. In addition to learning about flying and how to be part of an aircrew, wireless operators needed to learn how to look after, service and fix their radio equipment efficiently, as well as becoming proficient in Morse code, which they would likely have to use under intense pressure once operational. 'We would walk down the street putting the shop names into Morse,' says Roy Briggs.[21] 'We had to speed up and it helped.'

The wireless operator was responsible for maintaining contact between the aircraft and its base, which was important during take-off and landing on a busy bomber station. Like the other Lancaster crew members, a wireless operator had to go through general aircrew training, as well as specialist training for his trade. Sam Brookes chose the RAF when he was called up, and elected to train as a wireless operator. He reported to Lord's, for his induction into the RAF. 'I joined a squad of thirty likely lads,' he says, 'all destined to train as wireless operators.'[22] Sam was sent to an ITW, where he began his wireless training and started to learn Morse code. After this he went to No. 2 Radio School at Yatesbury, which was, he recalls, a huge wooden-hutted camp in the middle of nowhere, with a small grass airfield next door. 'We were all desperately keen,' he says, 'and training classes went on from 8 a.m. to 6 p.m., six days a week – Sundays off. Phew!' Sam had no problem with the theoretical side of the course but found it very difficult to achieve the speeds needed in Morse code. Despite this, he passed the course with excellent marks – 95 per cent for theory and 85 per cent for operating in the air – and proudly became a sergeant wireless operator, awaiting posting to an operational training unit (OTU).

Wireless operators also received instruction on wireless fault finding, Aldis lamp signalling, gunnery and emergency procedures. Wireless operators were responsible for their equipment, and checked and maintained it frequently and thoroughly. 'Every quarter of an hour we got a message containing a number,' Roy Briggs explains.[23] 'We had to keep logging them – it proved we were listening to the set. We also had to take readings from the electricals.' Roy remembers feeling lucky that in his position as wireless operator on the Lancaster, he benefited from the heat from the engines. Some wireless operators would get so warm they overheated and took off their heavy-duty flying boots. This was frowned upon, as if there was a sudden emergency, they would have to put them back on again very quickly or risk bailing out without any shoes on – not ideal if they landed in snow.

An Eighth Crew Member

Somewhat unusually, some Lancasters had an eighth crew member. In 1943, 101 Squadron converted from Wellingtons to Lancasters and began to use new technology and an eighth crew member to try to fool the Luftwaffe. The eighth man was a German speaker and a 'special operator' (SO), whose job was to disrupt enemy air communications by jamming Luftwaffe signals and to broadcast misinformation in German. Night fighters were guided toward Allied aircraft by ground controllers. The British Telecommunications Research Establishment at Malvern developed jamming equipment, known as 'Airborne Cigar', or 'ABC', that could be installed in Lancasters and used to identify German VHF frequencies and jam them.

The German-speaking SO could use the equipment to tune in to enemy radio communications. Speaking to them in their own language, he could then verbally direct the German night fighters away from the bomber stream and give them instructions that countered their real ones. His was a 'ghost voice', which could perfectly imitate the voices of German controllers. In a raid on Kassel, a German operator was so frustrated by the successful imitation of his own voice by an RAF SO that he had a 'violent outburst' over the radio waves. The SO responded: 'The Englishman is swearing now,' and the German controller replied, 'It is not the Englishman who is swearing, but me!'[24] The SO needed to know German to a reasonably high standard to be able to pull this off, and they needed to be skilled enough wireless operators to tune in to German frequencies when the Luftwaffe changed them. The SO also logged any information that would be relevant when the Lancaster returned home to an intelligence briefing.

While Sam Brookes was waiting for a posting to an OTU after completing his wireless training, something strange happened. One morning on parade, the NCO in charge asked anyone who had learned German at school to step forward. Sam hesitated for a moment, and then did so. He was soon told that his training would be cut short by a few months, and that he would be posted to a conversion unit to learn how to be a wireless operator on Lancasters. Sam was sent to No. 1 Lancaster Finishing School, where he accumulated ten hours as a passenger in Lancasters. 'The Lancaster was large, loud, fast and fierce,' he says.[25] Next, Sam found himself at No. 101 Squadron at Ludford Magna. He was going to be a SO. The first few days were spent on an introduction to the special radio equipment he would be using.

> To help identify the place to jam there was a panoramic receiver covering the same bands. The receiver scanned up and down the bands at high speed and the result of its

> travel was shown on a time base calibrated across a cathode ray tube in front of the operator. If there was any traffic on the band, it showed as a blip at the appropriate frequency along the line of light that was the time base. When a 'blip' appeared, one could immediately spot tune the receiver to it and listen to the transmission. If the language was German then it only took a moment to swing the first of the transmitters to the same frequency, press a switch and leave a powerful jamming warble there to prevent the underlying voice being heard. The other two transmitters could then be brought in on other 'blips'. If twenty-four aircraft were flying, spread through the Bomber stream, then there were a potential seventy-two loud jamming transmissions blotting out the night fighters' directions. The Germans tried all manner of devices to overcome the jamming, including having their instructions sung by Wagnerian sopranos. This was to fool our operators into thinking it was just a civilian channel and not worth jamming.

The ABC Lancasters had to be modified, and in addition to the jamming equipment they carried, complete with external aerials, they also had heavier machine guns than usual because the planes were particularly vulnerable. On a normal Lancaster there was a bed, but on an ABC Lancaster this was removed to make space for the eighth crew member and his equipment. The SO sat just aft of the main spar, immediately above the bomb bay and on the left-hand side of the aircraft. He wore a heated flying suit and heavy boots and gloves, which could make it tricky to operate his equipment – consisting of three transmitters and a cathode ray screen – and record information.

The SO needed to be able to concentrate for long periods of time, constantly listening, thinking and reacting to what was happening over the airwaves. A number of the SOs were German-speaking Jewish refugees, who were in particular danger if they were to bail out of the aircraft in an emergency and be captured in German-occupied territory. Before one mission, Reuben 'Ron' Herscovitz was quizzed by his friend and fellow SO J. A. Davies about why he carried a pair of civilian shoes slung around his neck on each of his thirty-six missions. He replied, 'My friend, if you are shot down, you will either be killed or taken to a proper prison camp under the control of the Geneva Convention. I am a Jew, and as the Herrenvolk would like to liquidate my race, I aim to get away from the wreckage as soon as possible. How can I possibly do that in heavy fur-lined flying boots?'[26] All of Ron's family had disappeared into Nazi camps, and as his RAF colleague Bruce Lewis said: 'The best way he could think of getting back at the Germans was to join Bomber Command.'[27]

Also a German-speaking SO, Leslie Temple completed thirty operations with 101 Squadron. Having spent four years in the Air Training Corps, he was conscripted into the RAF for aircrew duties. Leslie went through initial air training and a Lancaster conversion course and was trained as a wireless operator. 'I did all the examinations and so learnt Morse code pretty quickly,' he says. Leslie spoke fluent Yiddish at home and learned German at school. 'The fact that I had a knowledge of the German language made me that eighth member of the crew,' he says – he was posted to 101 Squadron.[28] SO work was top secret, and until he arrived at the squadron at Ludford Magna, he had no idea what he would be doing. 'I had my recording equipment and my equipment to listen in to the German transmissions, and I could hear the German language and I could understand what was going on, and I would transmit that to my skipper when anything was happening that was useful to us.' Leslie enjoyed working with his crew. 'We got on very well together,' he says.

Sam Brookes also enjoyed his time as an SO. He says:

> It was an absorbing time for keen, fit young men who thought only of the challenges and excitements of their task and little of the risks they were about to run ... Looking back I can see that all the things we were experiencing at this frenetic time were tremendous shocks to our systems.

> They left us ill equipped to take the apocalyptic decisions we were about to make and which, as it happened, would decide whether we lived or died.[29]

Special Operations

In addition to dropping bombs, Lancasters also participated in what were known as 'Special Operations'. No. 149 Squadron at RAF Methwold was one of the squadrons chosen for 'special duties'. This meant dropping supplies to the Special Operations Executive, an underground organization formed in 1940 to wage secret war in enemy-occupied territory. John Johnson was involved in preparing the Lancasters for these drops, ensuring each aircraft had a fully functioning and reliable radar set. He says:

> The containers being loaded on board were octagonal and a browny-orange colour. Each container carried its own individual number and also the total number of containers within that load, so that Resistance fighters would know exactly how many containers to look for in the dark.[30]

Sometimes, bombs that the Lancasters were supposed to be dropping would 'hang up', or not release from the aircraft properly. 'I can remember the concern the bomb armourers had that no hang-ups would happen on these trips,' John says, 'or some poor soul would be risking his or her life looking for a container that didn't exist.'

Wireless operator Tony Adams attended a ten-day 'battle course', designed to instruct aircrew in how to evade capture, how to contact an escape organization in an occupied country and the dos and don'ts if captured after being shot down. The course involved lectures, Tony explains, and 'getting photos taken in rough civilian clothes to be taken on operations with us so we could pose as farm workers on an identity card prepared by the Escape Organisation'.

Tony and his fellow aircrew spent dark nights crawling around muddy fields:

> Late one very dark night we had to go out on an escape exercise. This entailed being taken perhaps 30 miles away in a blacked-out truck or bus, being dumped on the roadside at some unknown place and being told to find our way back to Methwold by 4 p.m. the next day. Prior to leaving we were searched to ensure we had no money on us, dressed distinctively and given a card to carry that had to be marked by the Special Police, Home Guard and others who were notified of the role they had to play to 'capture' us. My bomb aimer and I were dumped near Wisbech, got captured about midnight and were very glad to reach Methwold by hitchhiking via King's Lynn after enjoying free beer from the patrons of a village pub who thought we had had to bail out ... and I'm afraid we didn't correct them![31]

Tony passed the course and was officially posted to 149 Squadron. 'We were told that it was a "Special Duties" squadron, very hush-hush, and under no circumstances were we to mention our activities to anyone. So my intention to keep a diary from that time was shelved for fear of a German spy finding it under all my dirty clothes in the bedside locker!'

Operational Training Units

After completing their training in their individual trades and being cleared for operational service, aircrew destined for Bomber Command were posted to an OTU for around ten weeks. Here, they would continue their training, learning to fly in their designated positions on real bomber aircraft, as opposed to the training aircraft they had flown so far.

This was a dangerous stage in the training process. OTUs were often given aircraft that were no longer fit for actual operational service, and the airmen were inexperienced in flying them. Even in their initial training, Bomber Command pilots were stretched and tested. In one particular incident, a skilful pilot, Owen Jones, was flying a Wellington over Wales on a cross-country navigation exercise. The aircraft suffered engine failure, and Owen's skills were tested as he flew it safely back to the base and made an excellent landing on one engine.[32] Some weren't as lucky, however, and more than 8,000 men were killed in training accidents and non-operational flying over the course of the war.

Navigator Peter Carpenter understood the odds. He spent around eight weeks at IOTU, training on Wellingtons, and during the training he completed a number of cross-country trips of over four hours in duration. On one such trip, Peter and his crew achieved fame by colliding with an enemy night fighter – a Ju88, in cloud at 18,000ft. 'I hasten to add that we were bang on track at the time,' he says. The pilot managed to turn back and land safely, despite having lost half the tail plane. 'This was dangerous stuff! In the event little was made of it and as a crew it certainly didn't affect our morale.'

It was at OTUs that crews were formed. Large groups of airmen arrived, all of different trades, and they would leave as organized aircrews for duty aboard specific aircraft – crews of seven men, in the Lancaster's case. Harry Parkins remembers the 'crewing up' process: 'The idea was you went into the bar, and there was a big area there where you mingled.'[33] To begin with, Harry found that airmen who had accumulated more flying hours weren't keen on accepting those with less experience. 'The first thing they would ask you is how many flying hours have you got,' he says. If an airman had none, they couldn't be sure he wouldn't get air sick or be too afraid to carry out his duties. Harry made sure he had some experience before it was his turn to 'crew up', by asking if he could accompany aircrews on practice flights.

Harry was approached by an Australian rear-gunner, who introduced him to a group of airmen from Australia and New Zealand.

When they asked if he would join them for a drink, Harry explained that he didn't drink at all. Then the mid-upper gunner offered him a cigarette. 'I don't smoke,' Harry said. The men looked at him, and the navigator asked, 'What the bloody hell do you do on Sundays?' 'That broke the ice,' Harry says, 'and I was in with the crew.' Pilot Benny Goodman says: 'Crews selected each other in what seemed a very haphazard manner, by talking to those we thought would be suitable, but I can't remember ever meeting any crew member who was subsequently dissatisfied and wanted to leave his original crew.'[34] Indeed, aircrews quickly formed close bonds. When Roy Briggs' crew assembled, they found that three of them were teenagers. 'So, we got together with a crew, and we stopped together,' he says.[35] 'That was very important.'

Heavy Conversion and LFS

As the number of Lancaster bombers available to Bomber Command increased, aircrew who had been flying other bombers essentially needed to be retrained to fly the new aircraft. For this, they were sent to Heavy Conversion Units (HCUs). When greeted by the Lancaster at his HCU, pilot Stevie Stevens was struck by the size of the aircraft. 'I thought, that's a pretty big aircraft, it was, of course, much bigger ...'[36] Flight engineer Harry Parkins had been flying on Stirlings: 'Then they said we were being converted onto Lancasters, and that was good because the Stirling was considered the flying submarine, and the Lancs could get up higher.'[37] Crews that were incomplete or had lost members at the point of leaving their OTU were completed at the HCU. For Peter Carpenter's crew, HCU was over in just ten days and consisted of two day cross-country trips and two night cross-country trips.

Flight engineer Bob Jay found he had been posted to an HCU ahead of the rest of his crew. This was usual for flight engineers, who had much more to learn on the new aircraft because of their responsibility for its systems and smooth operation. During training flights aboard Lancasters, the engineers practised three-engine landings, during which their skills would be heavily called upon. Bob's practice in three-engine landings later came in very handy, as on 27 March 1945 the Lancaster he was on lost an engine due to enemy fire during a raid on Hamm in Germany and he was forced to perform an emergency three-engine landing.

The more practice a crew could get in safety, the better chance they stood of coming home safely from operations. The HCU training flights included familiarization with the aircraft, circuits and landings, bombing practice, fighter affiliation and cross-country flying. These were usually conducted with experienced instructors aboard – usually aircrew who had completed a full operational tour – and were then repeated by the crew alone, without an instructor present. Flight engineers carried their emergency repair tool bags at all times, and filled in four-page flight engineer logs prior to, during and after every single flight.

After their time at the HCU, a crew destined to fly Lancasters was sent to Lancaster Finishing School (LFS). Aircrew often didn't have many hours logged in Lancasters before being released for operational flying. Peter Carpenter was sent to No. 1 LFS at Hemswell. 'This seemed to comprise little but circuits and landings (bumps),' he says, 'and took only three days to complete.' Immediately afterwards, with what he calls 'indecent haste', Peter's crew were posted to a squadron for operational service. Aircrew were trained to handle all sorts of emergencies aboard Lancasters.

Pilot Hugo Trotter attended No. 1 LFS at Hemswell. His logbook certified that he had 'completed lectures in, and is fully conversant with' the Lancaster's systems – including things like the fuel, oil and ignition systems – but that he was also fully trained in dinghy drill, abandon aircraft drill, crash landing drill, fire drill and bombing up drill. Recorded as an 'above average' pilot, Hugo had completed day circuits and night circuits, overshoots, feathering and stalling as both a second and first pilot in training. Still, having previously spent six months flying Wellingtons before converting to heavy bombers, he found Lancaster landings tricky. 'They dreaded my night landings,' he says of his crew with a chuckle. 'They were meant to be a proper three-pointer, but they were ghastly – kangaroo hops going down the runway.'

Once a crew had successfully converted to Lancasters, they were posted to an operational station. Bomb aimer Al Lovett was twenty-two when he arrived at RAF Methwold in January 1945 to begin his first tour of operations. Al's crew were told that they would belong to 149 (East India) Squadron. They were taken by train from Lindholme to Brandon in Norfolk and were picked up by a canvas-covered lorry – they had to stand up in the back throughout the journey. 'Upon arrival we reported to the guard-room at the main gate, then wandered around the dark and seemingly deserted airfield trying to find someone who would take an interest in our arrival. After a while we found the sergeants' mess and joined two WAAFs who were huddled around the kitchen stove. They kindly cooked some bacon sandwiches and gave us large mugs of tea which was most welcome.'[38]

A number of the station's aircraft were out on operations, and anyone not taking part was trying to get some sleep before the bombers came back. 'Soon we heard the engines of the Lancasters as they circled the now illuminated runways awaiting their turn to land. This was very new and exciting. We proceeded to the perimeter track near the control tower to watch the activities.' To the new crew's horror, one of the returning aircraft overshot the runway and crashed. 'Full of enthusiasm we ran towards it with the intention of assisting in any way we could,' Al says. 'To our surprise personnel were running in the opposite direction and in passing informed us that the aircraft had crashed on top of the bomb dump and that it may well blow up. Fortunately the crew escaped with minor cuts and bruises and the fire was quickly extinguished … This was our introduction to RAF Methwold and a foretaste of things to come.'

With such a short time spent converting to flying Lancasters and with relatively few hours of experience doing so, aircrews continued to learn and perfect their skills during their first operations. 'You had plenty of power,' pilot Stevie Stevens says.

> But when you were taking off with a bomb load and you had the wind coming across, the tail would swing, and it was quite difficult. You had to make absolutely certain you were strapped into the seat and really push hard on the rudder and sometimes use the trimmer as well, just to keep the thing straight on the runway. As soon as you'd started, the aircraft would take the air, but not stable air, and quite often it would blow off track, so you had to push hard to get back to where you wanted to go.

Like many pilots who flew the Lancaster, Stevie held the aircraft in high esteem. 'The Lancaster was an incredible aircraft, just superb. It was infinitely better than any other heavy aircraft.'[39]

CHAPTER FOUR

ON OPS

Before an Operation

AIRCREW ON BOMBER STATIONS DIDN'T KNOW if they would be flying on a given day or night until orders were posted on a noticeboard. 'It was a strange feeling,' wireless operator Bruce Rawling says, 'to see our crew's name up on the operations list…'[1] If aircrew were going on a daylight raid, they might be woken up as early as 2 or 3 a.m. 'You are woken from a deep sleep by a torch shining in your face', Bruce Rawling explains, 'and a voice saying, "Time to get up Flight Sergeant, breakfast in one hour and main briefing at 7 a.m." After dressing we would mount our trusty bikes and ride to the mess.'

Once they knew they'd be needed, the ground crews got to work checking over and preparing the Lancasters. Many aircrew had little rituals they kept to if they were flying. Wal Cryer says: 'I did what I did before every operation – I had a shower and put on some clean, fresh clothes. It lifts one's morale, but it was quite an ordeal. The month was December. The season was winter. There was a cold wind blowing and like all shower rooms in the air force it was air-conditioned by not having any doors.'[2] The planning and intelligence staff had prepared every detail of the operation they feasibly could, and what needed to happen when. From the intended estimated time of arrival of the bombers over the target, they worked backwards to calculate when the aircrews would need to be briefed, when they'd need to check over the aircraft and when they'd need to take off. They also worked out what Wal called 'egg eating time' – the time when an aircrew would eat before heading out on a sortie.

The cooks on bomber stations did a very important job, keeping the ground and air crews fuelled so they could carry out their duties with enough energy and strength. On a more sinister note, 'such a lavish meal (on British wartime standards) was considered necessary to sustain any crews that may be shot down,' airman Bob Cox explains.[3] If this happened over enemy territory, the crew would need to find their way home via escape lines, and they might not be able to eat for days.

Lucy Jane Lillie, the first WAAF cook to be appointed warrant officer, had been trained by her mother and was a 'very clever cook'. She joined the WAAF in 1939 and cooked at Bomber Command stations throughout the Battle of Britain and the Blitz, carrying on 'through bombardment with calm and courage'.[4] The cooks on bomber stations needed to be clever like Lucy, as they faced a daily challenge in making the ingredients they had go as far as possible while creating food that wouldn't dent morale.

No. 209 Maintenance Unit, which supplied RAF Elsham Wolds with everything they needed to maintain their Lancasters, had a very resourceful WAAF cook named Jessie. 'She really enjoyed her job,' her colleague Barbara Watkinson Bulleyment remembers:

> However, the rations were uninspiring and one day she decided to try out something she remembered from her childhood. Having soaked some raisins she then proceeded to string them at about 1 inch intervals along a strong piece of string, finishing up with several yards of line. In the woods nearby, and just before dusk, Jessie spread her line along a grassy pathway, having first tied one end of it firmly to a stake. Not until the following afternoon did an opportunity

> occur for her to visit her baited line, and as she approached she was startled by the sudden alarm call of a pheasant! Having fancied the raisins, it was now well and truly caught! Taking it back to camp Jessie then didn't have the courage to do the 'necessary' to the bird, and was almost ready to take it out to the woods again.

It was then that an RAF colleague arrived on the scene. He 'quickly dispatched the pheasant', Barbara recalls, and 'the officers very much enjoyed their tasty morsel – and were decidedly proud of having such an enterprising cook!'[5]

Domestic staff also helped to keep personnel on air stations well looked after. Spending so much time with aircrews, fearing for them when they went out on operations and counting the empty chairs when they did not return, these WAAF staff felt deeply the weight of loss on bomber stations. WAAF waitress Gladys Crittenden Scully remembers serving an evening meal in the officers' mess before an operation, when a young pilot officer asked her for some more sugar. 'I just hadn't any to give him,' she says sadly. 'Then serving them all when they came back, I found that he didn't make it. I had a good cry off duty … and all these years later when I think about it – I still cry.'[6]

The women went above and beyond to take care of 'their boys', aircrew in particular. Wal Cryer says: 'The operational egg went down very well, and we started to feel we could tackle anything.' It was thought that a good meal could stave off airsickness. Lancaster pilot Donald Knight frequently ate a large, greasy meal to help with the bouts of airsickness he suffered.[7] After the crews had eaten, they were summoned to the briefing room.

Briefing

On the day of an operation, the aircrews taking part were thoroughly briefed as to what exactly they were going to have to do and where they would be doing it. All the intelligence collected had been processed and formed the basis of the briefing. It was important at this stage – while information was flowing – to maintain a high degree of secrecy and to ensure absolutely no details of the operation could be leaked. Bomb aimer Al Lovett remembers a poster in the briefing room that said: 'It is better to keep your mouth shut and let people think you're a fool than open it and remove all doubt.'[8]

RAF police were on watch, particularly at the entrances and exits of buildings; the airfield would be locked down, no traffic would be allowed to enter or leave and telephones were locked down so nobody could use them. A few hours before take-off, aircrews were assembled in the briefing room and joined by the briefing staff – the commanding officer, flight and section commanders, the meteorological officer, the flying control officer and the intelligence, gunnery, navigation and armaments officers. A map of the target was concealed by a curtain. Once this was drawn back, the details of the operation were revealed to everyone present. 'Our first thought was for the large map on the wall,' Bruce Rawling says, 'and the length of red string which stretched from our base out over the route to be followed to the target, and if it told of a tough target the sinking feeling in our stomachs increased.'[9]

The CO would explain what the target was, if there was anything in particular they were aiming to hit, and usually why it had been selected. Once the target was known, the route to and from it was the next key piece of information. 'Intelligence told us why the route was not a straight line,' Wal explains. 'It was bent to take us around heavily fortified areas or cities. Also, it was hoped it would fool the Germans into thinking we were after a different target.' Bruce found the intelligence aspect of the briefing particularly interesting:

> The intelligence officer, with the aid of slides and large-scale maps and diagrams, described the route and target in detail, the type and intensity of defences, the location of the German fighter groups and their assembly points.

> He also gave a detailed analysis of the counter measures being mounted, such as spoof raids aimed at drawing off the fighter defences, the radio countermeasures being employed to jam and confuse the enemy radio and radar and the intruder operations by our fighters.

The navigation officer discussed timings and altitudes along the route, and the expected time and altitude to be over the target. The route home was also explained, and this was usually more straightforward than the route out. Next, the meteorological officer spoke to the crew about the expected weather conditions – of particular importance was information on cloud cover and how this might affect both Allied and enemy aircraft. The gunnery officer then talked the gunners through facing Luftwaffe fighters, and the armaments officer explained what bombs the Lancaster would be carrying. Maps and charts were given out, along with call signs and radio frequencies. These were sometimes printed onto very thin, edible rice paper, called 'flimsies', so if the aircraft was shot down, the crew could eat them and keep them out of the hands of the enemy.

WAAF Doris McCreight distributed the flimsies on her bomber station, wishing the aircrews good luck with an encouraging smile. Aircrews might also be given advice as to where to go if they were shot down over enemy territory. For Operation Margin, the crews were told: 'Anyone who is shot down over France should make for Bordeaux and go to the Black Cat café. If you come back OK, forget you ever heard of it.'[10]

To the Lancasters

A lot of superstition developed on bomber stations, and there were little things airmen *needed* to do prior to an operation. Some had mascots they collected from their quarters to take with them on operations and some had lucky charms, such as teddy bears belonging to their children. No. 617 Squadron pilot and Dambuster Micky Martin had a miniature koala given to him by his mother before he left Australia, which he always took with him when he was flying. Others had habits or rituals involving the ground personnel. Where airmen knew they might lose one another at any moment, the ground personnel represented a tangible constant to hold on to – they would always be there, a lighthouse to quite literally guide them home. After each briefing at WAAF map clerk Edna Skeen's station, the aircrew would pause to touch her shoulder as they filed out of the room. 'See you tonight, Edna,' they would say in a ritual they considered to be good luck.

Aware of the terrifying odds they faced, aircrews lived every day with the knowledge it might be their last. Before operations, they did what they needed to do to come to terms with this. Many wrote letters home, which they would leave behind for someone to pass to their loved ones if they should not return. Nineteen-year-old rear gunner Finlay McRae wrote a letter home to his parents, which was sent on to them when he did not return from his final mission in 1944:

> I thought I'd write this letter as we are going over tonight, and in case anything should happen to me. I want to thank you for everything you have done for me. I don't think I could ever repay you for what you have done and gone without to give to me. I know I have never lived up to what you wanted me to be. Some things I have done to hurt you that hurts me now when I think of them. If I come through this I am resolved to try to follow dadda's example. I know I scoffed often at him for his religion and that, but I can tell you I honour him for it now. And mamma, you always stood up for me in everything. How I have loved you always. I could not find a better mother. If anything happens to me I know it will break your hearts but the good Lord will look

> after you. Give my love to dear nanna and Flora, Wally and Rhoda. I'll have to go for now. God bless you, your loving son, Finlay.[11]

Just weeks after joining No. 619 Squadron, Australian Lancaster pilot Colin Flockhart wrote a letter home to his family to be sent to them in the event of his death. He wrote:

> Some impressions so that, if, by some chance, I should not finish my tour, you will know just how I feel about things and it may help to ease the suffering and sorrow you will endure at my loss. First of all let me say that I have enjoyed my air force service as I have enjoyed no other years of my life and I have been completely happy the whole time. I have travelled, made friendships and shared experiences which will stand me in good stead all my life ... This war was inevitable and I could never have been content unless I did my share ... I want you to know therefore that if I should die I shall not be afraid because my heart is at ease ... I love you all very dearly. Please don't think I'm pessimistic but I do realise what the odds are and I have seen too many of my friends pass on without leaving any words of hope or encouragement behind. Cheerio and keep smiling though your hearts are breaking.[12]

On 7 January 1945, Colin's Lancaster was returning from an operation against Munich when it collided with another aircraft. All the aircrew, on both aircraft, were killed.

Stevie Stevens' usual practice before an operation was to find a quiet corner of the airfield where he could go to pray. An RAF padre had given him a small leather-bound copy of the New Testament, which he carried with him whenever he was on operations. He marked the passage in John 14 that said: 'Let not your heart be troubled.' Just inside the book, he wrote a prayer which he had composed himself:

'God grant that I may never fail my crew, and that I may ever fulfil the trust and confidence they place in me.'[13]

As well as spiritual, there were practical matters to attend to, like making sure they used the bathroom. Though the Lancasters had Elsan toilets on board, the crew hated using them, as it could be extremely cold at high altitudes and they wore thick, heavy clothing, which made it tricky. Donald Knight recalled that when the Lancaster had to make evasive manoeuvres to avoid flak or enemy fighters, the Elsan tended to spill in the back of the fuselage, which was deeply unpleasant for all on board.[14] The airmen also had to collect their flying gear – including parachutes and life preservers from the parachute section, carefully packed by WAAF. They collected survival kits for the dreaded eventuality that they were shot down, and a helmet complete with oxygen mask and intercom equipment. They then went to the crew room to dress. This included the emptying of pockets and the removal of all personal effects, so that should they find themselves in enemy territory, nothing on their person would give them away as Allied airmen.

Then it was to the aircraft dispersal point. The Lancasters and other bombers were stationed on the airfield, usually at the perimeter, which could put them some distance from the briefing room. Sometimes aircrew needed to be driven out to their Lancasters, and often it was WAAF who did the driving, taking them out in trucks or buses. On one occasion, bomb aimer Al Lovett was walking to his Lancaster when a WAAF pulled up on a tractor, towing a trolley carrying a 4,000lb bomb. 'It was warm, and my flying gear was heavy, so I asked her if I could have a lift,' Al says. 'She agreed, and I climbed up and sat on the bomb like it was a horse.'[15]

Ground personnel handed out sandwiches, chocolate and flasks of coffee to the aircrew, who they knew would be in the air in cold, difficult conditions for hours. When the aircrew arrived at their bombers, it was common for them to gather around the aircraft's wheels and urinate on them. This was partly for good luck, but it was also a final attempt to stave off having to use the dreaded Elsan. 'On arrival at the planes the ground crew would be there to meet us', Bruce Rawling says, 'and give us any information we needed on the state of the plane.'[16] The ground staff had been hard at work completing checks and tests on the aircraft, and all had to be completed to the pilot and flight engineer's satisfaction.

The aircrew would make their own checks too. 'As the pilot,' Wal Cryer says, 'I would run up the four Merlin engines of the Lancaster and check each magneto [an electrical generator that uses magnets to produce alternating current] on each engine. Each crew member had his own equipment and responsibilities: the navigator his navigational instruments. The gunners would check the movement of their turrets and even fire a few rounds into a prepared sand hill.'[17] The flight engineer checked his instrument panel, the pressure, the temperature and the hydraulics. The pilot tested the intercom with the crew to make sure they would be able to communicate in flight. The wireless operator and the bomb aimer checked over their equipment.

Sometimes during the checks and preparations for a sortie, the ground and air crews discovered faults with equipment that needed to be rectified as soon as possible – the Lancasters needed to take off as close to their designated take-off time as they could, to avoid being left behind the bomber stream. Last-minute malfunctions could cause problems. On one occasion, an electrical fault occurred on Wal Cryer's Lancaster. The crew called for the electrician, but he could not find the problem without extensive investigation. The take-off time of 4.30 p.m. came and went, and the commanding officer granted a twenty-minute extension. When the problem was still not found, the crew were offered a replacement aircraft, which they took. Transferring to another Lancaster, they got soaked in the pouring rain. 'After the whole crew were settled into their respective stations there was this high-pitched scream from the intercom,' Wal says. 'This was caused by one or all of the crew having wet jackets and by inserting the jack into the plug it smeared the wetness and virtually shorted out. Shouting into my mic I managed to get each member of the crew in turn to pull their jack, give it a good wipe and then replace it. Finally we were able to communicate properly.'

When everyone was confident that the Lancaster was in good working order, the crew signed a form saying they were happy with the condition of the aircraft and handed it to the ground crew, who could now only stand back and watch their aircraft depart. 'When everyone was satisfied we shut down to wait for take-off time,' Bruce Rawling explains. 'This was the time for a last-minute smoke and relieving the old bladder. It was also the time when the tummy did most of its turning over.'[18] When take-off time arrived, the aircraft vibrated and juddered as one by one, each of the four Rolls-Royce Merlin engines would be started – No. 3 engine first, then 4, then 2, then 1. Each engine would give a little splutter with a puff of smoke as the propellors began to turn, and all four were soon singing in unison.

The pilot kept an eye on the gauges for the oil and engine coolant and on the temperatures, and worked through his take-off checklist. Each pilot had his own way of doing things, and some would have the flight engineer read out the list as well, to double-check that each task had been completed. Ex-Lancaster pilot Jack Currie recalls that 'for a successful take-off in a laden Lancaster you needed steady concentration, a little strength in hands and feet, and some degree of skill – nothing superhuman.'[19] It was time.

Take-Off

As a radio telephone operator at a bomber station, WAAF Doris McCreight worked in the control tower, from where she could see the Lancasters waiting to take off. The atmosphere could be tense before a raid. Doris stood before a blackboard which listed the names of the aircrews involved in the raid, along with their aircraft identification information and estimated times for take-off and return. She could not help but silently wonder which of the men listed – people she was used to seeing every day and had come to know as friends – might not make it home that night. Clare Kemp also worked in Flying Control, speaking and listening to the pilots over the radio before and after their operations. 'The pilots soon became familiar voices taking off,' she says.[20] Doris and Clare watched the Lancasters take off one by one, nervous for their crews and silently willing them to stay safe and come home.

Out on the airfield, the aircrew took their positions aboard their Lancasters, and the pilot ran a final comms check. At his allotted time, the pilot taxied the aircraft out to join the queue of bombers waiting to take off. 'There was a five-bar gate nearby,' bomb aimer Al Lovett says. 'The girls used to sit on it and wave to us as we taxied out.'[21] Bruce Rawling remembers watching the other aircraft take off ahead of his own:

> The pilot gives the signal to start the first engine. The whine of the starter motor, a cough followed by a roar and a large sheet of flame from the exhaust as the engine fired and continued to run. The next three followed and the plane had come alive and was a different thing. The planes ahead of us were pulling out of their dispersal pans onto the taxi ways and we followed them into the rapidly moving line. One after another they turned onto the runway, straightened up and receiving a green light from the runway control van increased the revs. Until the planes were shuddering against the brakes and then off down the runway to lift off into the sky.

The turn of each Lancaster came, putting an end to the aircrew's tense wait. Eric Grisdale describes taking off:

> Our speed gradually built up until eventually we were lifted smoothly by the four mighty Merlin engines into the evening sky. As we climbed to our allocated operating height, the time of take-off, gave us just sufficient daylight to see and appreciate the hundreds of other Lancasters and Halifaxes, starting off on the same journey. The disappearing view of

> the majestic old Cathedral of Lincoln gave us courage and faith that we would return.[22]

Often, groups of well-wishers would be there to wave the bombers off – the ground crew, WAAF and the squadron commander usually among them. John Jenkinson was very grateful for this:

> The one thing that remains firmly in my mind which I recall with great gratitude and affection – if they are the right words – were the groups of people who took the trouble to wave us off from the end of the runway by the caravan. The groups were of all ranks, trades and of both sexes. I also recall our ground crew of Sergeant 'Tubby' Barker, Arthur, Taffy and Eric who saw us off from the dispersal and were there to meet us on our return – even though some of them may have been off duty at the time. As a crew mascot we had a dog called Butch who was looked after by the F/L Engineer's Leader while we were flying.[23]

The bombers took off in quick succession. The air became thinner as the Lancasters climbed, and the pilots instructed their crews to put their oxygen masks on at the appropriate time. Take-off could be a dangerous time during an operation. 'If you were taking off with a full bomb load and a strong cross wind, and the aircraft blew off course, it was very difficult to correct,' Stevie Stevens says.[24] Once, when Al Lovett's crew were taking off in their Lancaster, the outer port engine failed and caused the aircraft to swing badly to port. 'Fuel was streaming from the wing root and the RAF personnel who had assembled by the flight van to wish the crews good luck prepared to take cover in case we crashed at the end of the runway. However, the skipper feathered the port outer propeller and managed to get the aircraft safely into the air.'

In the Air

Once airborne and at the required altitude, the bombers headed to a predetermined assembly point, where they would join the other bombers in their group. The aircraft did not fly in formation, but they did fly together in a 'stream'. The navigator started working immediately after take-off, and throughout the flight the crew would tell him if they saw significant landmarks, to help him confirm where they were. Once they had crossed the sea, the pilot would call, 'Enemy coast ahead.' Everyone on board took a deep breath. The swarm of bombers was much more likely to face anti-aircraft fire and enemy fighters from this point on. The pilot banked the aircraft frequently, helping the gunners to see more of the sky, and every crew member who could see out of the aircraft strained constantly to see signs of enemy fighters as early as possible.

Once the Lancaster reached the target, the crew could begin the bombing run. They closed in, the bomb aimer giving course corrections to the pilot because he could see directly down. To drop its bombs as accurately as possible, the aircraft needed to be straight and level – which made it much easier for enemy fighters to hit, so crews aimed to do this as quickly as they could. Bomb aimer Al Lovett explains:

> Just before reaching the target I set the bombsight, made preliminary corrections for the final release and opened the bomb doors. I then made further final corrections as the target came into the sights, held my breath and pressed bomb release. We felt the Lancaster shudder as the bombs cleared and a final jerk as the 4000lb 'cookie' was released. The jettison bars were operated to ensure that all the bombs had gone. After a few seconds the camera proceeded to operate and photographs of the target area were taken. The bomb doors were then closed and the bomb bay checked for hang-ups with the aid of an Aldis

ABOVE: Prototype Avro Lancaster BT308 at Ringway, January 1941.

BELOW: Roy Chadwick (*holding a model of the Avro York and pointing at it*) in his design office with his colleagues, 1942.

ABOVE: Prototype Avro Manchester L7246 at Ringway, July 1939.

LEFT: Women workers 'doping'. Not all components were skinned with aluminium; some control surfaces were still skinned in fabric. A close-fitting fabric 'bag' was stitched around the component and a doping solution applied which caused the fabric to tighten and set hard as it moulded itself to the structure.

RIGHT: Main wing structure being assembled in its jig.

ABOVE: The mass production of Lancasters was simplified by Roy Chadwick's design.

BELOW: Lancaster Mark I, L7578, KM-B, of No. 44 (Rhodesia) Squadron, flying low over Lincolnshire, 14 April 1942. Practice for the low-level attack on the MAN diesel works at Augsburg, which would take place on 17 April.

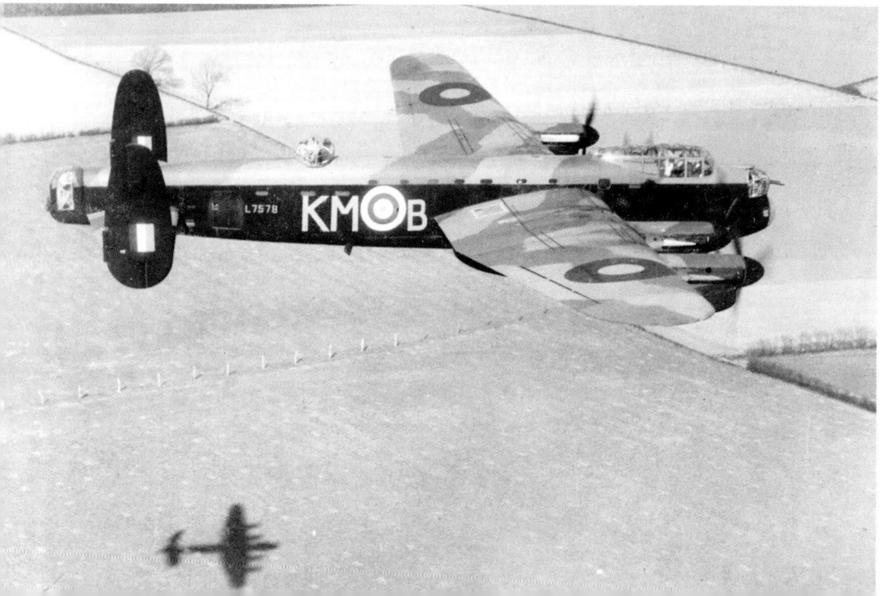

ABOVE: Ground crew at work on a Lancaster Mk2. The two on the wings are refuelling the aircraft.

LEFT: P/O Hugo Trotter DFC, Lancaster pilot.

BELOW: WAAF cook Lucy Jane Lillie.

BELOW: WAAF Officer Fay Gillon debriefing a bomber crew after an operation.

LEFT: Bomber Command navigator Peter Carpenter.

BELOW: Wing Commander Guy Gibson guided the King and Queen on their visit to meet members of 617 Squadron after the famous Dambusters raid. Here, the King examines reconnaissance photographs.

RIGHT: Lancaster pilot Charles Owen faced many difficult situations during his time flying Lancasters.

BELOW: WAAF Aline Wakefield (*far right*) continued to work in Bomber Command after her fiancé was killed on operations.

ABOVE: Rear gunner Bob Howes (*second from right, seated*) in debrief with the rest of his crew following an operation.

> lamp. I leaned back and breathed again. No one was more surprised than I that everything had gone without a hitch. When the words 'bombs gone, bomb doors closed' were spoken a sigh of relief from the rest of the crew was heard over the intercom.[25]

As the bombs left the Lancaster, it would lurch upwards from the sudden loss of weight. 'Then I'd say, you can take her home again now,' Al says, 'and the crew would cheer.' The aircraft was now lighter and could move faster, and the navigator followed the set course home as far as possible, avoiding known enemy defences. The bomb aimer, who could see the world outside the aircraft clearly through its Perspex nose, would sometimes assist with navigation. Sometimes there had to be deviations from the prescribed course – perhaps because of unexpected enemy defences, which would keep the navigator and the bomb aimer busy.

The crew were tired and were often prescribed amphetamines to help them stay awake. If their coffee and sandwiches hadn't frozen, they could have them on the way home. It was a relief to be headed home, but they could not relax – it was vital to stay alert and on guard against enemy fighters and flak. 'At night, you'd get a fighter aircraft flying in the afterglow, with his lights on,' Al Lovett explains. 'We didn't fire unless fired upon – we kept an eye on them.' Squinting for long periods of time in the darkness, trying desperately to keep the aircraft safe from any lurking predators, the worst thing Al and his colleagues could spot were Luftwaffe night fighters. 'They had upward-firing canons, and could come underneath us and fire at the belly of the Lancaster,' he says. *Schräge Musik* (a German colloquialism for jazz music) was the name given to the upright cannons, which were feared by Bomber Command aircrews. 'Once, a fighter suddenly came level with us,' Al recalls, 'and there were two flashes from underneath his wings. One shot went under my compartment, and the other went over the top.'

There was also the risk of colliding with another Allied aircraft, with so many of them flying at once at similar altitudes and in the same location. When it was dark, the crew would see momentary flashes of light. Sometimes this was a flak gun going off below. Sometimes it was an enemy fighter or an Allied bomber exploding in the air, or on the ground having been shot down. Sometimes it was two aircraft colliding in mid-air. It was vital to avoid searchlight beams, and if caught in one, a pilot carried out evasive manoeuvres at speed. Inevitably, sometimes operations didn't go according to plan due to technical issues on board the aircraft. Wireless operator Arthur Atkinson recalls one such raid – his new crew's first flight together: 'We were put on the list to go to Stuttgart, our first op. This was a disaster completely from start to finish. We took off, we hadn't been flying long and it was fairly obvious our DR compass wasn't working properly. Anyway, we pressed on.'[26]

After what seemed like hours, the crew still had not arrived over Stuttgart and found themselves 'wandering all over Europe'. Eventually the rear gunner thought he had spotted the enemy coast, which would allow them to plot an approximate course to England. He was mistaken, however, and it wasn't until a little while later that the enemy coast actually appeared. 'The skipper said, "Well that's all right but I don't think we've got enough fuel to get across the Channel now,"' Arthur explains. He asked the crew to make a decision – they could choose to bail out over enemy territory, and if they survived they would become prisoners of war, or they could try to make it across the Channel and ditch if necessary. The universal decision among the crew was to try to get home. They flew over thick cloud, waiting for a break so they could look for land below. They spotted a flashing beacon, but Arthur's radio equipment wasn't working, and they couldn't establish where they were. The pilot flew around the beacon while the crew tried to decide what to do, and suddenly an airfield lit up beneath them. 'There it was, full runways, perimeter, the lot, marvellous – we'll land there.' They prepared to land, but the landing gear would not come down and the flaps wouldn't work. They came around again. 'This time we blew the wheels down with a compressed air tank,' Arthur explains. 'Fortunately, they came down and locked and with the flight engineer pumping like mad on the flaps he managed to hit the ground and roll along.' Arthur went to the back of the aircraft and opened the door, and was greeted by a man on a bicycle. 'I said, "Aye mate, where's this then?" The man replied, "Westonzoyland." Arthur was convinced they'd landed in Holland. It sounded Dutch to me. "Westonzoyland!" I said, "Where's that?" The man said, "Somerset."' They were home.

Lancaster pilot Gordon Cleminson also experienced a raid where everything seemed to go wrong. Pre-flight tests on the Lancaster, which was close to maximum weight, did not reveal any problems. Gordon started the take-off run, but just before they reached flying speed, one of the engines died. It was too late to abort take-off – to do so would have been deadly, so they left the ground and tried to climb as best they could. The huge weight and decreased power of the Lancaster made this very difficult, and Gordon was troubled by the fact that he'd known an Australian crew suffer the same problem – they were killed when their aircraft couldn't quite clear the trees in its path. Gordon managed to stay straight and level and build enough speed to climb safely. Standing orders for such an occurrence were to fly to German Heligoland and dump the bombs there. On their approach to Heligoland, they discovered that the Lancaster had no hydraulics to open the bomb doors. The aircraft was crippled, and to make matters even worse, it became clear it was defenceless – there was also no power to the gun turrets.

Standing orders for aircraft unable to dump their bombs at Heligoland were to use the Wash – a bay in East Anglia – as an emergency bomb dump. By now the crew had managed to get the bomb doors open using a pump, but when they got to the Wash the whole area was a mass of fishing boats. The crew hand-pumped the bomb bay doors shut again and had a rethink. Standing orders didn't account for situations such as these. They reduced their fuel load and headed back to their air station, intending to land with the bombs on board. On the way there, the crew hand-pumped the hydraulics to lower the landing gear, but they couldn't be sure that the wheels had gone fully into place. Despite all the problems, Gordon managed to land the Lancaster safely, its huge load of bombs still on board – and with a dodgy wheel. It was, he said, 'the best and gentlest landing of his whole flying career'.[27]

One of the most difficult things aircrew faced was watching fellow Bomber Command aircraft in difficulty, unable to help them. Sometimes there was nothing to be done, and they could only watch as friends and colleagues met their ends. Sometimes, however, they were able to assist. On one occasion, bomb aimer Al Lovett's Lancaster was returning to base when the crew observed a damaged Lancaster on their starboard side, with one engine out of action. 'We descended and flew alongside,' Al says. 'It was one of our squadron aircraft and was flown by an Australian pilot, F/O Michaels and his crew. The skipper decided to escort the damaged aircraft back to base so that in the event of it having to ditch in the North Sea its position could be reported. The aircraft was gradually losing height and we had descended to approximately 5,000ft.' Flying over occupied territory in the Netherlands, both Lancasters began to take anti-aircraft fire, and their pilots put them into a dive to gain speed and get out to sea. Both Lancasters made it home safely.

The dangers were many on bomber operations, and the atmosphere in a Lancaster could be heavy with unspoken fear, pressure and an awareness that death and destruction could come at any moment. Crews found little ways to relieve the tension, even if only slightly. 'Despite the seriousness of bombing raids,' says Canadian pilot Arthur Bishop,

> we actually had competition between crews to see who had the most fuel left in his fuel tanks at the end of a raid. My flight engineer was exceptional and he handled his duties with skill and ingenuity. He came up with the idea of feathering an engine on the way back over the Dutch coast. We usually came out of the target at 17,000ft plus, so we had some height to lose before arriving over base. Let's

> 'feather an engine', he said, and so it was that we developed the practice of feathering an engine over the Dutch Coast and restarting it over base for landing. In this way we always won the competition and the rest of the pilots on the Squadron have – to this day – never figured out how it was accomplished.[28]

Homeward Bound

Once back over Britain, the aircrews could relax a little. When they reached their airfield, the bombers with the least fuel and with injured crew or damage to the aircraft were given landing priority. To land, the bombers entered a circuit and called control for landing instructions. A radio telephone operator in Flying Control would answer the call, relieved to hear the aircrew were back. WAAF R/T operator Maureen Miller explains:

> On return, the first plane to radio in was told to 'Pancake', using the station call sign. No names were ever used; the call sign for Wigsley, for instance, was 'Biddy', and Scampton was 'Heron'. The second aircraft to call in was told, 'Aerodrome one thousand', which meant he should circle at 1,000ft. Subsequent arrivals were stacked at 500ft intervals at different heights so that they landed in turn, avoiding confusion and collisions. If an aircraft radioed in that it was in trouble or had been badly damaged, the others were called collectively and asked to stand by. They were held in the air while the plane in difficulties was called in first. In between, we used to listen out for what we called 'Darkie' calls, now known as 'Mayday' calls.[29]

WAAF Doris McCreight remembers waiting to pick up SOS signals from aircraft that had been shot down or badly damaged. If a last-known location was given at sea, there was a chance that a boat or ship could be directed to pluck the crew out of the water – if they had managed to bail out. 'There were always those who did not return,' she says, 'and I would spend the rest of the night listening out for a mayday call. When all hope was gone, it was sad to see the blackboard wiped clean.'

Other times, pilots needed help finding their way home in dense fog or mist. 'Sometimes a stray aircraft would call up and ask where he was,' Maureen explains.

> When that happened, you would go through the procedure of asking him where he came from and letting him know his position. 'Darkie' calls could be very exciting. If pilots were lost or disoriented, we had to talk them down safely. When this happened, it could be a very, very difficult job for the control officer, who might be on the balcony outside firing a Very pistol [flare gun] and communicating all the time on the R/T. I was on duty one night when the control officer was a Canadian. I remember that particularly because a pilot had made a 'Darkie' call, and it took ages for the poor chap to get down. I can't remember if he was running out of fuel, but he avoided a crash, and he was so grateful to us for getting him down safely that he came up into the control tower afterwards and thanked us. Moments like that made being an R/T operator very satisfying and worthwhile. All in all, it was a wonderful job, and I thoroughly enjoyed it.

From the crews' perspective, it was a great relief to hear the calm voice coming from the tower to welcome them home. '"Pancake" was the word every bomber pilot longed to hear over his radio,' Stevie Stevens says. 'It was the final instruction to land after an aircraft had joined the airfield circuit and was approaching the runway.'[30]

Each aircraft was, in turn, given the 'prepare to land' notice, and the pilot switched the nose light on.[31] The crew were beyond relieved when they felt the aircraft touch down. Sometimes the bombers could not make it to their own airfields because of lack of fuel, damage or heavy fog. Pilot Hugo Trotter recalls an instance when his Lancaster was diverted:

> With Lincolnshire, the mists rise. We were on the way back and the wireless operator got a message to say that Lincolnshire was pretty well closed down and they'd given us a diversion. We came to the aerodrome – I approached and landed, and the penny suddenly dropped that the wireless operator had sent us to a B-17 Eighth Air Force Fortress base. We parked up and opened up the bomb bays, and it was quite amusing. It was very early in the morning and quite light – maybe 5 a.m. – I wanted to give them the chance to see what a Lanc's bomber bay is like. I think they were quite intrigued – for a bit of showmanship you couldn't get better.[32]

Peter Carpenter's crew was also diverted to an American base, on Christmas Eve 1944. It had been snowing in Lincolnshire, and they landed at Old Buckenham in Norfolk to avoid the bad weather at Elsham Wolds. Old Buckenham was the home of the US Army Air Force's 453rd Bomb Group from December 1943, its personnel, who flew B-24 Liberators, holding a distinguished flying record. Peter and his friends shuffled out of the Lancaster, trembling and bleary, and were welcomed wholeheartedly by the Americans. Peter's crew were sad to miss their mess Christmas dinner and party, but their hosts were very kind and treated them to Christmas 'American style' – 'all of the courses in the same container ... pud next to turkey'.[33] Arthur Wolstenholme, the mid-upper gunner, remembers how the Americans reacted to the Lancaster: 'Incidentally the crews were amazed at the Lanc, both the room inside and the bomb bays.'[34]

No matter where they landed, once safely on the ground the pilot taxied the Lancaster to a designated point and powered down the aircraft. Upon exiting, the aircrew were often shocked to find extensive damage to the plane that had brought them home safely. It was over – and they had survived. Ambulances took any wounded airmen to be treated, and RAF or WAAF drivers ferried the aircrew to the Ops block. There, mugs of warm sugary tea or cocoa were handed out, as well as rum and cigarettes, to steady the airmen's nerves. It wasn't uncommon for them to experience a delayed reaction, once the adrenaline stopped pumping and they were safe. There was just one more stage of the operation to get through – the debriefing.

An intelligence officer would interrogate the crew, drawing out useful information while it was still fresh in their minds. The officer would ask them to recount their experiences of the operation – what kind of enemy defences had they encountered along the route? How well defended was the target? Had they hit it? If so, how much damage had they caused? What were the approximate losses, for the Luftwaffe and for the RAF? Quizzing the crews after an operation could yield information on how successful it had been and therefore what kind of follow-up action might be needed. Returned aircrews were often exhausted and emotionally spent – and sometimes traumatized, having watched friends and colleagues be shot out of the sky to an unknown, but likely terrible, fate below.

To begin with, debriefs and crew interrogations were carried out by male RAF officers, as it was felt that the young airmen might find it difficult to open up about such things in front of female colleagues. There was also the worry that if the WAAF were to carry out such a task, they might break down in hysterics at hearing such terrible things. As Bomber Command's workload increased, however, and more and more crews needed to be debriefed, the RAF trialled using WAAF interrogators. They were found to be very effective in the role, and where it had been feared that their supposed emotional sensitivity might be a disadvantage, the women were able to use empathy, patience and kindness to coax the airmen into talking about what they had seen and experienced. By piecing together the information provided by each member of the crew with aerial reconnaissance photographs

– including those taken on the bombing run – the intelligence officer could produce a report which was detailed and accurate, providing information on the effectiveness of an individual operation.

After the debrief, it was time for a meal. If back from a night operation, this would be a hearty breakfast of bacon, eggs and chips, with extra milk and sugar rations, and maybe even some fruit juice. The airmen sat together, acutely aware that some of the chairs in the cafeteria were empty – there were missing friends and colleagues who had not returned that night. They hoped desperately that they had been forced to land elsewhere, or that they might have bailed out and were on their way home, either on a friendly ship or via the escape lines in Europe. Perhaps they had been taken alive as prisoners of war – even that was better than being gone forever. The men were exhausted, physically and emotionally, and often fell asleep straight away. They had survived another operation – but their fight wasn't over. They would have to go out and do it all again. And again.

Repair and Repeat

After the agonising wait for the return of their Lancasters from operations, ground crew got to work repairing aircraft that had suffered damage due to enemy fire and accidents. Mechanics, electricians, metal workers, fabric workers and welders used their specialist skills to get the damaged aircraft – some of which had just about limped home in need of extensive repairs – back into good working order. Sometimes they were shocked by the condition in which they found the Lancasters and the equipment they carried, and were perturbed at imagining what the aircrew – their friends – had been through. 'Many of the squadron aircraft received heavy flak damage,' Al Lovett explains.

> Our Lancaster was hit numerous times by pieces of shrapnel from near-misses. It was found that the port inner engine

> oil-tank had been hit allowing the oil to escape, the bomb doors had been holed in several places, the port under-carriage leg damaged and the rear of the fuselage was also badly holed. A member of the ground staff, Tosh Williams, despite the very hot oil, managed to retrieve the piece of shrapnel from the tank and presented it to the skipper.[35]

John Johnson once spent a full thirty-six hours repairing a single aircraft – 'Heavenly Hilda', or OJ-H, NF 972 – to bring it back to full operational condition. 'It seemed that everything went wrong … When I eventually "signed off" I returned to the Nissen hut, not having had any sleep … The beds were built in two halves, to slide together and so take up less floor space during the daytime. My three "biscuits" – the mattress, folded blankets and paillasse were stacked on top. I sat on the frame, leaned back on the stack and fell asleep.'[36] John was so tired when he completed his work on the Lancaster that he'd left his hat onboard, just inside the door. That same day, NF 972 was one of twenty aircraft that participated in a raid on the oil refinery at Gelsenkirchen. It never returned, being seen to go down in the Wesel area following a fire and explosions on board.

Ground crew were faced with stark reminders of the horrors faced by their aircrews. It might be that empty .303 cases littered sections of the aircraft and needed to be cleared away after the gunners had fired at pursuing night fighters. It might be much worse. John Johnson climbed aboard another Lancaster, OJ-J, NG 224, after it had carried out a raid over Gelsenkirchen, encountering heavy flak. Eleven of the squadron's aircraft were hit, and NG 224's bomb aimer was killed by shrapnel that had hit him in the face. 'As yet I hadn't heard of the tragedy,' John says.

> I saw the smashed bomb aimer's panel and then I was asked by the sergeant on the flight line to hold my inspection for a little while. The aircraft fitters were stripping out the light green vinyl covered sponge pads on which the bomb-aimer

> laid, which were soaked in blood, and whatever else that they could take out of the nose that was blood spattered, and these were buried in a pit alongside the dispersal. The aircraft then went off to the maintenance hangar to be repaired and transferred.

Despite the constant weight of the grave losses suffered in Bomber Command, close relationships developed between ground personnel and aircrews. 'There is a terrific bond which develops,' wireless operator Bruce Rawling explains, 'and they would worry like hell if you were late getting back.' Pilot Doug Harvey says: 'You had to understand ground crew … They would literally do anything for you, accept any task, if they knew and understood why it was important, and if they knew you understood their problems.'[37] Air gunner Arthur Browett's ground crew put a particularly special finishing touch to his Lancaster. 'Each time we flew in our aircraft B-Beer, a carpet was laid the full length of the aircraft, and pictures were on the walls inside. A certain pub was playing hell because someone had taken all their stair carpet, and pictures off the walls on the landing. We had a good ground crew!'[38]

There needed to be a high level of trust between ground and air crews. The airmen were relying completely on their ground personnel to keep the Lancasters and other bombers in safe working order. They needed to be able to have total confidence in their aircraft, and that meant having total confidence and trust in the people who maintained them. The ground crew were also painfully aware of this and worked hard every day in the knowledge that the aircrews lives were, to some extent, in their hands. 'The first-class maintenance bestowed upon the Lanc was on many occasions the reason we returned to base safely,' Al Lovett says. 'Ground crew "owned" the bomber,' pilot Doug Harvey says.

> While the aircrew might think the bomber belonged to them, and painted witty sayings, pictures and bombs on the

> nose of the bomber, the ground crew knew differently. It was their aircraft, and they had a fierce pride of ownership. They wanted their bomber to work to perfection, and this was apparent to any interested aircrew ... If, as aircrew, you understood that the bomber belonged to them, and that you only borrowed it for flying purposes, the trust between the ground and air sides developed beautifully.[39]

The atmosphere on a bomber station could be very tense. There was a constant and common awareness of the immense strain under which aircrew lived, and that strain spread across everyone working toward Bomber Command's operational objectives. John Johnson voices it: 'One can imagine the emotional stress that each and every member of a bomber crew felt knowing that each raid that he went on could be his last day on earth.'[40] If bombers were lucky enough to return after operations, no one could afford to relax, because off they would go again the next day or night, back into the fray with terrifying odds. Ground crew were apprehensive as they prepared the bombers to go out, carrying huge responsibility and determined to do all they could to ensure the safety of the aircraft and their precious crews – their friends.

While the aircraft were gone they waited nervously, surrounded by silence and darkness. Then they faced the horrors of war that so cruelly and profoundly affected the men and the aircraft they lived and worked with when aircrews returned – and especially when they did not. The aircrews showed tremendous, mind-boggling courage in the face of terrifying danger; the ground crews bore the great burden of grief when their aircrews did not return. 'It was the ground crew who wept for the missing aircrew as they waited through the long, cold nights for their bomber to return,' Doug says. 'For the ground crew it was a sad time when most of the bombers had returned and their dispersal stood empty ... Some ground crew lost ten or more bombers and each had its effect on their behaviour. A pilot gets to love a particular aircraft, for, like a car, it has its own idiosyncrasies; but a ground technician gets to revere it and to give it human qualities.'[41]

Though they loved their aircraft, some ground crew struggled with the reality of life in Bomber Command. Engine maintainer Kenneth Warburton found that 'witnessing a repetitive destruction of life in the machines whose power source he engineered did not sit well'.[42] Despite the difficulties of their work and the tense environment they existed in, the ground crew somehow found it within themselves to go about their duties in an upbeat way, in the silent knowledge that their airmen needed them to put on a brave face. 'Perhaps the most surprising thing about them was their cheerfulness,' Doug says.[43] For this, he seems to have been grateful. Benny Goodman of 617 Squadron was quick to praise the ground crews he worked with:

> Working out in all weathers, often in wind, snow and rain-swept dispersals they were always there to ensure the serviceability of our aircraft. Despite working long hours, they were always there to see us depart, and waited in uncertainty, eager to witness our return ... and woe betide us if we damaged their aircraft! For 365 days and nights they made it possible for us to do our job. All of us who flew knew their worth ... We would have been wingless wonders without them.[44]

Of the ground crew at RAF Methwold, Air Vice Marshal Blucke said in June 1945: 'To aircrew is due the highest praise but let it not be forgotten that their feats of skill and gallantry were made possible only by the tireless energies and devotion to duty of each man and woman, no matter how great or how small their allotted task … The squadron worked and lived as a team, and it only helped to win the war because it was a good team.'[45] The same was true on bomber stations all over the country. After they had finished a tour of operations, aircrews were keen to show their appreciation for the ground personnel who had made it possible for them to carry out their work and come home safely. 'Shortly after our last op,' wireless operator Tony Adams says, 'we showed them our appreciation by taking them to the Red Lion in Hockwold. The publican, Wally Russell, had organised a poacher to get a rabbit or two and Mrs Russell cooked a delicious rabbit pie which, with suitable liquid refreshment, ensured that we had a wonderful conclusion to our partnership.'[46] Wireless operator Bruce Rawling remembers coming back from his final operation:

> Looking back to see the sky covered with flak bursts, bombs falling from the planes still bombing and the clouds of smoke and dust that were rising into the clear air. It was hard to realise that with a bit of luck it was all over and we had lived through it. We swooped low over our dispersal and could see the ground crew waving to us. Then down onto the deck and it was all over but for the party in the mess that night and taking the ground crew into town for a night out in the traditional aircrew farewell.[47]

CHAPTER FIVE

THE LANCASTER GOES TO WAR

Operation Margin

THE AVRO LANCASTER WENT INTO OPERATIONAL service with the RAF in 1942. The first operational Lancasters took part in various small operations, but their first major sortie would be a very specific, very secret mission, codenamed Operation Margin. A number of aircrews from 44 and 97 Squadrons were specially selected for the operation, and the crews were given instructions to practise flying in formation. This was odd – bombing raids were usually conducted at night, and it was difficult and unusual to fly in formation in the dark. It pointed to the operation taking place in daylight.

They were given lengthy practice routes, which also indicated that they would be flying a long distance – probably deep into enemy territory. When the crews left their quarters at RAF Waddington in the morning on 17 April, the sky was clear and bright. The aircrews of 44 Squadron showed their ID cards at the door of the briefing room and assembled for the pre-raid briefing, in which they would finally be privy to the plan. Over at Woodhall Spa, 97 Squadron's chosen crews were also being briefed. The main goal of the operation, it was stated, would be to make a crucial contribution toward the Allied fight in the Battle of the Atlantic. When the curtain concealing the route map was pulled back, the target was revealed to be Augsburg, a city in the south of Germany. At Waddington, there was an audible gasp. At Woodhall Spa, 'there was a roar of laughter instead of the gasp of horror', said Rod Rodley, a pilot with 97 Squadron. 'No one believed that the air force would be so stupid as to send twelve of its newest four-engined bombers all that distance inside Germany in daylight. We sat back and waited calmly for someone to say, "Now the real target is this." Unfortunately it was the real target...'[1]

There was silence. Glances were exchanged and worries went unspoken. Everything had pointed to the flight being a long one, including the fact that the fuel tanks were being filled to capacity. Augsburg, though? It was a roughly 1,500 mile round-trip from Waddington. The Lancaster was the only aircraft capable of pulling it off with any degree of accuracy. The plan was for the heavy bombers to cross the coast of France and proceed deep inland. Their path would be made smoother by 'well-co-ordinated diversions' carried out by other bombers and fighters. The attack itself would be executed at dusk, so the journey home could be made under the cover of darkness. It was to be a precision raid, and the target was to be a strategic industrial one. 'At that time it was touch and go in the North Atlantic between Britain having enough to eat and not having enough to eat,' explains 97 Squadron pilot Rod Rodley.[2] German U-boats had been wreaking havoc in the Atlantic, sending vital Allied supplies and ships to the bottom of the ocean and claiming thousands of lives in the process. If they were left to continue causing such carnage, the consequences for Britain and the Allies would be very serious. U-boats were powered by diesel engines, which were being manufactured in Augsburg at the Maschinenfabrik Augsburg-Nürnberg, or MAN Works. It was these works that were selected as the target for Operation Margin.

The stunned airmen lit cigarettes and did their best to concentrate as the information on their imminent raid was given. By the end of the briefing, 'the crews were determined that these diesels should not go forth in submarines', Rod says. Their aircraft were to fly in two sections, and those in each of the sections were instructed to remain close together – that explained the practice in formation flying. After heading out over the English coast, the force was to remain below 500ft, which would keep them from being detected by enemy radar. Towns and areas likely to be defended with anti-aircraft measures and Luftwaffe airfields were to be avoided at all costs. Once they reached the northern end of Augsburg, the formation would turn left and reduce their altitude, making straight for the MAN works. The attack was to be carried out at low level, with each aircraft carrying four 1,000lb bombs. It was vital to get clear of the target before they detonated.

In some ways this was an experimental raid. The Lancaster had been designed with long-range missions in mind, and this would be a real test for the aircraft. A daylight bombing attack on a significant industrial target deep in German territory, the operation order acknowledged, would hopefully also cause 'considerable alarm and despondency among the population' in Germany. The aircrews listened carefully as they were bombarded with information during the briefing. It was a lot to take in and remember. Pilot Patrick Dorehill, who was used to flying Hampdens, felt confident in the Lancaster in a way he never had in other aircraft. 'We did a week or two of low-level training beforehand and I confess before operations on Hampdens I was always a bit nervous. But prior to this mission … I wasn't nervous at all.'[3] The ground crews at both stations carried out their checks and preparation on each Lancaster, and the aircrews prepared themselves as best they could for what lay ahead. All too soon, it was time to go. Each Lancaster followed the previous one up into the clear, warm sky, their crews concentrating on doing their jobs to the best of their ability. Operation Margin had begun.

Led by Rhodesian pilot Squadron Leader John Nettleton and his Lancaster B-Baker, 44 Squadron reached the French coast flying under the radar. Flying close to Beaumont-le-Roger, an airfield used by the Luftwaffe, they got a nasty surprise. The diversionary circuses had attacked ahead of schedule, and the Luftwaffe fighters sent to intercept them were on their way back to base – just in time to find 44 Squadron passing by. 'The bombers, the bombers!' German radio operator Otto Happel flew out of his chair in the commander's office at the airfield and watched through the window as six huge British bomber aircraft passed over, flying low. Major Walter Oesau, the commandant of the Luftwaffe's Jagdgeschwader 2 Richthofen fighter wing, stood beside him and watched as the alarms blared.[4]

Happel put out a warning over the radio while Oesau ran to his ME109, intent on intercepting and engaging with the airborne enemy intruders. He was not the only one – several German fighters had not yet landed from intercepting the circuses and retracted their landing gear to remain airborne and deal with the Lancasters. It was the first glimpse the Luftwaffe would have of Britain's new bomber, as between twenty and thirty fighters closed in on 44 Squadron's Lancasters. The German fighters soon realized that the only defensive armaments these new aircraft sported were .303 machine guns, and they adapted their tactics to use their canons against the planes, making sure to stay just out of range to avoid taking damage while they attacked.

No. 44 Squadron did not fare well. Pat Dorehill remembers seeing one of the Lancasters go down: 'The worst experience was when Dusty Rhodes on our right … was on fire and his plane just sort of … you could see the flames in the cockpit … it just sort of swooped, and we raised up a bit to try and escape from being hit by him and of course that was a real disaster.'[5] After the engagement with the Luftwaffe, four of the Squadron's six Lancasters had been shot down. The other two continued on to Augsburg. 'With the whole Luftwaffe after us, I never thought we would get there at all,' Pat says.

Led by Wing Commander John 'Flap' Sherwood, 97 Squadron's Lancasters had fared better. All six Lancasters managed to remain undetected by the enemy, clearing hundreds of miles of occupied territory and arriving at Augsburg without any losses. 'Occasionally you would see some Frenchmen take a second look and wave their berets or their shovels,' Rod Rodley remembers.[6] 'A bunch of German soldiers doing PT [exercise] in their singlets broke hurriedly for their shelters as we roared over. The next opposition was a German officer on one of the steamers on Lake Constanz firing a revolver at us. I could see him quite clearly, defending the ladies with his Luger against 48 Browning machine guns.'

Once over the target, however, both squadrons met with savage anti-aircraft fire. No. 44 Squadron's remaining two Lancasters released their bombs over the target – but then one was struck in a fuel tank. The pilot did his best to crash-land it – three crew members were killed and four survived. No. 97 Squadron's six aircraft now attacked the target. Sherwood's aircraft, however, was struck, and the wing caught fire. He continued to lead the other two Lancasters in his formation away until he could control his own no more. Rod Rodley saw what happened:

> I looked down at our leader's aircraft and saw there was a little wisp of steam trailing back from it. The white steam turned to black smoke, with fire in the wing. I was slightly above him. In the top of the Lancaster there was a little wooden hatch for getting out if you had to land at sea. I realised that this wooden hatch had burned away and I could look down into the fuselage. It looked like a blow lamp with the petrol swilling around the wings and centre section, igniting the fuselage and the slipstream blowing it down. Just like a blow lamp. He dropped back and I asked our gunner to keep an eye on him. Suddenly he said, 'Oh God, Skip, he's gone. He looks like a chrysanthemum of fire.'[7]

All on board were lost, except for Sherwood, who was catapulted clear of the explosion, still strapped into his pilot seat. He would spend the remainder of the war as a prisoner of war. Two more of 97 Squadron's Lancasters were hit, but they managed to strike their target before one aircraft exploded. The other limped home, severely damaged. The operation's aim had been achieved and the factory had been bombed – but at great cost. Of the twelve Lancasters that had set out, only five made it home. Of the eighty-five men who had taken off for the mission, forty-nine were posted as missing.

Operation Margin revealed strengths and weaknesses of the new bomber. The Lancaster had done what it was designed to do. Those that returned to Britain had covered a remarkable distance and dropped a sizable payload on an industrial target in southern Germany in a precision raid. It was one of the most audacious raids Bomber Command had attempted yet, and ultimately, it was considered a success. On the other hand, the damage to the factory had been fairly minimal, and it was not out of action for long. Luftwaffe fighters had soon figured out the limitations of the Lancaster's defensive weaponry, which was no match for their canons. Unprotected, the bombers that had been detected by the enemy had been decimated, and the losses were high.

Squadron Leader John Nettleton became the first person to be awarded the Victoria Cross in action involving Lancasters – nine others would be awarded to Lancaster crew members during the war.[8] Operation Margin served as an important lesson to future special operations in which the Lancaster would take part. Two months after the mission, in June 1942, Roy Chadwick, the designer of the Lancaster, stated that it was an aircraft 'in which I naturally take great pride, and believe that it will prove to be a deadly weapon in the hands of the Royal Air Force'.[9] As time went on, he would be proven correct.

A Show of Force

The Augsburg Raid had demonstrated that in the Lancaster, Bomber Command possessed an aircraft that was capable of striking targets deep inside Germany. In addition to the new aircraft, there were also exciting and much needed developments in technology that went some way toward solving one of the command's biggest problems. As mentioned previously, in the early part of the war, Bomber Command's crews had had trouble all striking the same town or city, let alone the same factory. The War Cabinet accepted that precision bombing just wasn't possible and in 1942 sanctioned 'area bombing', the targeting of entire cities to ensure that strategic targets within them were destroyed. Area bombing was deemed necessary if the Allies were going to defeat Germany, and Air Chief Marshal Arthur Harris believed that such tactics had the power to tip the scales and win the war.

Significant problems persisted with navigation and target identification, however, including poor visibility due to cloud, weather and smog. At the end of 1941, four 'vital needs' were identified in the bomber force, one of them being 'the introduction of navigational aids'.[10] Fortunately, progress in radio and radio direction finding (radar) technology made it possible to develop the navigational aids needed, providing a means for bomber crews to navigate with improved accuracy in cloud, bad weather and at night.

One of these was called 'GEE'. Invented by R. J. Dippy of the Telecommunications Research Establishment, GEE (or 'Ground Electronics Engineering'), was a system which allowed the navigator to calculate the position of his aircraft by measuring the time taken to receive pulse signals from three different ground stations. Radio signals were emitted from a number of stations in Britain, sent in such a way that the navigator could use them to calculate the position of his aircraft where the beams crossed each other. It had a relatively short range – about 350–400 miles – which meant it could only really be useful in western Germany, and anti-jamming measures had to be developed to prevent the enemy interfering with the system. Still, the Air Staff stated in February 1942 that 'the introduction of this equipment on operations should be regarded as a revolutionary advance in bombing technique which, during the period of its effective life as a target-finding device, will enable results to be obtained of a much more effective nature'.[11]

The 'cardinal principle' of using GEE was 'the complete concentration on one target until the effort estimated to be required for its destruction has been achieved'.[12] By mid-1944 there were five chains of GEE signal-emitting stations around Britain, and these continued to be set up in

Europe as the Allies moved into it after the D-Day landings in June 1944. GEE remained in use for the rest of the war.

It was clear to Harris, though, that even with the most modern heavy bombers like the Lancaster and new equipment like GEE, unescorted daylight raids were just not feasible as a regular tactic at this stage in the war. Over half of the aircraft sent to Augsburg had not returned, which was an unacceptable and unsustainable rate of loss. This was especially true when taking into account the resources needed to fight the Battle of the Atlantic and to continue fighting in multiple theatres of war. Harris had taken up the reins of Bomber Command with a series of attacks against Rostock and Lübeck, as well as a precision raid on the Renault facility in Paris.[13] What he wanted to do, though, was to demonstrate as clearly as possible that his Command was capable of fulfilling its purpose, and to this end he began to plan a mammoth operation.

On 18 May 1942, he shared his idea with the Chief of the Air Staff, Sir Charles Portal: to send 1,000 bombers to Germany at once. Along with the Prime Minister, Portal approved it. The decision-makers who could determine Bomber Command's fate were watching – and so were the British public. Harris hoped that the 'Thousand Bomber Raid', codenamed 'Operation Millennium', would gain public support for his command. It would not be easy to gather enough bombers to achieve the target of 1,000. This number was important to Harris because it sent a very clear message – it was as much a psychological move as a physical one and would demonstrate to the German people that their government could not protect them. It would also boost morale, he hoped, in Britain, in the RAF and in Bomber Command itself.

There was a lot of work to do. In May 1942, there were only four operational squadrons fully equipped with Lancaster bombers. The plan required Harris to borrow all the operational reserve aircraft he could from operational training units and conversion units, and to ask other services and RAF commands in possession of suitable aircraft if he could borrow what they had. In the end, Harris ended up with 1,047 aircraft, including Wellingtons, Halifaxes, Stirlings – and seventy-three Lancasters.

Now, the aircraft needed crews, and every man who could be spared was gathered. A number of crew members came from OTUs, with the result that some forty-nine aircraft were piloted by pupils who had not yet completed their training. Many other men were inexperienced, and for everyone involved an operation of this size was new and out of the ordinary. On 30 May, the 1,047 aircraft took off, comprising the largest force deployed by Bomber Command in a single night of the war to date.

The target was the Rhineland city of Cologne. Harris deployed new tactics for the raid – the aircraft would fly in a stream of bombers, all following the same route, at the same speed, on the way to and from the target. With so many aircraft flying at once, there would, of course, be a risk of collision and accident. To help reduce this risk, each aircraft was given a specific altitude and time slot, to keep them all in place and out of each other's way as far as possible. The operation would be led by more experienced crews, who would locate and pinpoint the target for the following bombers. They would lead in aircraft equipped with GEE. German defences in Cologne, it was hoped, would be completely overwhelmed by the sheer number of attacking bombers, and rendered ineffective. The bombers would approach in waves, all of them dropping their bombs in a period of ninety minutes, overwhelming the emergency services in the city below. This new way of operating formed the basis of Bomber Command's main tactics for the remainder of the war.

On the night of 30/31 May, the first wave in the bomber stream located Cologne with ease thanks to GEE, and once the first bombs had been dropped on the city, it was illuminated for those that followed. Of the 1,047 bombers involved in the raid, 868 dropped their bombs on the city, and forty-one aircraft were lost. German records show that 469 people were killed, and Cologne suffered considerable damage. Tens of thousands of buildings – a mixture of residential, commercial and industrial – were destroyed or damaged, as were various utilities, such as water and gas mains, electricity cables and telephone circuits. More than 45,000 people were 'bombed out' (lost their homes), and around 150,000 (out of a population of almost 700,000) left Cologne after the raid.

Luftwaffe Commander-in-Chief Reichsmarschall Hermann Göring had famously boasted that no enemy bomber would fly over the Reich. The first Thousand-Bomber Raid was a huge propaganda success, proving Göring wrong in front of the Nazi leadership, the German people and the rest of the world. Two nights later, a second Thousand-Bomber Raid was carried out, this time with 956 bombers targeting the industrial town of Essen. This raid achieved relatively little in terms of damage but reinforced the psychological impact of the raid on Cologne. On 25 June a third raid, involving 960 bombers, targeted Bremen. The level of destruction was higher than that in Essen but lower than Cologne, with most of the damage being to residential areas.

The Thousand Bomber Raids were considered a success, boosting morale in Bomber Command and proving that strategic bombing had an important role to play in Britain's approach to fighting the war. Harris received a knighthood in recognition of his work in turning the command into an offensive force to be reckoned with, at a time when one was so badly needed.

The Pathfinders

Another answer to the problem of bombing accuracy was the development of specialized crews who could mark the targets clearly and lead the bombers to them. In March 1942, the 'Shaker' bombing technique was introduced and tested in a raid on Essen on the night of 8 March. Certain aircraft were designated 'illuminators' – their job was to drop flares on the target. Some were 'target markers' – they dropped incendiaries onto the area the flares had illuminated, further highlighting it. The rest were 'followers' and were guided to the lit area to drop their bombs. A number of aircraft carried GEE and were trained to arrive in several waves over the target at three-minute intervals. The results were promising, but there was significant room for improvement.

Calls for a specially trained precision force that could guide the bomber stream persisted. The Air Staff decided that a specialist group of 'Target Finders' was what was needed, and on 11 August 1942 it was created. Australian airman Don Bennett was chosen to lead it on 5 July 1942, but Arthur Harris was not supportive of the idea. Bennett writes:

> He did not believe it was right to weaken the command by taking its best crews in order to form a corps d'élite as a leading body. He thought it was unfair to other Groups, and he had, therefore, done everything he could to stop the idea of a Path Finder Force. However, he had been given a direct order from the Prime Minister through the Chief of Air Staff, and since it was forced upon him he insisted that I should command it.[14]

Harris could not stand the name 'Target Finders' and instead named the group the Pathfinder Force (PFF). Though he was not in favour of its creation, he assured Bennett that he would support him 'in every way'. Bennett possessed 'an understanding of the many problems of long-range flying which was probably unique in the Service. He was an acknowledged expert on the subject of air navigation and he knew intimately the job which each member of a bomber crew had to undertake'.[15] Harris said of Bennett: 'His technical knowledge and his personal operational ability was altogether exceptional.'[16] He could also, however, be impatient, and 'some people found him difficult to work with. He could not suffer fools gladly, and by his own high standards there were many fools…'

Bennett got to work straight away:

> I immediately began work on every aspect of the problem … The divisions of the problem were fairly clear. The human element was undoubtedly the most important,

> and the selection and training of crews was my most vital consideration. Second was the development and production of the very best navigational equipment available. Third, I had to provide the means of illuminating and/or marking the target in such a way that the main force crews could identify it in spite of all the decoys and dummies and the diversions that the enemy might provide.[17]

Tackling the human element – the aircrew – meant finding the most skilled pilots and navigators, and the obvious place to look was to the men already serving in Bomber Command, who had been fully trained and had accumulated valuable operational experience, their skills already proven. Later in the war, as losses mounted and the need remained, the most promising students in OTUs were recruited straight into the PFF.

A post to a Pathfinder crew came with higher rank and an increase in pay, and aircrew were keen to earn the right to wear the group's gold eagle insignia. However, it also came with an increased number of operational tours – at least forty-five, compared to the thirty flown by the main Bomber Command force. The only break would be a standard week of leave every six weeks, or 'survivor's leave' if they were unlucky enough to have to bail out, ditch their aircraft at sea or crash. The men who joined the Pathfinders were volunteers, and they understood that the odds of survival were not good. Around 20,000 young men served as Pathfinders, most of them in their early twenties or younger, and more than half of them came from Commonwealth countries and overseas locations, such as the US, Norway and Hong Kong.[18]

The PFF faced long flights, which were monotonous at best, and at worst were terrifying. They encountered bad weather which shook and rattled their aircraft or made it difficult to see anything at all, and they were preyed upon by enemy flak and fighters, constantly lurking to pick them off in the darkness over enemy-occupied territory. The Pathfinders were at the head of the raid – the front line against enemy defences, often exposed to terrible danger for longer than the main force, as they had to circle the target area to mark and re-mark the target, so the incoming waves of bombers could see it clearly. If they were shot down, they faced capture and death at the hands of the Nazis or angry locals, or being interned in a prisoner of war camp. Their timing had to be perfect, and the pressure was intense.

On Bennett's second element – technology – the Pathfinders looked to radar and radio developments and advances. GEE had proven a very useful navigational aid, but it wasn't wholly adequate in accurately locating targets and it could be jammed. Bennett was convinced that 'the hope for Pathfinders' lay in new technology. In December 1942 'Oboe' was used for the first time operationally, helping bomber crews to find and hit their targets with a much higher degree of accuracy. The bombers would fly along a fixed radio beam – a radar pulse, which was audible to the pilot – and their position would be tracked by two ground stations. Variations in the pulse, which were easily recognizable, signalled variations from course. The ground stations could locate with a high degree of precision where on the main beam the aircraft was located. A second signal was sent to the aircraft as it approached its target – a series of dashes and dots – that gave the crew exact information about when to release their bombs. When the signal stopped, the bomb aimer released the bombs.

Oboe was a significant development. GEE was helpful, reducing the margin of error to a matter of a few hundred yards, but Oboe enabled 'blind bombing' to be carried out with a much higher degree of precision. If an aircraft was over a target in heavy cloud cover or the haze caused by industrial facilities, it could still drop bombs on a specific target and hit it. Like GEE, Oboe had limitations – for one thing, its range was limited by the curvature of the earth, and it could be jammed. But the new technology enabled the Pathfinders to achieve a higher level of accuracy in target-marking, which translated to improvements in the accuracy of bombing for the main force.

On Bennett's third point, the force was also equipped with specially designed 'target indicators', developed with the help of fireworks experts. These were extremely bright flare markers, coloured red, yellow and green, designed to be dropped onto the target to illuminate it clearly for aircraft hundreds of feet above to see. They were so bright they could even be seen through cloud and in conditions of low visibility. Lancasters both served as part of the Pathfinder Force and were guided by the Pathfinders to their targets in some of the most significant operations in the air war. The Pathfinders transformed Bomber Command into a mighty and remarkably capable offensive weapon, able to carry out mass bombing raids and precision strikes on diverse targets. Thanks to them, the number of bomber crews reaching within 3 miles of their targets increased from as low as 25 per cent in some operations in August 1942 to 95 per cent in some operations in April 1945. As Bomber Command's effectiveness increased, it made a vital contribution in the build-up to D-Day and in the Allied advance into western Europe after the landings.

However, the success of the Pathfinders came at an enormous cost. Of the 20,000 men recruited into the special aircrews, more than 3,600 were killed in action. At the height of the Battle of Berlin, the Pathfinders lost at least 210 crews on operations or in accidents and crashes, and in one terrible six-week period, eighty-seven Pathfinder crews – more than 600 men – were listed as missing or killed in action. The two squadrons that took the heaviest losses in Bomber Command were both Pathfinders.

Leader of the Pathfinders Don Bennett issued a victory message to his men on VE Day. 'The Path Finder Force has shouldered a grave responsibility,' he wrote. 'It has led Bomber Command, the greatest striking force ever known ... I want to thank you each man and woman of you personally and to congratulate you on your unrelenting spirit and energy and on the results you have achieved.'[19]

Operation Robinson

In Operation Millennium, the Lancaster had further proven its ability to strike deep into Germany itself. Bomber Command was becoming a force that could reap massive destruction, and with increasing numbers of Lancasters being produced and new technology to improve bombing accuracy, the command stepped up the offensive against Nazi Germany. Operations were carried out against Hamburg, Stuttgart, Munich, Mannheim and other cities in 1942. Germany was using factories in occupied territories to manufacture war materials, and these were also logical targets for Bomber Command. The Schneider Armaments Factory at Le Creusot, for instance, was targeted in October. This particular plant in France was producing materials for the railway network and weapons. It was a high-priority bombing target, and it was thought that hitting it would damage German war production and enemy capabilities.

Bombing such factories at night would inevitably mean casualties among the civilian populations in areas where civilians had not chosen German occupation and did not support the Nazi war effort. It was decided that the raid should be carried out in daylight, to increase bombing accuracy and decrease the likelihood of harming local people in occupied areas. With the significant losses of the Augsburg raid (which had also been carried out in daylight) still lingering in the mind, the attack would be undertaken with caution.

To reach the Schneider factory, the aircraft would have to fly across a significant chunk of occupied territory. The risky task was assigned to Bomber Command's 5 Group – the only group to have completely converted to using the Lancaster. The new bomber could fly a longer, evasive route due to its remarkable range, and it could fly fast, which gave it a fighting chance against enemy defences. Its huge bomb bay could hold the type of bomb load that could do significant damage to the factory. On 17 October, ninety-four Lancasters – nine squadrons' worth and the entire complement of No. 5 Group Bomber Command – took off from their respective airfields in the middle of the afternoon. Operation Robinson was underway.

Having practised flying in formation, the Lancasters made their way together across the Channel and over France at very low altitude, level with the treetops for some of the journey, to avoid detection by enemy radar. Eighty-eight of the Lancasters were tasked with bombing the factory, and the other six would target a transformer station at Montchanin to prevent it supplying the factory with electrical power. Arriving over the target at dusk, they had just enough light to positively identify the factory. Climbing to between 2,500 and 7,500ft, the squadrons all released their bombs in under ten minutes. With almost no flak, there were no aircraft or men lost on the Schneider factory raid, and only one aircraft was lost in the entire operation, having clipped a building at Montchanin and crashed.

The crews of No. 5 Group reported an accurate and successful raid. The factory closed down for three weeks, and the necessary repairs were carried out over eight months – the raid had, to some extent at least, been successful. Photographic reconnaissance after the raid revealed, though, that not as many bombs had struck the target as had been hoped. It was still relatively early days for the Lancaster. No. 5 Group's crews had been trained quickly to fly under different circumstances than they were used to, and the Lancasters were underarmed, with around 4,000lb each in their bomb bays. The aircraft was still yet to really flex its muscles.

In addition to Bomber Command's operations, Lancasters were also loaned to Coastal Command for anti-submarine operations. In the summer of 1942, for instance, No. 61 Squadron was twice detached from its base in Cornwall and loaned to Coastal Command to assist with anti-submarine operations in the Bay of Biscay. On 17 July, the crew of 61 Squadron's Lancaster R5724 became one of the first Bomber Command crews to prove irrefutably that they had sunk a U-boat at sea.[20] A photograph taken from the Lancaster showed the crew of U-boat U-751 swimming away from their sinking vessel, after R5724 had struck it with depth charges.[21]

Also in the summer of 1942, Bomber Command started to work with the Americans. The US had entered the war in December 1941 following the Japanese attack on Pearl Harbor in Hawaii, and the decision was taken very early on that the Eighth US Army Air Force (USAAF) would work in Britain with Bomber Command, forming a combined strategic bombing force. The Eighth began to arrive in the summer of 1942, with General Ira Eaker in command. On 8 September 1942, a joint directive was issued. The RAF was given the responsibility for night bombing and the USAAF would conduct day bombing. Working together, the two forces would develop the 'Combined Bomber Offensive', establishing 'around the clock' bombing of the enemy. The combined force would, it was hoped, be able to bomb on such a scale that the German ability to fight back in the air would be worn down and, if possible, eliminated.

The Battle of the Ruhr

In January 1943, the Western Allies met in Casablanca to discuss their strategy moving forward in the war. British and American leaders were determined to continue the heavy bombing of German targets, resulting in the 'Casablanca Directive' on 21 January. The directive called for the 'progressive destruction and dislocation of the German military, industrial and economic system' and was supported by both Winston Churchill and the American President Franklin D. Roosevelt. German industry – particularly submarine and aircraft industry – would be targeted, as would fuel facilities and communications. The Eighth Air Force would continue to bomb by day, and Bomber Command by night.

The first contribution of Bomber Command to the combined bomber offensive would be in the 'Battle of the Ruhr'. In considering strategically useful targets, Bomber Command had identified early in the war that the Ruhr region of Germany – a centre of war industry – was a very important one. The 1941 Butt Report (see Chapter One), however, had highlighted Bomber Command's inability to accurately hit targets in the region. Still, its location in the west of Germany meant the Ruhr was easier to get to than other targets, and its significance to the German war effort made it a key area of focus. Being of such significance it was very heavily defended, which made Bomber Command's job of targeting it much more difficult. In addition to strong ground defences, the industrial nature of the area meant that there was often thick smog hanging over it, making it even trickier to carry out raids.

There were, however, a couple of factors that enabled Bomber Command to launch a fresh aerial bombing campaign in the Ruhr. The command had grown and now possessed more aircraft – and most importantly, more four-engined bombers like the Lancaster. The aircraft now had new systems to assist with accurate navigation and bomb-aiming. As well as GEE and Oboe, in the summer of 1943 a new radar system was introduced that could be fitted to a bomber and would essentially create a radar picture of the ground below. This new innovation was called H2S, and it used a radar scanner in the aircraft to send and receive pulses to study the terrain below, spanning miles around the aircraft. The picture it produced showed features of the landscape, including towns, rivers, lakes and coastlines. H2S had fewer range limitations than GEE and Oboe, and it was useful in thick cloud, fog and haze. Like GEE and Oboe, however, it was not without problems – the apparatus could be temperamental and the information it provided could be difficult to interpret. In November, a new version was introduced which could provide a much sharper image of the features of the landscape below, and H2S continued to be installed in increasing numbers of aircraft.

With new aircraft and new equipment, Harris was sure that his bomber force could be effective in the Ruhr and launched an intensive bombing campaign. On the night of 5/6 March 1943, the Battle of the Ruhr began with a raid on Essen. That night, 157 Lancasters were part of a force of 442 aircraft targeting the city, led by eight de Havilland Mosquitoes using the new Oboe system. In particular, the raid sought to damage the Krupp Works, one of the largest and most significant factories in the Ruhr, which was making steel and armaments.

A mixture of high explosives and incendiaries were dropped on the steelworks, causing damage to fifty-three of its buildings. Over 3,000 houses were destroyed and more than 450 civilians were killed. Even with imperfect visibility, the bomber force had devastated Essen.

On the night of the 12th the Krupp Works was hit again, in a raid carried out by 457 aircraft, 156 of them Lancasters. Between early March and the middle of July, sustained aerial attacks continued in the Ruhr region, and all the major cities in the region were bombed. The Battle of the Ruhr was the start of Bomber Command's main offensive against German cities and industrial targets. The campaign was deemed a success, as German production – particularly in the areas of steel and aircraft – were majorly disrupted.

The Dambusters

As well as taking part in Bomber Command's general operations, Lancasters were also used in specific, precision operations. For these they sometimes had to be modified to carry special weapons. The most famous raid of this sort was carried out during the Battle of the Ruhr in May 1943, under the codename Operation Chastise. In looking at potential targets, the RAF had selected three dams in the Ruhr region that supplied water and hydroelectric power for both civilian and industrial purposes. To damage the dams would mean these industrial facilities were cut off from their power and war production would, it was hoped, be significantly disrupted.

Hitting the dams, though, was no easy task. They were heavily defended, with torpedo nets in the water which prevented explosive devices getting near the dams and anti-aircraft guns pointed to the sky. The dams had been on the RAF's list of potential targets since 1937, but no weapon existed that could do the necessary damage under such conditions. In 1942, however, that changed. British engineer and inventor Barnes Wallis developed a mine that could 'skip' across water. Initially developed with naval and shipping targets in mind, the mine was tested for its potential use against the Ruhr dams. Testing revealed that if dropped from a height of around 60ft, at a ground speed of 232mph, the mine would spin backwards, and skip across the surface of the water and over the torpedo net. Once it hit the dam it would sink, and when it reached a certain depth underwater, it would explode like a depth charge against the wall of the dam. The weapon was called 'Upkeep' and is known today as the 'bouncing bomb'.

At last possessing a weapon that made a raid on the dams possible, Bomber Command needed the aircraft to transport it and the crew to fly it. In March 1943, a new squadron was formed to carry out the operation. Initially codenamed 'Squadron X', 617 Squadron would fly Lancasters specially modified to carry and drop Upkeep. Led by twenty-four-year-old Wing Commander Guy Gibson, 617 included aircrew from Britain, Australia, New Zealand and Canada. The squadron practised low-level flying at night, initially unaware of the details of the operation.

Harris was not happy about the secret mission, viewing it as a waste of precious resources and an unnecessary risk. Flying in formation at such low altitude was not something Bomber Command's airmen had much experience of, and they would need to do this over dangerous, unfamiliar territory. The huge losses at Augsburg lingered in his mind. The dams would not be easy to hit accurately, even with the new Upkeep mine. The Möhne dam was a curved gravity dam, 40m high and 650m long. Due to the fact its reservoir was surrounded by hills covered in trees, 617's aircraft would be exposed on their approach. The Eder dam was very similar, the only approach option being from the north, where again, the aircraft would be exposed. The Sorpe dam was a different kind of dam, with an upright central wall supported by sloping earth supports. The approach was tricky in that there was a church spire directly in the flight path.

Operation Chastise would demand skilled flying and navigation, and extreme courage from the aircrews involved. In order to give them as much of a chance of success as possible, a tremendous amount of thorough preparation was carried out before the operation. Information was gathered on the terrain the aircrews would be flying over. It was hilly and littered with obstacles, and the more the aircrews knew about it in advance, the greater their chance of executing the raid successfully and returning home. In addition to maps and photographs, detailed models of the dams and the surrounding areas were constructed and used in the briefings for the raid.

WAAF intelligence officer Joan Baughan collected information on enemy defences in the area, and Edna Skeen provided maps of the Ruhr valley. Edna was so crucial to the planning of the operation that for the week before it took place, she stayed in her office all day and night, the door locked, and if she left it to use the bathroom the key was given to Guy Gibson or the station commander, both of whom needed to know where she was at all times. Though she did not know the details of the operation, Edna supplied maps to the aircrews right up until the night of the raid.

There was one WAAF officer, however, who 'knew all there was to know of the proposed raid'. The only woman included in the detailed planning of Operation Chastise was twenty-one-year-old intelligence officer Fay Gillon. Fay attended all of 617 Squadron's briefings and worked closely with the aircrews as they trained. She was given the difficult job of liaising with the organizers of the flying training programme and with HQ 5 Group, clearing low-flying routes for 617 Squadron. The aircrews needed to train at very low altitudes, which upset people both on the station and in the local area. Fay's job was to placate them without giving away any secret information about the operation. Gibson recognized that this would be difficult and stressful, and to reward her for her superb efforts he invited her on a training flight with the squadron.

When the operation was given the go-ahead by the Chief of the Air Staff on 14 May 1943, Gibson ran a tactical exercise designed to be as like the real operation as possible. Fay was again invited along. She describes the flight:

> A signal from the wing commander [Gibson] and all three of us simultaneously creeping down the runway and gathering speed. The terrific roar and power of the engines, then the last bump and we are airborne. Me clambering into the flight engineer's seat and watching eagerly and intently as we go

> rushing out to sea over Mablethorpe, and into the gathering dusk, gliding right down, practically into the drink. Dropping a smoke float to check the wind, and then a burst of firing from the WC's plane, followed by a burst from all three of us, missing each other by inches. Then, suddenly, the target, glistening in the moonlight. The voice of the wing commander coming over the VHF ... Then a huge explosion and a flash of light. Right on target. Then our turn. Mick doing a big circle to get into position, grim determination on his face, and Jack and I with our noses glued to the Perspex. Down, down, 20ft more, 10ft more, 5ft more, steady, steady on an altitude of 60ft and the run along the water. 'Bomb's gone!' from Bob, and then pull up, up into the sky at full revs.[22]

Fay observed the crew that night after the aircraft had landed. 'The crew bursting out with cracks and jokes and clambering out into the waiting bus. Looking around at their faces and noticing happiness and satisfaction on all of them. Wonderful, absolutely wizard. Back to the mess and a pint of beer and eggs and bacon for supper with the boys. Then the wing commander arriving with a beam of appreciation on his face. "Bloody good show boys."'

Just before 9.30 p.m. on 16 May, after around ten weeks of training, nineteen Lancasters and 133 aircrew of 617 Squadron took off in three waves to make their way to the Ruhr, and Operation Chastise began. Map clerk Edna Skeen watched the aircraft take off and thought to herself: 'This will make history and I have had a part in it.' Vera Tassell was on duty as a watchkeeper that night and recalls that it was 'by far the most exciting and impressive' experience of her WAAF career. Vera and Edna had watched 617 training for this moment and wondered, as the aircraft took off, why the bomb doors of the Lancasters did not seem to be able to close over the oddly shaped bombs in their bellies.

Each aircraft carried an Upkeep, and Guy Gibson led the way in the first wave. His Lancaster was the first to bomb the Möhne, which, after it had been struck by five aircraft, was breached. The Eder suffered a similar fate, collapsing just before 2 a.m. The Sorpe was bombed by the second and third wave of Lancasters and also suffered damage. Vera Tassell went on duty in the operations room back at Scampton to find an atmosphere of 'suppressed excitement', which intensified with the arrival of Commander-in-Chief Arthur Harris. There was 'dead silence' in the operations room, until the code word signifying the success of the attack on the first dam was used by a signals officer. Harris gave a 'slight grimace', which Vera presumed to be a smile, and he asked her to 'get Washington' on the telephone.

The results of the raid were complicated. The squadron suffered terrible losses – of 133 aircrew, fifty-three were killed and three were taken as prisoners of war. The breaching of two dams caused flooding in the Ruhr valley, and around 1,300 people were killed, including a number of prisoners of war. The industrial impact was minimal, and Operation Chastise certainly did not cause the kind of damage that would seriously affect Germany's war capabilities. It took time, resources and money to carry out repairs to the dams, however – and this was time, money and resources that were not being used elsewhere in the German war effort.

The impact on British morale was also significant, and the 'Dambusters', as 617 Squadron came to be known, were hailed as heroes and became celebrities. Guy Gibson was awarded the Victoria Cross. Chastise had demonstrated the new capabilities of the reformed Bomber Command and showcased advances in aviation technology and the operational skills of the force using it. The Lancaster had proven its ability as a capable aircraft in the execution of specialist precision raids, and it would continue to play an integral role in Bomber Command's operations.

CHAPTER SIX

FROM THE DAMS TO BERLIN

Combat

A Lancaster was not a comfortable place to be. First and foremost, it was a warplane, and touches of comfort were extremely lacking. There was exposed metal everywhere, and the crew needed to be careful not to get snagged on anything when moving around the fuselage in their bulky flying gear while carrying portable oxygen units, which they needed because the aircraft wasn't pressurized. Cold was a constant enemy to all who flew on Lancasters. The crew's heated flight suits could malfunction due to electrical faults and damage to the aircraft, which left them vulnerable to the extremely low temperatures at high altitude. It could get down to -40°, the rear of the aircraft getting especially cold, and frostbite could cause the loss of fingers. Physically, it was a tough environment in which to do an already dangerous job. Mentally, though, operations on Lancasters were unimaginably difficult. 'It was pretty obvious that we couldn't all survive,' writes Lancaster pilot Stevie Stevens.

> And when you looked around the table at a briefing for 18–20 crews, you knew darn well the next day that at least two or three wouldn't be coming back, and perhaps more. As the Captain, you would come out and try to make a joke or a comment just to lighten the mood and to keep up the morale of your crew. Many would go out after briefing, light up a cigarette or take a lucky pee against the tail wheel. The Tannoy would click, and we'd be sitting outside, waiting for it, but pretending not to be interested.[1]

No one expected airmen to be unafraid on bombing raids – such a thing would be unreasonable beyond doubt. Courage was not the absence of fear, but the mastery of it. Airmen who had not yet experienced enemy fire couldn't be sure how they would react – and wouldn't know until it happened. Wireless operator Roy Briggs says: 'The first time I really saw anti-aircraft fire coming up, I didn't know whether I was dreaming. I was twenty then, and I couldn't believe a twenty-year-old boy from Battersea was flying in a Lancaster over Germany. You always thought you were going to come back, and the others weren't.'[2] Roy remembers the distress of having to watch another Lancaster be shot at by the enemy. 'I could stand up in the astrodome with a long lead and listen to the set, and I said to the skipper, "Plane's been hit to the right" – we moved over. We don't know if he was hit again, but there were bits flying off of it. We saw three chutes coming out. It was hard to watch.'

Some airmen experienced terrifying near-misses – close brushes with death. 'Some raids were very easy with little or no opposition,' says RAAF wireless operator Bruce Rawling, 'while others were gut wrenching.'[3] Bruce was on his third operation in Lancasters when things went horribly wrong:

> Our target was a synthetic oil plant. We were in heavy cloud practically all the way and finally emerged at about 22,000ft. The bomber stream was all over the place. As we were

> turning out of the target a Lanc was hit and blew up. We were carrying a load of propaganda leaflets which I had to push out of the flare chute, which was down near the tail, the lever on the compressed bottle of carbon dioxide on my Mae West life jacket caught and released the CO_2 and inflated my jacket which, being under my tight parachute harness gave me a hell of a shock and nearly choked me. I staggered back and unknowingly pulled the oxygen lead out of the plug. Next thing I knew I was almost passing out with lack of oxygen and called out 'help' in a tiny voice. Jock, our engineer, came back with a portable oxygen bottle to see what was wrong and at the same time Bill put the nose down to get a lower altitude. At about 17,000ft we ran into severe icing and the plane flipped over and went down in a vertical dive. All I remember was floating around in the middle of the plane being hit by all the loose stuff and Jock got hit in the head by a Very Light pistol that had broken free. While this was going on Bill was struggling to regain control of the plane ... he and Les were heaving back on the control column, Bill with his feet on the instrument panel to get more leverage. We broke free of cloud at about 7,000ft heading back the wrong way into Germany and they just managed to slowly pull out of the dive. The airspeed indicator had gone off the clock but we estimated we must have been doing 400mph.

On another occasion, Bruce's crew were on a daylight raid on Witten in the Ruhr when they were set upon by enemy fighters:

> Fighters seemed to be going in all directions. Ted called to Bill to corkscrew port but I saw the fighter coming down at us on the other side and yelled to go the other way. The fighter flashed over the top of us and shot down the Lancaster just ahead. He went down in flames. Bill was calling for directions

> and Ted said, 'Get into the cloud.' Unbeknown to him, as he was facing to the rear, we had reached the edge of the frontal cloud and it dropped sheer away to about 6,000ft. Bill put the plane into a falling leaf to simulate having been hit and dived for the cloud at about 320mph. We dropped our bombs somewhere near the target on the way down. A fighter shot down another Lanc and came tearing after us. We only just reached the cloud cover ahead of him and he couldn't find us. Unfortunately we were smack bang in the middle of the Ruhr at 6,000ft and we came out of cloud right over the middle of Duisburg. Boy was I scared. They tossed everything but the kitchen sink at us and I'm not too sure they didn't include that. Finally we cleared the town and passed over the Rhine in a hail of bullets. It was a scared and weary crew that made it back that afternoon.

Some aircrews were involved in firefights multiple times in their tours. Rear gunner Bob Howes recorded several instances in his logbook where his Lancaster encountered and engaged the enemy. In a raid on Darmstadt on 25 August 1944, for instance, he wrote, 'ME110 destroyed'. On 6 October 1944, he recorded, 'Combat Ju. 88', and on 26 November that year he documented that the Lancaster was 'attacked on bombing run'. Such experiences could have long-lasting effects on the men involved. Bob suffered nightmares long after the conclusion of the war and 'machine-gunned' in his sleep.

Then there was the psychological impact of suffering a 'near-miss', a brush with death. Finlay McRae recorded a near-miss in his diary after his crew fought off two enemy fighters:

> On the way home we got lost and as we were very short of petrol Johnnie warned us that there was a strong possibility of us 'ditching' [performing an emergency landing on water]. The crew behaved fine. We were for four hours over the sea when we sighted land. We were never so pleased to see

> the coast. We had only five minutes of petrol left when we landed and were given up for lost. The whole crew has been recommended for their endurance and as they say, 'devotion to duty'. Afterwards Johnnie told me that if any of us had panicked he would have gone off his head. I believe him.[4]

Sometimes a near-miss occurred between two friendly aircraft. Crews would look up through the Perspex turret and find, to their horror, that a fellow Allied aircraft was hovering above their own, its bomb doors wide open. Sometimes evasive manoeuvres were necessary to avoid being hit by bombs carried by friends and colleagues and collisions were frequent – especially when a Lancaster released its payload and lurched upwards, sometimes by as much as 500ft, which could cause it to collide with another aircraft. Norman Wilkins describes surviving a collision with another aircraft:

> One time over Germany there was a whacking great bumph. The whole aircraft started rocking and when we'd all recovered ourselves and decided that our trousers were still clean, George said to me, 'Norman. What do you reckon?' 'I've got no radar,' I said, 'It must have been something to do with the radar. I'm going to put an oxygen bottle on and go back and see if I can find what damage was done.' Well ... all we'd got back there was a big hole. The radar had collided with something and had gone. During debriefings we heard that a Halifax had lost a tail and had landed successfully. So, two things were put together. The Halifax had taken our radio off and our radio had taken one of his fins off. That was the worst feeling that we had.[5]

For his part, navigator Peter Carpenter refers to what he calls 'unrecorded great escapes', where his crew narrowly escaped serious injury or death:

> At Caen it was watching bombs from a Lancaster above us miss our own wings by no more than a few feet. This was in daylight. Records show that there was intense flak – but I remember those bombs. [On another occasion we were] being engaged by the night fighters over the Baltic – very near to Peenemünde. We were one of six 103 planes 'gardening' in the Baltic that night. I was in the navigation compartment tracking our position on the H2S screen when some enemy fire with trace was so near and so bright that everything flashed daylight. We were about three and a half hours from base, the plane was full of acrid fumes from our own guns – and I felt that we all knew how vulnerable we were. Nobody spoke.[6]

Benny Goodman and his crew in 617 Squadron took a hit to the nose of their Lancaster during one raid. 'Everyone seemed okay, but after landing back at base the bomb aimer discovered that both heels of his flying boots were pitted with shrapnel. An inch or two either way?' His crew experienced another near-miss:

> On another raid the wireless operator was tuning his radio and leaned a little closer to the set. As he did so, a large projectile or piece of flak entered one side of the fuselage and exited the other. After we landed, the wireless operator sat normally in his seat and we measured the two holes and the position of his head. If he had been sitting in this position at the time of the attack, the projectile/flak would have pierced one side of his head and exited the other.[7]

Survival often came down to being at the right place at the right time – and in the right position – inside the aircraft. Rear gunner Bob Howes, of 207 Squadron, stood up as best he could in his turret, stretching his legs after a long period of being sat down scanning the sky for signs of the enemy. Just as he did so, a bullet entered the turret and hit him. In a moment of sheer luck, the bullet had hit the strap of Bob's belt, and though the belt had a slit in it, Bob himself was unharmed. When the crew returned to base, they used a rod to measure the trajectory of the bullet from where it had entered the rear turret. They concluded that if Bob had not stood up when he did, he likely would have been seriously injured or killed.[8]

Similarly, Jock Bunten was alarmed when he returned from a sortie to find that his Lancaster had eighty-nine holes in it, and one was 3ft away from where he had been sitting. There was one 'vital ingredient' in bomber operations, Peter Carpenter said – 'luck'.

One of the hardest things Bomber Command crews had to deal with was watching as other aircraft, with their friends and colleagues on board, were shot down or decimated right in front of them. 'It was an awful sight to see a plane get hit by a 4,000lb bomb, it just disintegrated in a giant fireball,' said Australian wireless operator Bruce Rawling.[9] Tony Adams was on a daylight raid on Homburg when the group of Lancasters started to take anti-aircraft fire:

> Approaching the target in a clear sky a Lancaster formed up on each side of us as one in front was blown up and then the one on our starboard, 100 yards away, got a burst underneath and went down with four engines flaming. I believe it was from a New Zealand squadron ... Of the 100 or so wireless operators on that raid I had been selected to report the result by coded message. I hope they could read it as my hand on the Morse key was very shaky. Since then I have wondered if the ack ack gunners were told to aim for the leader of the formation and missed us.[10]

Wireless operator Arthur Atkinson remembers one occasion when he was working on his wireless set aboard a Lancaster, and suddenly there was a brilliant white flash:

> I wondered what the hell it was, it was like daylight in the cockpit. I jumped up on the step and stuck my head out the

> astrodome just in time to see a wing sailing past with two engines on it, and the propellers going round. An aircraft had blown up just in front of us, and the skipper [was] pulling back on the stick trying to miss it so we didn't hit the damn thing.[11]

Watching Lancasters and other bombers explode, disintegrate and fall out of the sky, the crew of surviving aircraft were utterly helpless to do anything to help. 'I remember flying up towards the target one day and seeing a Lanc below us,' pilot Hugo Trotter says, 'and a German fighter chasing him. I did put the nose down, but he was too far away.'[12] Most of the time, airmen wouldn't know until they got back to base if their friends and squadron mates had made it – the empty chairs in the mess would reveal the answer. People just disappeared, and heartbreakingly, some of them would never be found.

John Johnson remembers a ride on a crew bus with a just-returned crew:

> Bomber crews were notoriously superstitious, and many carried lucky charms of one sort or another with them, often something connected with their wife, girlfriend, children or family. After completing my inspection of the returning aircraft I'd occasionally hitch a ride back to the technical site in a crew bus, the interrogation room being not far from the radar section. On one such ride back the rear gunner of the crew had just completed his last mission. He sat in the back of the crew bus with his arms wrapped around a teddy bear, no doubt his child's, with tears of relief just pouring down his cheeks, obviously totally unable to speak.[13]

It is recorded that around 5,000–6,000 airmen experienced serious 'combat stress' caused by exhaustion and fear, but the number is much higher if more minor cases are included – and as with any war, exact figures will never be known. Billy Strachan realized on his forty-fifth trip that his nerves couldn't take bombing operations anymore:

> I remember so clearly. I was carrying a 12,000 pound bomb destined for some German shipping. We were stationed in Lincolnshire and our flight path was over Lincoln Cathedral. It was a foggy night, with visibility about 100 yards. I asked my engineer, who stood beside me, to make sure we were on course to get over the top of the cathedral tower. He replied: 'We've just passed it.' I looked out and suddenly realised that it was just beyond our wingtips, to the side. This was the last straw. It was sheer luck. I hadn't seen it at all – and I was the pilot! There and then my nerve went. I knew I simply couldn't go on – that this was the end of me as a pilot! I flew to a special 'hole' we had in the North Sea, which no allied shipping ever went near, and dropped my 'big one'. Then I flew back to the airfield.

Some airmen were so affected by combat stress on operations they became 'flak happy' or released their bombs early so as to get away quicker. When treated with rest, around a third of these men returned to duty. If they could not recover, they were removed from their station so as not to undermine the morale of others. Unfortunately, some were treated harshly by their colleagues and were given the dreaded label, 'LMF' – 'Lack of Moral Fibre'. For many airmen, the humiliation of being branded LMF was worse than actually having to fly.

Pointblank

In June 1943, the combined Anglo-American bombing directive was altered to account for the improvements in German air defences. Codenamed 'Pointblank', the new directive cited the German fighter force as the 'immediate target', and the combined bomber force was tasked first and foremost with destroying it. So, on the night of 20 June 1943, sixty Lancasters took off and headed for Friedrichshafen in Germany. In the old Zeppelin sheds – which Avro 504s had bombed in the first strategic air raid in November 1914 – was a factory where radar equipment was being manufactured for use in the Luftwaffe's fighter defences. The Lancasters were guided by Pathfinders equipped with H2S, and the 'Master Bomber' technique was used – a controller in one of the Pathfinder aircraft would lead the way, and target indicators would be dropped to show the rest of the bomber force where to drop their bombs. In Friedrichshafen, the Pathfinders dropped their target indicators successfully, guiding the main bomber force to where they released their bombs.

Lancaster pilot Roy Yule remembers taking part in a raid where the Master Bomber technique was used. When his aircraft arrived at the target, there was a layer of cloud at around 5,000ft and the order came for the bombers to descend to below it. Roy complied, closing the throttles of his Lancaster and putting it into a dive, getting under the cloud and levelling off at 4,000ft. 'This turned out to be one hell of a dangerous bombing run,' Roy says. 'Over half the main force did not come below cloud but bombed through it on the fires and flares that could be seen through the thin layer.' Around 140 Lancasters had obeyed and descended, and they now converged on the target markers that the Pathfinders had dropped. The Master Bomber, his voice 'clear and casual', ordered the aircraft to bomb to starboard of the red target indicators. 'Then I had to dodge under another Lancaster coming from our port side,' Roy says, 'looking up into its yawning bomb bay with its rows of 500lb bombs and a cookie. I jabbed the left rudder to slide clear of it. Stan, who could not see the other Lanc, had started his run-up patter giving me "Right," and shouted agitatedly, "Right, not bloody left!"' He describes the carnage:

> The scene ahead was fantastic. Red and yellow tracer shells were criss-crossing from the flak batteries outside the town. They seemed to be coming from eight different positions and looked like 20mm and 37mm, which are nasty blighters at the height we were at. Strings of bombs were falling through the cloud from the Lancs above. Flashes from the

> exploding blockbusters on the ground were blinding. A stricken Lancaster crashed on its run-in, blowing up with its full bomb load. Large columns of thick black smoke rose from the town up to 3,000ft. Stan gave, 'Right, right, steady, bombs away.' Then our aircraft was bucking and rearing as the pressure waves hit us. 4,000ft was reckoned to be the absolute minimum height for dropping a blockbuster. At last we were through the target and turning south over the Rhine and my stomach muscles started to relax. We landed back at Wickenby at forty-two minutes after midnight. At debriefing, Frank, the mid-upper gunner, said that a string of bombs with a wobbling blockbuster dropped past our starboard tailplane as our own bombs were leaving.[14]

Operation Gomorrah

In July 1943, the Lancaster was deployed on one of the most destructive bombing raids of the Second World War. The city of Hamburg was an obvious industrial target, as there were numerous manufacturing and transport facilities there, as well as shipyards where U-boats were being built. It had been targeted before, but now a huge operation was ordered against it, codenamed Operation Gomorrah in reference to the biblical city devastated by fire.

At around 10 p.m. on the night of 24 July, 791 bombers, Lancasters among them, took off in near-perfect conditions and headed for Hamburg. The aircraft flew in six waves, each containing 100–120 bombers. For the first time, Bomber Command deployed a new radar countermeasure called 'Window'. It didn't look like much – bundles of thin strips of aluminium foil – but when dropped from an aircraft, Window disrupted and jammed German radar so the radar operator would find it near-impossible to distinguish actual aircraft from 'echoes' on their screens caused by the strips. No. 76 Squadron was selected to use Window over Hamburg, and the aircrews were taught how to drop it out of the aircraft's flare chute, using a stopwatch to time each drop perfectly. The tactic worked very well, confusing the radar-guided enemy defences thoroughly and preventing night fighters from finding the real bomber stream.

In a single hour, 2,300 tons of bombs were dropped on Hamburg. These included 8,000lb blockbuster bombs and 4,000lb cookies. Years of experiencing and carrying out bombing fed into the development of a new theory or technique: the explosives would shatter roof tiles and blow holes in roofs, and incendiaries could then drop into the holes, causing fires of unimaginable strength and destruction inside buildings. More than 350,000 individual incendiary bombs were dropped, along with the high explosives, and it was these that caused most of the devastating fires. Much of the destruction was caused by intense firestorms: fires of such high intensity that they created and supported their own wind systems.

One such firestorm was created on 27 July. The day had been hot and dry in Hamburg, and firefighters were busy tackling fires from earlier raids that were still burning. When night came, around 780 RAF bombers arrived to continue the pummelling of the city. The high explosives dropped, blocking roads and making it much more difficult for the already-stretched emergency services to move around the city and fight the fires that were coming. The city turned into a furnace and a firestorm developed. Winds blew at up to 150mph, and temperatures reached 800°C (1,472°F) and upwards. People were sucked toward the fire, and hot air caused the combustion of clothing. Rescue efforts were largely futile, and it was a fight simply to survive.

Kate Hoffmeister was nineteen and remembers struggling to run against the wind in the street: 'There were people on the roadway, some already dead, some still lying alive but stuck in the asphalt. They must have rushed on to the roadway without thinking. Their feet have got stuck and they had put their hands out to try and get out again.'[15] Kate's face, arms and legs were badly burned. Henni Klank fled her apartment with her husband and baby as the curtains caught fire and a crack appeared in the ceiling. Henni describes the 'thundering, blazing hell' that had replaced the city she lived in. 'The streets were burning, the trees were burning and the tops of them were bent ... The air was burning; simply everything was burning.'[16]

Operation Gomorrah continued until 3 August. Over eight days, RAF and USAAF bombers near-annihilated Hamburg. More than 30,0000 civilians were killed. There were more casualties in ten days than there were in the entire Blitz in Britain. In terms of Bomber Command's strategy, the raid accomplished its aims. Almost 600 industrial plants were destroyed, along with the docks, more than 250 Nazi Party buildings and facilities – and U-boat production facilities were affected too. A large portion of the population that was left fled the city, and other German cities feared they would be next. The effect on German morale was significant, with calls from civilians for better protection against attacks from above.

Harris's aim was to end the war as quickly as possible, and with as few British casualties as possible. He, like many others, wanted to avoid the large-scale, terrible rates of bloodshed and loss of the First World War – there could be no more stalemates or battles like the Somme. Attacks like Gomorrah were, he reasoned, the way to achieve this, and he planned further raids, turning his attention to Germany's capital city next. Some concentration camp inmates were forced to help clear the bodies in the wake of the bombing of Hamburg. One of them – Victor Baeyens – was surprised at the level of destruction. 'When listening to those horror stories we no longer broke into cheers as we did during the raid itself,' he says. 'What a curse war is.'[17]

Operation Hydra

By June 1943, the British government had received evidence from various intelligence sources, including aerial reconnaissance, which confirmed that significant secret weapons development was taking place at the Peenemünde research establishment on the Baltic coast. Peenemünde was playing an important role in the development of jet-propelled aircraft, long-range weapons and, it was revealed, objects thought to be rockets. The facility could not be allowed to continue its work on these weapons, and so a heavy bombing raid on the site was ordered. On the night of 17/18 August 1943, 596 bombers took off and made their way to Peenemünde, 324 of them Lancasters. That night, 101 Squadron's Arthur Orchard climbed aboard his Lancaster for his first operation. The station at Ludford Magna was 'buzzing' before the operation. 'Since the petrol load was a relatively large one, we knew it was going to be a long trip, but we hadn't the least idea where. Not till briefing time did we know, and the news was not conducive to the morale of a sprog crew.'[18]

The night of the 17th there was a full moon. 'We gasped,' Arthur says. 'We would be seen by every German fighter between the Channel and the Baltic. Worse, we were to bomb from only 7,000ft and our bomb size were blast effective at that height. So, we knew the raid had to be effective at all costs.' After the briefing and the 'precious fried egg', Arthur and his crew set off for their target in their heavily laden Lancaster. This was to be a precision raid on relatively small targets – the most important areas to hit, the crews were told in their briefing, were the factory itself, the research centre and the area where the scientists and technicians were living. These were identifiable from a smuggled-out map which British intelligence had in their possession. Arthur remembers the sortie well:

> As we neared the target, the Lancaster started to heave and pitch in the slipstream of other aircraft which we could see clearly in the full moon. An unholy mess of flak came up from the target area below. Small bits clattered against our aircraft, but our bomb aimer got the load away successfully and we headed for home. There were fighters in the offing, so we jinked about a bit in the usual evasive action and finally settled down to the long trip back and in the early morning hours landed safely back at Ludford Magna. Seven hours exactly was the duration of that operation.

The bombers attacked in three waves. The first two waves were relatively unharassed, but the third wave faced German night fighters, and forty-one aircraft were lost in total (twenty-three of them Lancasters). The raid had mixed results. The factory area was not damaged as much as had been hoped, and due to mistakes in target marking the accommodation where foreign labourers were housed was bombed and several hundred were killed. The residential area was struck and a significant number of scientists, technicians and engineers were killed, but others escaped, including Wernher von Braun – a leading figure in the development of rocket technology in Nazi Germany.

The raid was one factor in the forced relocation of efforts to develop secret weapons – and these efforts continued. On the morning of 13 June 1944, a stubby-winged little aircraft appeared in the sky above London. It was emitting a peculiar buzzing sound – until it suddenly went quiet. The aircraft plummeted to the ground, smashing into a railway bridge and exploding. Six people were killed. 'It was when it went silent that you really had to worry,' Londoner Mary Knight remembers. 'When the engine cut, you had seconds to run for cover.'[19] Nicknamed 'buzz bombs' and 'doodlebugs' by the British people, these missiles were one of the most frightening weapons deployed against Britain in the Second World War. One of Nazi Germany's *Vergeltungswaffen* – vengeance weapons – the V1 was a menace. Between June 1944 and March 1945, 6,725 V1s were launched against Britain. Of these, 2,340 hit London, and 5,475 people were killed. A further 16,000 were injured and many were rendered homeless by the destruction wrought. There were also V2 rockets to worry about. V2s were first launched against Britain in September 1944, and 517 of them hit London in the space of a few months. V2s were not as accurate as V1s, but they were harder to detect because they travelled at the speed of sound, emitting no warning noise before impact, making it impossible to protect against them.

The Allied air forces went about removing the threat at the root by bombing the launch sites. Though the sites were small and quite difficult to hit, the raids were surprisingly successful and significantly reduced the number of V1s being launched against Britain. By 1945, the threat from the V-weapons had been eliminated by the bombers and the liberating forces on the ground.

Back to Happy Valley

Now on his eighth operation, Arthur Orchard discovered in the briefing room that his crew would be targeting the Ruhr Valley – or 'Happy Valley', as aircrews referred to it. On the night of 19 September 1943, Arthur's crew boarded their 'old faithful' Lancaster, E-Easy, and made their preparations for the raid. This would be a 'lightning strike' sortie, and as the papers reported the next day, it was 'Out after tea, back for supper raid on Germany'. 'We were downing our egg and bacon to a backcloth of brittle cheerfulness and idle chatter,' Arthur remembers.

> This prelude [was] the worst of all – and we were thankful when the Bedford truck arrived to take us out to the aircraft. We looked a strange motley piling into those trucks dressed in our various garb – boys really appearing to be men with their bulbous flying jackets and heavy boots ... Our Lanc stood there in its drab camouflage paint – stained with oil, threadbare in parts through erosion by the elements as if waiting for this truck load of unruly beings who would alone make it live again.

They were soon off, climbing as fast as their heavy load would permit 'into the comfort of the ever-darkening sky', eager to join the bomber stream and fall under its protection before reaching occupied territory. Part of the Pathfinder force, Arthur's Lancaster was to drop four flares to illuminate the target, as well as its load of high explosive bombs. Arthur continues:

> Over the target area it was a three-minute run up to the aiming point – straight and level. The pilot ordered bomb doors open and there we were, exposing our naked underbelly, holding some 6.5 tons of explosive to a hail of red-hot metal – filling the sky around us. It seemed an eternity before Booker seemed to scream 'Bombs Away'. Within seconds the bomb doors closed, and we started once again our jigging and weaving. An ugly orange glare lit the dark sky only 50 yards away. It was sufficient for us to see that one of our own four engine bombers would not be returning to base. I suppose such an end is accepted by aircrews but I'm sure each of us were saying quietly and simply to ourselves that, 'I was glad it wasn't me.' No sooner was the thought out of my mind when the aircraft was struck by a blinding flash sending the aircraft in a steep dive completely out of control. But 8,000ft later, fortunately, the skipper together with assistance from the flight engineer got it under control. As soon as we cleared the target area we found, following a check at all stations, no damage – that is as far as we could see. We all breathed again with relief.

This relief, however, was misplaced and short-lived. Arthur's right leg had gone numb, and he felt a clamminess. Looking down, he discovered that the heating elements in his heated flight suit had burned out, and the right side was getting colder in the freezing altitude. Then the altimeter stopped working, so there was no way of estimating the Lancaster's altitude. Then the radio stopped working, cutting the crew off from the world outside the aircraft. They continued on dead reckoning, aware from the Met officer's briefing that cloud cover was expected on their return. To make a dangerous situation worse, they were low on fuel.

The radio operator had managed to get a call for help off to nearby RAF Downham Market, which had been received, and the airfield sent up flares to try to guide the crew. The Lancaster was slowly descending – without its altimeter – to get below the advised weather report of 3,000ft cloud base. The aircraft cleared the cloud cover and Arthur saw the flares, 'but to our horror', he says, 'the giant aircraft could not have been flying more than 15ft off the ground as we could see tops of trees above us.' If they had been able to make contact with their airfield, the crew of E-Easy would have been diverted to another airfield because of the thick fog rising up from the ground, as there was zero visibility, which was extremely dangerous. 'I had the feeling the old plane was trying to claw its way back into the sky,' Arthur recalls, 'but alas the next thing I remember was opening my eyes unable to move looking up into that black night sky that was a comfort to us not many hours before.' They had crashed around half a mile from the Norfolk town of Downham Market, in a village called Wimbotsham. Two weeks later, in the hospital Arthur was told that he was the sole survivor of his crew. Arthur suffered a concussion and a badly broken leg, which would leave him disabled for the rest of his life. 'Little did any of us know at tea time there would be no supper for any of us that night,' he says.

The Battle of Berlin

As Germany's capital city, Berlin was an obvious and important political target. It was also a difficult one to attack, due to its size, its distance from Britain and the heavy defences protecting it. The more than 1,000 nautical-mile journey there and back was wrought with danger, with anti-aircraft guns and flak towers along the way and concentrated around the target, as well as night fighters lurking in suspicion that their capital would inevitably come under attack. Various raids were carried out over Berlin by Bomber Command – including one on the night of 4 September 1943.

The crew of Lancaster F-Freddy, of 207 Squadron, took part in the raid. As the aircraft closed in on the target, the navigator advised the pilot that they would be on target in thirty seconds. The pilot asked the flight engineer to increase the revs, noting the fighter flares in the distance. The bomb doors were opened, and the bomb was released, causing the Lancaster to lurch upwards. 'Chaser behind us!' came the dreaded call over the intercom. 'Where is the rear gunner? Can you see him?' the pilot asked. It was important that the pilot remain calm, so as to keep his crew from panicking. A few seconds later, the rear gunner replied, 'He's come down!' The crew cheered as the hit was confirmed – the rear gunner had managed to shoot down the fighter pursuing them. 'He's got him! Right in the middle! Bloody good shot!' Now dealing with flak, the pilot called for calm. 'Don't shout all at once,' he said, adding: 'Good show lads, now keep your eyes open.' Also on board F-Freddy was Wynford Vaughan Thomas of the BBC. He described the raid in real time, with soundman Reginald Pidsley recording it as it happened:

> The main searchlight is probing for us all the time. Our pilot weaving, getting out of it. Down goes the nose of the Lancaster, we feel ourselves being flung around, wings dipped ... that main beam is getting further and further away ... we're out of it and once we are through that searchlight ... I got a glimpse of that furious glowing carpet of light and all we can now see is Berlin. So we set course for home and all the time I kept looking back at the glow in the sky until miles away I recorded our last glimpse of Berlin. At last we're out of the searchlights, we've left the whole boiling cauldron behind us. We all breathe a heartfelt sigh of relief. Now I am looking back right over the giant tail fin, and that's our last sight of it – just a great glow in the sky, and around that glow a feathery spray of searchlights, and all that is 50 miles away. And now we have 600 miles to go for home. Well that 600 miles was coloured in a very different spirit than the outward journey.[20]

The bomb aimer notified the navigator once they were over the British coast. 'It's good to see England again,' he said. The pilot agreed. 'That's a sight for sore eyes, that is.' Wynford Vaughan reflected on the trip after they had landed. 'We were home – Pidsley and I from a single trip, but the crew of F for Freddie, and thousands of others like them, would be preparing to set out again. Well, I can only say that next time both of us hear this roar of English bombers over the countryside, we'll feel a new, and a very deep respect for the crews who man them.'

In November 1943, Bomber Command launched a sustained campaign against Germany's capital city. After the destruction of Hamburg in Operation Gomorah, Harris believed that a similar attack on Berlin might break Germany's will to continue the war and end the conflict. 'It will cost us between 400 and 500 aircraft,' he said. 'It will cost Germany the war.'[21] Twenty-year-old pilot Charles Owen took part in a raid on Berlin in November and recorded his experience in his diary:

> Another trip as second pilot, this time with P/O Montgomery. Many fighter flares on route in, and we saw several aircraft shot down. There was a little cloud over the Big City, but hundreds of search lights and very heavy flak. We overshot the target on our initial run, and so turned back and bombed against the stream. I did not like it at all, and made up my mind never to do it again if I could help it.[22]

Like in Hamburg, firestorms ravaged the city, causing widescale destruction and death, with more than 100,000 civilians left homeless.[23]

Charles was sent to Berlin again: 'Streets and buildings could be seen lit up by fires,' he wrote in his diary. 'Large pall of smoke observed covering target area. Hundreds of searchlights and very heavy flak.' When Charles and his crew got home, they found several bullet holes in the starboard wing and cockpit roof of the Lancaster, and the bomb aimer had been wounded in the leg. After another raid on Berlin, rear gunner Finlay McRae wrote in his diary: 'It takes guts to be a gunner, to sit out in the tail when the Messerschmitts are coming, and the slugs begin to wail.'[24] After another, he wrote: 'Very tough time. Had to fight like wild cats. Probably destroyed one fighter.'

Rear gunner David Inglis took part in the 498-aircraft raid on Berlin on 16 December.[25] His Lancaster met with flak over the coast of Holland and engaged fighters close to the target. On the return flight, the crew took a northerly route over Denmark to shake off the fighters and returned to England after successfully completing their mission. Once they got home, however, they found that the weather was much worse than expected, with low cloud base over high ground. The crew attempted to find their airfield, but David's Lancaster crashed just before midnight, with the loss of everyone on board. On that night alone, twenty-five Lancasters either crashed or were abandoned by their crews, who parachuted out.

Over the course of the campaign, 9,111 sorties were flown over Berlin by Bomber Command, and 492 aircraft were lost. In excess of 3,500 Bomber Command aircrew were killed or taken prisoner, and the losses were felt painfully by those who survived. The sustained aerial campaign against Berlin caused extensive damage, but it was not the success that Harris hoped it would be. It distracted the German military and forced them to use resources they then could not use elsewhere, and many buildings, civilian and industrial in nature, were damaged. The Luftwaffe, however, had previously been shaken up by Operation Gomorrah and had improved its defence system. Using better integrated air defence – a combination of radar and good ground controlling – it fought back, with German night fighters attacking the RAF's bombers as they flew in their stream. The resulting Allied losses were simply not justifiable or sustainable. This was especially true with the planned Allied invasion of occupied Europe, which would now become the main focus of the fight against Nazi Germany.

CHAPTER SEVEN

OVERLORD TO DRESDEN

Toward Overlord

In January 1944, raids against German targets continued. Pilot Charles Owen and his crew faced more difficult circumstances aboard V-Victor. On 2 January, they were involved in another raid on Berlin. 'New Year but same target,' Charles wrote in his diary.

> Very quiet on way in, and 10/10 cloud over target. Flak was moderate. Got jumped badly by fighter on way home across France. Both gunners were wounded, the rear gunner seriously, and the starboard outer engine caught fire. Found it impossible either to extinguish fire or feather prop, and had to have rudder tie by engineer to maintain straight flight, as the rudder trimmers had been shot away. Limped into Tangmere and swung off runway on landing, due to starboard tyre being holed by canon shell. End of V-Victor I.[1]

Charles and his crew received another aircraft – V-Victor II – and on 5 January (Charles' twenty-first birthday) they took part in a raid on Stettin. 'A grand trip in bright moonlight,' Charles wrote.

'Target was very clear and covered in snow ... A very pleasant trip, but very long, and hardly the way to spend a 21st.' On 21 January, the crew of V-Victor II experienced a near-miss in a raid on Magdeburg: 'No fighters, but nearly got bombed by another aircraft,' Charles' diary reads. 'Saw his cookie go down past the wing. Very shaking.'

Bomber crews continued to take the fight to the enemy in the first half of 1944, while, behind closed doors, a major push into occupied Europe was being planned. Operation Overlord – the Allied invasion of occupied western Europe – would be a mission of gigantic proportions, involving land, sea and air forces. A high degree of effective cooperation would be needed to ensure success, and Bomber Command would be integrated into a huge Allied effort.

For the air component, an Allied Expeditionary Air Force (AEAF) was established, with Air Chief Marshal Sir Trafford Leigh-Mallory in command. The AEAF would support Allied armies in the initial invasion of Europe and would then continue to move with the armies as they pushed further and further into German-occupied territory. Just how the heavy bombers – the most powerful element of the RAF and the USAAF – fit into this plan, though, was a subject of much discussion among Allied planners. There was the Luftwaffe to consider, particularly its fighter capabilities and defences in western Europe, which posed a threat to the invasion force. It was important to identify ways in which the bombers could make it much more difficult for German forces to get to the invasion area. It was likely that German troops would travel via train, for instance, so the railway network was a significant strategic target.

Then there were battlefields to think about; the bombers, army commanders argued, could be useful where battles actually played out. Head of Bomber Command Harris was not convinced and argued instead that attacks on German industrial cities should continue. The USAAF agreed that striking targets where manufacturing was taking place would continue to inhibit Germany's ability to fight back, and under Pointblank the Allied air forces had been directed to damage

Germany's military and industrial capabilities, which would weaken it ahead of the invasion.

Before any Allied invasion of occupied Europe, the Allied air forces needed to secure control of the air – this was crucial, and without it, it was far less likely that the invasion would be successful. Toward this goal, Allied air commanders planned a large-scale bombardment of the German aircraft industry. In February 1944, Operation Argument was launched, targeting German aircraft assembly plants. That week – also known as 'Big Week' – the RAF and the US Eighth Air Force carried out systematic raids on aircraft assembly plants. The factories themselves were not damaged as catastrophically as the Allies had hoped, and initially positive results did not lead to long-term disruption to German aircraft production, which returned to normal relatively quickly.

The Luftwaffe, however, was lured out, and aerial battle ensued. Trained pilots were difficult and time-consuming to replace, and a substantial number of experienced German pilots were lost during Big Week. Replacement Luftwaffe pilots had much less training than their RAF and USAAF counterparts, and German losses continued, causing a major headache for the German Air Force. The American fighters had performed well against the Luftwaffe, and now Lieutenant-General Carl Spaatz, who was responsible for American strategic bomber forces in Europe, pushed to maintain the pressure on the German Air Force – particularly on its fuel supply. Harris, however, remained uninterested in what he called 'panacea' targets and maintained that the wider bombing of German cities was more likely to achieve the total destruction of the enemy's war-fighting capabilities. This was the way to win the war, he said. Bomber Command pilots continued to carry out bombing raids accordingly.

Once an aircrew member had completed their tour of thirty operations, there was no expectation or obligation for them to begin another, and they could remain in the RAF as an instructor. Some, however, did volunteer for a second tour. Kenneth Bickers, a pilot with 103 Squadron at Elsham Wolds, did so despite being engaged to be married. He wrote to his parents: 'As soon as I received news that we were on our way back (to recommence attacks on Germany) I nipped smartly down to Leicester to see Joan – she's still going to marry me at Easter and wouldn't hear of any postponement. I'm glad!'[2] His fiancée, Joan, had given him the job of deciding where they would spend their honeymoon. 'Was supposed to have come to a decision last week,' he wrote, 'but haven't had a real opportunity to think.'

Kenneth had been promoted to Squadron Leader and had a new Lancaster. 'I have a very good crew and a very good aircraft. The aircraft C-Charlie is brand new, it took some wrangling, but we got it in the end!' He commenced his second tour on 15 March, with a raid on Stuttgart. In his letter home on 17 March – less than a month before his wedding – he asked his father if he would attend and ended with: 'Well I think I had better close so cheerio for now. My love to Bunty [his small sister] and God Bless you all. Your loving Son, Ken.' This was to be Ken's last letter home. On 24 March, C-Charlie took off, part of the last large-scale attack on Berlin by Bomber Command. Forty-four Lancasters were lost that night – C-Charlie was one of them. Ken was one of the youngest flight commanders to be killed in Bomber Command during 1944.

On 30 March, Bomber Command targeted Nuremberg, a site of political significance where many of the infamous Nazi rallies had been held in the 1930s. Pilot Charles Owen recorded the raid in his diary:

> Moon far too bright for comfort, and the sky swarming with fighters. Saw combats all over the sky right from the coast to the target, and a very large number of aircraft shot down. I weaved a lot more than usual, and was not attacked, although we saw fighters attacking other aircraft. Target was partially covered by cloud, and bombing was rather scattered. Ran into heavy cloud soon after leaving target, and stayed in almost to French coast. Not at all a pleasant trip.[3]

Australian wireless operator Bruce Rawling remembers flying as part of the main force, working with the Pathfinders targeting Nuremberg:

> Daylight soon faded and as we flew over France there seemed to be flak everywhere. When passing Stuttgart we saw some fighter flares (flares used by the German fighters to highlight the bombers) and one of our planes go down in flames ... The first of the Pathfinders made their presence felt by flying right over the centre of the city and laying a lane of brilliant amber coloured parachute flares. Then another came in at 90 degrees and laid another lane. The city was lit up like day in an eerie amber light. Then we heard the voice of the Master Bomber calling the Primary Marker planes in to bomb the aiming point which they did laying down a cluster of brilliant red ground markers. He then called in the backers-up who laid down their green markers around the primary reds. Of course the Germans were well awake by this time and hurling plenty of ironmongery into the air. The Master Bomber then called the main force in to bomb the target indicators. As we ran in on our run we could see the shock waves of the 4,000lb Cookies going off and the thousands of sparkling silvery dots as the incendiary bombs took hold. It was a most evil and yet beautiful sight.[4]

The results of the Nuremberg raid were not what the Allies had hoped for. The target was only lightly damaged, and the raid resulted in the highest aircrew losses for any single air operation in the Second World War. Of the 779 bombers that were sent on the raid, over 100 were lost, along with the men who crewed them.

The Allies continued to fight for air superiority in western Europe. The Americans worked towards Pointblank's objectives, helped tremendously by their new long-range P-51 Mustang fighter aircraft. On 14 April 1944, Bomber Command and the US Strategic Air Forces in Europe were placed under the direction of General

Eisenhower and the Supreme Headquarters Allied Expeditionary Force. On 17 April 1944, a directive was issued by Allied Supreme Headquarters which listed the primary objective of the heavy bombers in the build-up to Overlord: they were to destroy the Luftwaffe's air combat strength and target railways to keep the invasion area in Normandy from being accessible to German reinforcements. Other targets could be hit if there were time and resources left around this primary objective.

In April and May, Bomber Command worked toward the 'Transportation Plan', bombing railway targets in France, Belgium and Germany with a higher degree of accuracy than expected. Bridges, railway lines, repair depots, locomotives, wagons and other significant rail targets were hit with significant damage and destruction, achieving the objective of making it much more difficult for German reinforcements – particularly panzer divisions – to get to Normandy during the invasion. Airfields and aircraft factories were also hit, and mines were laid in the enemy waters surrounding the invasion corridor in an effort to prevent the Kriegsmarine, the German Navy, from being able to interfere.

The Allied bombers were very effective in their mission, damaging Germany's ability to fight back against the invasion. An attack on 3/4 May 1944 on a German Army base near the French village of Mailly, for instance, destroyed parts of the base, armaments, tanks and motor vehicles and put Wehrmacht soldiers out of action – these were German resources that now could not contribute to the fight against the invasion.

Bombers also aimed for radar sites, anti-aircraft equipment and gun emplacements to try to reduce the risk to the aerial component of the D-Day invasion. On 7 May 1944, an ammunition dump near Orléans in France was targeted, and two days later a ball-bearing factory was hit at Annecy.

ABOVE: The German battleship *Tirpitz* – a deadly threat to Allied shipping.

RIGHT: Bomber Command bomb aimer Al Lovett.

ABOVE: Lancaster ground engineer Kenneth Ball (*back row, fourth from right*).

BELOW: Aerial reconnaissance photograph taken over Dresden in Germany, showing the fires still burning following two devastating attacks carried out on 13/14 February 1945.

ABOVE: Rear gunner Finlay McCrae (*far left*) and his crew. Finlay was killed on operations just a few weeks after his nineteenth birthday.

LEFT: Wireless operator Arthur Atkinson experienced an operation where everything went wrong.

BELOW: A Lancaster dropping a Grand Slam bomb.

LEFT: A Lancaster flies through flak tracers in a bombing raid on Hamburg.

BELOW: Lancaster pilot Stevie Stevens and his new wife, WAAF Maureen (née Miller).

ABOVE: Lancasters are loaded with food for Operation Manna.

BELOW: The personnel of 514 Squadron, pictured with an Avro Lancaster bomber in Waterbeach, Cambridgeshire, in 1945. Formed in September 1943 and disbanded in August 1945, the squadron flew food supplies to Holland as part of post-war Operation Manna.

RIGHT: Bomber Command wireless operator Roy Briggs took part in Operation Manna.

BELOW: Bomb aimer Al Lovett (*seated, fourth from left*) and his crew with their ground crew. The crew took part in Operation Manna.

RIGHT: 149 Squadron rear gunner Jock Bunten and members of his crew. Jock took part in Operation Exodus.

ABOVE: Ex-prisoners of war board Lancasters to get home during Operation Exodus.

RIGHT: Ex-prisoner of war Private Lawrence Leishman of the Royal Berkshire Regiment was transported home to England on board a Lancaster.

LEFT: Wartime Lancaster pilot Hugo Trotter DFC visiting RAF Coningsby, where current BBMF Lancaster pilot Seb Davey and 12 Squadron's Ashley McKenna introduced Hugo to Lancaster PA474.

ABOVE: 'Thank you boys' is spelled out in empty sacks by Dutch civilians who have received food dropped by British bombers during Operation Manna.

Taking Fire

Some bomber crews were lucky enough never to experience enemy fire, while others experienced it night after night. Finlay McRae recorded a hair-raising experience during a raid on Germany in his diary:

> Caught by about fifty search lights. Flak was bursting all around us. Estimated that there were about 100 guns concentrated on us alone. We shoved the nose down til we were doing over 300mph and then made a 90 degree turn out of them. By good luck we got out. Were attacked by two Ju88s over target but after we fired they went off to find an easier prey.[5]

Special operator with 101 Squadron, Leslie Temple recalled the worst operation he went on:

> The Lancaster was blown slightly off course over the North Sea so the bomb aimer had to ask that they fly round for a second time over the target to ensure accuracy, which was always extremely hazardous. As we did not jam over the actual target, I could watch everything from the astrodome. ... There was a solid curtain burst and hellish flak, wall of search lights across the sky. Other bombers all around waiting to release their bombs, and predatory German night fighters spitting canon fire. Finally we dropped our bombs on target, but were suddenly nailed by a master search light on the way out. Immediately, a dozen others combed us at 20,000ft ... German flak opened up and we were scarred with shrapnel which simply passed through the airframe, over our two port engines and burst into flames. I feared the worst ...[6]

Being Jewish, Leslie was particularly at risk if the Lancaster were to crash in or near to occupied territory. The quick-thinking pilot,

Canadian Eric Neilson, put the Lancaster's nose down and pulled out of the beam at 5,000ft. The flight engineer managed to extinguish the flames, despite having limited power due to two cut engines, and the skilled navigator used a sextant and the stars to get them home. When they arrived back at their base, their problems were not over – they could not get the wheels to come down. They crash-landed at Ludford Magna on two engines, with over 100 holes in the aircraft. 'After debriefing,' Leslie says, 'I laid on my bed and could not stop shaking for twelve hours. The MO [medical officer] said the best cure was simply to get back up again soon and of course we did … No counselling in those days, so that was a pretty difficult situation.'

Lancaster pilot Bruce Giles recalls a similarly terrifying situation during a raid on Gelsenkirchen:

> FLASH, BANG, CORDITE FUMES, all together! The usual wince, blink, eyes open, relief at not falling out of the sky. Then over the intercom from the Nav – 'I've been hit! I'm dying!' Me in reply – 'Rubbish, you're not dying' (sheer hopeful speculation). 'Get cracking bomb aimer and wireless operator, give him a hand and don't forget your emergency oxygen supply.' The prospect of two would-be nurses draped unconscious over the seriously wounded Nav didn't bear thinking about. What to do? Two smashed up legs, loss of blood, shock etc. Two to three hours back to base. No, not good enough.[7]

It was late in the war, and Bruce decided to land in France or Belgium to find help.

> Next to lose 20,000ft in a hurry without breaking any ear drums. That done, skittering across what turned out to be Belgium at 1,000ft looking for a runway. ANY runway, please! Within about ten minutes – it seemed like an hour – up comes a steel mesh strip (looked very short) marked A26

> and lined up with P-47 Thunderbolts. It crossed one's mind, will this stuff take the weight of a Lanc? Well, here goes, a tender touch down, no worries.

An American ambulance met them at the end of the strip and the crew could only watch, hope and pray as it drove away carrying their friend fighting for his life.

Due to the nature of the job, it was inevitable that some aircrew would sustain severe injuries, including burns. In July 1941, the Guinea Pig Club was formed to support aircrew who had suffered severe burns. Surgeon Archibald McIndoe, a pioneer of plastic surgery, cared for and operated on the young men, rehabilitating them both physically and mentally. He encouraged the airmen to live full lives and not to let their disfigurements stand in the way of doing so. By 1945, 80 per cent of the 649 members of the Guinea Pig Club were from bomber aircrews.

John Hughes and his crew were 20 miles short of their target – Nuremberg – when their Lancaster was hit by anti-aircraft fire. It became necessary for them to jettison the bombs so they didn't explode in the Lancaster, but a fire had broken out on board and some of the bombs were jammed in the bomb bay. John stood on the burning metal of the bomb racks, staring into the thousands of feet of space beneath him, and stamped on the remaining bombs to release them. His feet were badly burned, but the crew survived.

D-Day

Finally, on 6 June 1944, Operation Overlord was launched. The Allied air forces supported the invasion in various ways – not all of them involving bombing. The Germans had been expecting an Allied invasion, but they did not know when or where it would be. Taking advantage of this, the Allies launched an impressive deception operation, codenamed Operation Fortitude, to lure the Germans away from Normandy, the real site of the invasion of France. 'Fortitude North' would convince them, it was hoped, that an attack would take place in Norway, and 'Fortitude South' would make it look like the Allied invasion force would land north-east of Normandy in the Pas-de-Calais region.

The deception plan was the stuff of Hollywood movies. Real tanks were replaced by dummy inflatable ones and a fake force was created – the First US Army Group (FUSAG) – which made it seem like there were more troops than there really were. Fake radio traffic was generated to make it seem like something big was afoot. Spies and double agents were used to deliver false information and reinforce the deception to Germany. The Lancaster played its part in the deception too. To reinforce the idea that the invasion was happening elsewhere, 617 Squadron carried out Operations Taxable and Glimmer. Flying along the French coast in their Lancasters, 617 dropped Window from the aircraft to disrupt and jam German radar, and on 6 June 1944 they were used to mimic an invasion force. Used in high enough quantities, Window appeared on radar screens as a large number of aircraft, and on this occasion it tricked the Germans into thinking an invasion force was moving further north along the French coast than they actually were.

The vast Allied deception campaign was so successful that for several weeks after the invasion had taken place, the Germans were still expecting a second wave in the area around Calais. On 6 June 1944, pilot Charles Owen and his crew took part in a raid against a coastal battery at Saint-Pierre-du-Mont: 'We thought the briefing sounded a little odd for this trip,' Charles writes.

> And sure when we broke cloud over the French coast the Channel was full of ships ... D-Day was on. We bombed at 05.00 just as it was getting light, and had a grandstand view of the Americans running in on the beach. First-class prang on the battery, but saw Jimmy Carter shot down by a Ju88 over the target. Marvellous sight coming back as the

> sun came up. We on the way back and the Americans on the way out. Landed back in time for breakfast, but very disappointed that there was nothing on the 8 o'clock news.[8]

Bomber Command – its Lancasters included – helped to keep German reinforcements away from the invasion force in Normandy, both on 6 June and after as the liberating Allied forces moved inland. Two days after the landings, four Lancasters from 83 Squadron approached a railway tunnel in France, through which a complete panzer division was expected to travel on its way to assist with fighting the Allied invaders. Three Mosquitoes marked both ends of the tunnel clearly, and the four Lancasters illuminated the target so twenty-five aircraft from 617 Squadron could bomb it. This they did, releasing their bombs accurately on the target. This was the first attack in which the 12,000lb 'Tallboy' bomb was used. Another creation of Barnes Wallis, who had created the bouncing bomb used in the Dambusters attack, Tallboy was an extra-large specialist weapon designed to penetrate deep into the earth, creating a sort of subterranean cavern into which the area above would collapse. Any structures still standing in the vicinity after it had struck would suffer extensive damage to their foundations. Wallis had been working on such a weapon for years but lacked an aircraft capable of carrying it. The Lancaster, with its huge bomb bay and lift capacity, solved that problem.

When Tallboy was used for the first time on 8 June 1944, it caused devastation to the Saumur railway tunnel by slamming into the hillside, spilling thousands of tons of earth onto the railway line. The attack was successful in preventing German reinforcements from reaching Normandy.

Bomber Command's Lancasters continued to support the Allied invasion as it moved further inland. On 14 June, 221 Lancasters set out, guided by thirteen Mosquitoes, to carry out a daylight raid on Le Havre. There were U-boat and E-boat pens at the port, which posed a threat to Allied ships bringing supplies to the invasion force in France. The raid was carried out in two waves, including twenty-two of 617 Squadron's Lancasters carrying Tallboys. It was a major success – the bombs hit with a high degree of accuracy, and one Tallboy even managed to smash through the 15ft-thick concrete roof of one of the E-boat pens. After this one attack, the threat posed by E-boats to Allied shipping was significantly reduced. Bomber Command also assisted the ground forces by targeting troop positions, communications targets and enemy supplies, continuing to make it difficult for the German forces to co-ordinate and function effectively against the invasion. They played a vital role in Overlord and the weeks that followed, as the Allies pushed further and further into Europe, wrenching territory back from the enemy.

Now that the Normandy invasion had taken place and the Allies were moving into occupied territory, Lancasters and their crews would continue to work hard to hasten the end of the war. The Lancasters at its centre, Bomber Command was a force to be reckoned with. Germany continued to take a battering at the hands of the Allied bomber force. Both in daylight and at night, specially selected strategic transportation and fuel targets continued to be bombed to further prevent the German forces from being able to effectively move and fight, and cities were continually bombed in an effort to obliterate German manufacturing toward the war effort. Almost half of the bombs that fell on German cities did so between August 1944 and May 1945. Though the tide of war had turned against Nazi Germany, however, Hitler showed no sign of backing down.

Sinking the *Tirpitz*

Though it was initially instructed to hit tactical targets, Bomber Command's main priority was changed by the Combined Chiefs on 25 September to oil targets and transport was designated second most important. Harris was unconvinced, maintaining that bombing industrial cities was the quickest way to bring an end to the war. In

October, the Combined Chiefs ordered two operations, the common objective being 'to bring home to the enemy a realisation' of the overwhelming superiority of the Allied air forces and 'the futility of continued resistance'.[9]

Hurricane I planned for the 'concentration of effort in time and space against objectives in the Ruhr', aiming for the 'maximum disorganisation of the Ruhr and the denial to the enemy of essential facilities and particularly its communications'. It was hoped that 'administrative chaos' would follow the material destruction of industrial targets. Hurricane II, meanwhile, would employ the 'maximum effort' of RAF Bomber Command and the USAAF against 'the major oil targets throughout Axis Europe', with particular attention paid to the 'Ruhr-Rhineland synthetic oil plants'. A sort of compromise had been reached.

By now, Bomber Command was big enough that it could be in multiple places at once and perform well. As well as carrying out its own strategic bombing operations, it could also support ground offensives and reconnaissance and special operations such as those carried out by the Special Operations Executive. It also assisted in the war at sea. On 12 November 1944, a major threat to the Allies was removed from the ocean. The *Tirpitz* – sister ship of the mighty *Bismarck* and one of the most feared battleships in the Kriegsmarine – had a top speed of 34 knots and sported 38cm guns with a range of 22 miles.[10] At 52,600 tons when fully loaded, it was the heaviest ship ever built by a European navy. The *Tirpitz* had long been a thorn in Churchill's side, lurking as a constant threat to the Allied convoys making their way to Murmansk in Russia.

The RAF and the Fleet Air Arm had been trying for years to sink it, with multiple attacks by aircraft, midget submarines and Chariots (manned torpedoes). Though they had managed to damage it, repairs were always carried out and it remained afloat. On 15 September 1944, Lancaster bombers from No. 9 and No. 617 Squadrons were sent to locate and bomb the *Tirpitz*. Hidden at anchor in a Norwegian fjord, the *Tirpitz* had been sighted and its location passed to Bomber

Command. Setting out from northern Russia, the Lancasters headed for its last known location. When they arrived, it was difficult to see the *Tirpitz*, as bad weather and a smokescreen from the ship obscured their view. Bombs were released in the general vicinity, and one struck the ship in the bow, severely damaging it. Hitler ordered that the crippled *Tirpitz* be towed to Tromsø, where she would be used as a floating gun battery.

The ship was now closer to Britain, and with extra fuel tanks the Lancasters of 9 and 617 Squadrons could reach it from British airfields. Flying from Lossiemouth in Scotland, thirty Lancasters located the *Tirpitz* and bombed it, their bomb loads including Tallboys. The ship capsized and was finally removed as a threat to Allied shipping. As well as a material success, it was also a morale win – the *Tirpitz* had been deemed 'unsinkable' by Hitler and was a jewel in the Kriegsmarine's crown. Crippling it proved Hitler wrong in front of the German people, and the sinking was a blow to the German Navy's reputation.

FIDO

The danger to bomber crews was not ended once they had arrived back over Britain. In thick fog, it could be very difficult to see the runway clearly enough to land safely, and while GEE could help them to locate their airfields, it could not mark out the runway itself. Bomber Command warned that fog over British airfields could be as much of a menace to bomber crews as flak over Germany. This was where FIDO – 'Fog Investigation and Dispersal Operation' – could be critical to survival. By December 1943, FIDO was operational at three airfields: RAFs Graveley, Fiskerton and Downham Market, and it would go on to be installed at fifteen airfields around the UK.

To the uninitiated, FIDO looked quite alarming. Long pipes were installed along the sides of the runway and were pierced with holes. The pipes contained petrol, which would spurt out when the system was in operation. A member of the air station's ground crew would literally set fire to the spurting petrol, and the result was lines of fire illuminating the runway. The heat dispersed the lethal fog and cloud, and the fire provided a flarepath for the pilot to follow. As he did with most new equipment he encountered, Donald Bennett, AOC of the Pathfinders, insisted on personally testing FIDO: 'I took a Lancaster myself from Oakington over to Graveley one night, and did the first landing with FIDO burning. I had vague thoughts of seeing lions jump through a hoop of flame at the circus. The glare was certainly considerable, and there was some turbulence, but it was nothing to worry about.'[11] Of course, the pilot had to be careful not to run off the runway into the flaming petrol.

Lancaster pilot Arthur Bishop and his crew were warned that the weather might be a little 'iffy' on the way back from an operation in the Ruhr. 'The wireless operator was required to listen out at certain times for any diversions to another airfield,' he says.

> Somehow this communication failed and we arrived back over base at 20,000ft. It was socked in from that height to the ground. What to do? Before we had time to consider, Middleton-St George gave us a diversion to a FIDO airport ... We descended through 20,000ft and just as we reached the 800ft level, a huge glow appeared in the sky, dead ahead. There was our FIDO landing strip. Our circuit was made at 800ft and we landed without incident.[12]

By the end of the war, over 2,500 aircraft had used the FIDO system.[13]

Dresden

As the war entered its final year, the Lancaster continued to take part in bombing operations. On 27 January, cities were once again designated high priority as bombing targets. A new operation was ordered, codenamed 'Thunderclap'. It was designed to support a Soviet offensive in the east and to prevent the movement of troops and materials in central and eastern Germany as they fought to cope with the mass of refugees fleeing the Soviet advance.

It was not Harris but the Air Ministry that had come up with the idea, supported by the Joint Chiefs of Staff and by Churchill. A new joint strategy tasked the British and American bomber forces with various attacks against German cities. One of those cities was Dresden.

Bomber Command and the USAAF's Eighth Air Force were both ordered to target the city. It was a strategic target – the site of over 100 factories working to supply the German military with war materials, marshalling yards, barracks and a major rail hub for the movement of German troops. Some 800 RAF aircraft, hundreds of Lancasters among them, targeted the medieval city on the night of 13 February. Ron Pain remembers his aircrew being given cards with Union Jacks on, to hang around their necks in case of landing behind Russian lines.[14] The bombers encountered little resistance in the sky or from the ground, and dropped huge amounts of high explosives and incendiary bombs on the ancient city. The bombs set in motion waves of high-pressure air, and a firestorm was ignited in the densely populated centre.

A few hours later, a second wave stoked the raging fires, and the next day the Flying Fortresses and Liberators of the USAAF delivered their blow. The firestorm was so intense it could be seen from 100 miles away by crews on their homeward journeys. The results were apocalyptic. The fires were so hot they melted metal and puffed stone into powder. Human beings in the path of the fires stood no chance at all of survival, and there was little the city could do to protect itself.

Tom Tobin of 153 Squadron took part in the raid on Dresden. He remembers a strong wind that night, which fanned the inferno and created the perfect conditions for a firestorm. It also made it difficult for the Lancasters to fly, however, and affected fuel consumption. On the way home, Tom and his flight engineer, Jock Smart, shut down the two outer engines to conserve fuel. With no bombs on board and only a little fuel left, the Lancaster could fly well enough on two engines – they feathered the props and limped home. They were so low on fuel that they had to ignore the instruction to complete a circuit prior to landing, touching down immediately with almost nothing left in their fuel tank.

The next day and the day after that, Dresden was bombed again – this time by the USAAF alone. The city burned for weeks. Allied prisoners of war were forced to help pull bodies out of the rubble, and these were burned as quickly as possible to prevent disease from seeping into the devastated city. The figures vary, and it is difficult to know exactly how many people were killed in the operation against Dresden. Recent figures suggest that around 19,000 lost their lives.[15]

An End in Sight

From mid-February the Allied bomber forces were directed to concentrate on tactical targets as they supported the ground offensives below. No. 617 Squadron were called upon once again to carry out precision raids on targets that would make it difficult for German troops to move around. They were the only squadron to use the new 22,000lb 'Grand Slam' bomb, sometimes referred to as the 'Earthquake bomb', which worked in a similar fashion to the Tallboy but on a larger scale. To carry Grand Slam, 617's Lancasters had to be modified, and the bomb would sit in a doorless bomb bay.

Grand Slam was first used in March 1945, when it was dropped on the Bielefeld viaduct in northern Germany. It caused more than 100 yards of the viaduct to collapse. No. 617 Squadron also used it against a ring of bridges in the Ruhr. In April, Lancasters from Nos 6 and 8 Groups targeted coastal gun batteries in the Frisian Islands, and members of No. 5 Group bombed an oil refinery in southern Norway. No. 617 Squadron were called upon again, this time to hit the Valentin U-boat pens and assembly plant near Bremen. Valentin was one of Germany's largest military projects in the Second World War, and one of the biggest U-boat facilities it possessed. Covering over 35,000 square metres, it was shrouded in reinforced concrete. From 1943 to 1945, thousands of people – a mixture of civilians, concentration camp detainees and prisoners of war – were forced to work on its construction. More than 1,100 of them lost their lives because of the terrible working conditions and Nazi malice, succumbing to illness, starvation and arbitrary killings.

By March 1945 the facility was around 90 per cent completed, and it was due to become fully operational just a few months later. The Allies could not allow the continuation of U-boat manufacture, and the Dambusters, the masters of precision bombing, were tasked with putting it out of action. In April, 617 Squadron's Lancasters set off to bomb the high-level target, some of them carrying Tallboys and Grand Slams. During the raid, two Grand Slams struck the bunker, burying themselves in the reinforced concrete, where they exploded. The facility never produced a single U-boat, and just a few weeks later it was occupied by British troops.

The last raid on Berlin took place on the night of 20/21 April, and on 25th a daylight raid was carried out against Hitler's 'Eagle's Nest' in the Bavarian Alps at Berchtesgaden. The Allies felt that it was important to remove it as a potential location for a 'final stand' by fanatical Nazis. Hitler was not at Eagle's Nest when the 359 Lancasters from Nos 1, 5 and 8 Groups attacked it, along with the SS barracks at Berchtesgaden, but the raid was still considered highly effective.

The final attack made by Bomber Command on Germany was on 2 May, when Kiel was bombed to prevent German ships from carrying troops to Norway where they might try to continue to fight.

CHAPTER EIGHT

FOOD AND FREEDOM

Operation Manna

As the end of the war drew near, some Lancasters were given assignments that were very different to their usual task of bombing. One such assignment was a massive humanitarian operation in the Netherlands. In the summer of 1944, the Allies had launched Operation Market Garden, an airborne operation to try to secure the River Rhine crossings, to enable an advance into northern Germany. In anticipation of Market Garden's success, the Dutch Government in Exile urged railway workers in Holland to strike, and they did. Market Garden failed, however, and the German occupiers treated the Dutch harshly because of their support for the Allies. The transportation of food was stopped for weeks, and railway rolling stock was seized and taken to Germany. Winter was approaching, and the canals and rivers froze, making the transportation of food even more difficult.

The situation in the Netherlands was dire – 20,000 had already died of starvation, and a further 980,000 were considered malnourished. Some were even eating small animals, including pets, scraps found in bins and tulip bulbs, leaves, flowers, berries – some of which could be poisonous – trying desperately to stay alive. On 29 April 1945, 242 Lancasters took off and headed for the Netherlands – and this time, they weren't carrying bombs. Instead, they carried 535 tons of food, which they would drop to the people below as they executed the first airborne humanitarian relief mission in history: Operation Manna.

In order for the RAF to be able to safely drop the vital food supplies, there needed to be a ceasefire and an agreement with the Germans to ensure that the Lancasters would not be fired upon. Air commodore Andrew Geddes worked to secure the ceasefire and tackled the vast logistics involved in an operation of this size and scale. This included plotting air routes to designated drop zones and figuring out exactly how the food would be stowed in the Lancasters and then dropped safely so as not to destroy it. Initially, various different schemes were tried by different squadrons. Flight Lieutenant Bill Langford of 153 Squadron was involved in a trial drop on 21 April:

> I flew V-Victor to Netheravon [in Wiltshire], carrying a mixture of goodies in sacks, slung from ropes on a Heath Robinson device in the bomb bay. We were to demonstrate to an assembly of RAF and army brass just how food would be dropped to the starving Dutch. Approaching the airfield at around 200ft, wheels and flaps down for minimum flying speed, we lined up the white cross on the ground and pressed the button ... when it all went wrong! Sacks of peas, tins of spam, and all sorts of containers rained from the sky, scattering the assembled brass in all directions. Not what was envisaged![1]

Eventually panniers were developed – called 'blocks' – which could be fitted in a Lancaster bomb bay. Each block held a certain number of individual sacks containing the food, which included sugar, dried egg powder, margarine, salt, cheese, tinned meat, flour, dried milk, coffee, cereals, tea, high-vitamin chocolate and potatoes.

Crews practised low-level flying and simulated drops, which weren't so very different to the techniques used in low-level bombing.

Preparations also meant making sure there would be no attacks on aircraft taking these routes. Though the Germans were suspicious, an uncomfortable agreement was reached. On 29 April, two test flights were carried out to ensure the Lancasters could pass over the Netherlands in peace. The Germans placed anti-aircraft guns at some drop zones, just in case the Lancasters dropped troops or bombs instead of the promised food. The aircraft flew in at low level and dropped the food as the British government had said they would. The next day a ceasefire was signed, and over the next ten days the Lancasters were guided to their drop zones by Mosquitoes, which marked the targets.

'The food would be dropped from 500ft,' John Johnson of 149 Squadron, who took part in Operation Manna, says. 'Just as on a bombing run, onto clearly marked sites.' People on the ground also assisted with alerting the Lancaster crews as to where to drop food – Jock Bunten of 149 Squadron remembers 'a chap walking up and down a field with a Union Jack to signal to us where to drop'. Wireless operator Roy Briggs also participated in the first day of Operation Manna on 29 April. That morning, he sat down in the briefing room as usual. 'They said, "You're not going to bomb today, you're not carrying bombs, you're carrying food. We're only sending a few of you over and we're going to tell the Germans and the Dutch that you're coming."'[2] The next day, he went into the briefing room again, and his superiors said: 'We got away with it, so we're going to send more today' – then Roy and his friends heard that the ceasefire was in place.

Norman Wilkins also participated: 'We made several runs over the city at low level and finally dropped several panniers of food into the main square. One could see the Dutch people waving with happy smiling faces. An incredible sight never to be forgotten.' Bomb aimer Al Lovett remembers seeing people below with prams and wheelbarrows, looking to the sky and waiting for the food to drop. Flying low, Norman and Al could also see German flak guns trained on the Lancasters, tracking them as they went by. Years after the war, a Dutch policeman told Norman: 'We were starving … People were actually falling down in the street, from starvation.'[3]

Many aircrew packaged up their flying rations, attaching them to little parachutes made from handkerchiefs and dropping them with notes that said: 'For the children'. After dropping their loads, many pilots decided to put on a show for the crowds below, flying low and waggling their wings. Bomb aimers flashed 'V' for victory on the Aldis signalling lamp. This was a very different sort of operation for Lancaster crews – and one they greatly enjoyed, without the extreme danger of their usual work. 'It was one of the best parts of the war,' Al Lovett says. 'It gave great satisfaction to the aircrews involved. For the first time they could contribute to construction instead of destruction. We were told that the deaths from starvation had risen to about 400 a week. No wonder we received such a very enthusiastic welcome, flags waving and thousands of people thronging the dropping zones.'[4]

Several aircraft were found to have bullet holes upon return to base, and despite the ceasefire individual German soldiers were assumed to have shot at them. Three aircraft were lost during Operation Manna – two of which collided and a third which suffered an engine fire. The USAAF also carried out an aid drop – named Operation Chowhound – on 1 May, delivering a further 4,000 tons of food. The next day a ground-based relief mission followed, called Operation Faust. It is estimated that the Allied food drops saved around a million lives, delivering a total of almost 7,000 tons of food.

Hans Onderwater, a leading expert on Operation Manna, was born in 1946 and says his mother was 'only a shadow of herself' after the war. His father had been in hiding for a long time, wanted by the Nazis for assisting underground resistance work. Operations Manna and Chowhound were about more than food and staving off starvation, Hans says:

> When they saw the Lancasters and the B17s coming over and when they saw the food drops in Rotterdam they knew that now the war was at an end. Because it was not only the

> fact that there was food coming for the people. No. It also meant that when these aircraft that we had seen and heard for four years at a very high altitude at night and during the day are now so low that we can actually see the aircrew sitting in the planes, waving at us. Well, the Germans now must be at the brim of defeat to allow them to do that. So, it was also a morale booster.[5]

For the Dutch, the Lancaster was a symbol of hope – of life and of freedom from and victory over their oppressors.

The Dutch were very keen to show their thanks to the aircrews and did so in a variety of ways. They wrote messages on the roofs of barns and used empty sacks to spell out things like 'Thank You Boys' in fields, so the low-flying Lancasters would see it on their next drop. The gratitude of the Dutch people lasted for decades after the war, and Operation Manna remains a happier part of the Lancaster's legacy. Hans Onderwater calls himself 'a result of the food drops', because without them his parents would have starved and he would not have been born.[6] Hans worked with Dutch officials to establish the Food and Freedom Foundation in 1981, which sought to invite former aircrew involved in food drops to visit the Netherlands. In 1983, the first visit took place, with around fifty RAF personnel travelling from Britain. It was a great success, and another trip was organized in 1985 – this time the invitation extending to aircrew who participated in Manna from Canada, the US, Poland, New Zealand and Australia. The visits became a regular occurrence until 2015, when it had become too difficult for former aircrew to travel due to their age. 'First and foremost, what struck me', Hans says, 'was the reaction of Dutch people.' He describes seeing a Lancaster at one of these events:

> When they heard far away the sound of the Merlin engines of the Lancaster. It is an overwhelming experience when you suddenly see people who you consider to be of the

> age of your own parents to get so emotional because of the sound of aircraft. That's it. People who start crying. People who start waving like mad at a Lancaster. Calling the Lancaster 'she'. Saying, 'There she is.' And then of course, the meeting between the Dutch recipients and the Allied givers who will embrace even though they don't speak each other's language, who will be so happy to meet and who will become friends and they have been friends since the first time they met.

One of the most poignant memories I have of these meetings is when we were at a town called Vlaardingen, where an American tail gunner met a Dutchman who had received food from the Americans and the Dutchman was saying all the time in Dutch thank you, thank you. '*Dank je, dank je, dank je*,' and the American, who didn't speak any Dutch of course, with tears in his eyes was saying, 'It's OK. It's OK. It's OK.' And in the end these two elderly gentlemen embraced each other and gave each other a kiss and well, that moment I was in tears. So, yes, the remembrance and the commemoration of the food drops to the Dutch people who lived in those days is still something that makes the heart beat twice as quickly.[7]

Norman Wilkins, who had participated in Manna as aircrew, went on one of the visits and stood with his Dutch hosts as a Lancaster flew over. He was given laminated drawings done by Dutch children, to use as placemats in his home. 'The townspeople … were fighting each other to get on the coaches to hug the men that had brought them food,' he recalls. 'That was a very emotional business that … None of us stopped crying the whole time.'[8]

Operation Manna inspired friendships that would last a lifetime. Roy Briggs remains friends with a woman from Rotterdam, who was in the city when the life-saving food was dropped. They remain friends today and meet up regularly.

Bailing Out

Another task given to Lancasters toward the end of the war was to bring home Allied men who had been interned in German-occupied areas as prisoners of war. If a Lancaster got into trouble on an operation, it was hoped that the crew might be able to 'bail out', or exit the aircraft to avoid being killed when it crashed. If a Lancaster made a water landing or the crew bailed out over the sea, an emergency signal would be activated before they left the Lancaster, and survivors found themselves bobbing in a dinghy in freezing, rough waters, desperately hoping the signal had been seen by someone and help was coming. If forced to bail out over land, it was a very different story. They might be captured and killed, or interned as prisoners of war, but even that gave them more of a chance of surviving than staying in a flaming aircraft.

Bailing out was not easy. Lancasters were not easy to move around in at the best of times – there wasn't much room with the equipment and the crew in an enclosed space, and the bulky flying suits crews wore to keep warm made it even more difficult. If it became necessary to bail out, chances were there would be absolute chaos on board – darkness, fire and smoke, the aircraft falling or banking and potential injuries with panic and confusion. Apart from the main door, the only other exit on the aircraft suitable for parachute escape was the narrow forward hatch underneath the bomb aimer's position in the nose. This was small, and wearing a parachute and flight suit it would have been difficult to fit through it in an emergency. That was if they even managed to locate it in the dark, and speed was of the essence – to have even a chance of survival without incapacitating injury, the crew needed to exit above a certain altitude and before it became impossible to do so. If they did manage to jump, the crew would need to make sure they didn't become caught on the aircraft or dragged into the engines.

Approaching Mannheim, nineteen-year-old Ron Pain's Lancaster was hit by a single shot of flak between the two starboard engines and a fire broke out on board. The pilot said, 'Jump for it boys,' issuing the order to bail out. Ron was down in the nose with the bomb aimer, Charlie, his usual seat being occupied by a trainee pilot. Charlie helped him to jettison the escape hatch door. Ron made sure his parachute was fastened and wriggled through the small hole in the floor into the night sky.

> After counting to five and straightening my body, I pulled the handle and must have been knocked unconscious by one of the harness buckles as the chute opened. When I came to with a cut and a large bump on the forehead, all I could see of K-King was a few tank cap covers floating about. I looked for other parachutes but saw nothing although I would have expected other members of the crew to have jumped.[9]

Several German policemen were following Ron's progress as he floated down through the sky, his parachute billowing above him. He landed in the middle of a privet hedge, 6 inches away from some iron railings. He was in Heidelberg. Ron would swiftly be taken prisoner.

During a night operation, at around 2 a.m., Eric Grisdale's Lancaster was suddenly raked by bullets on the port side. The port fuel tank was ruptured, and the aircraft caught fire.

> I immediately threw the aircraft into a corkscrew manoeuvre, a completely reflex action. There was no further attack, nor any crew reports of sighting the fighter. I operated the fire extinguisher on the port inner engine, but this had no effect whatsoever. The whole thing was burning fiercely, the aircraft was becoming impossible to handle and was not responding to my action. A quick survey showed that the navigator and the wireless operator had both been killed by the first burst of gunfire. I realised that the position was hopeless and gave the order to abandon aircraft.[10]

No man could predict how he would react in this situation. Eric says:

> I was convinced that my final moment had arrived, and that I would shortly know what it was like to die. There was no feeling of panic, only one of inevitability and acceptance. I do not suppose that it was more than a few seconds, when there followed another more violent explosion, and the next recollection I have, is that I was free from the aircraft. I do not know how long I had been free-falling, but I was falling backwards, looking up at my feet and laughing at the realisation that they were my feet. This was quickly followed by the more serious realisation, that I had to do something about it. I pulled the ripcord on my parachute, which opened immediately, and within five seconds I touched earth. During the whole of this time, my fiercely burning aircraft appeared to be immediately above, and seemed to be falling on top of me. It was far too close for comfort, and crashed to the ground in a searing ball of fire, only about a hundred yards from the spot where I landed.

Years after the war when Ian Davies visited a Lancaster with his father, who had been a flight engineer with the Pathfinders, he asked him about this. '[He said:] "I vividly remember clambering over the main spar, in ordinary clothing, questioning how one would do it in the dark with the aircraft under attack and possibly on fire, if one had to bail out." Dad paused for a moment, let out a small sigh and just said, "bloody quick".'[11] Only 15 per cent of airmen safely exited stricken Lancasters.

Prisoners of War

Eric Grisdale's 'greatest moment of despair' was lying alone in a field in occupied Europe, listening to the sound of about 400 Allied aircraft fading into the distance. His Lancaster bomber was burning fiercely nearby, and Eric suspected that his crew were dead. 'With each decreasing decibel of that sound,' he says, 'my heart and spirit sank lower and lower into the lowest depth of despair.'[12]

For airmen who managed to bail out of bombers over enemy territory, their struggle had only just begun. If they managed to land without injury, they faced days of evading capture by the SS and the Gestapo or by angry civilians who wanted revenge for the bombing of Germany's cities. If caught, they might be executed or sent to a prisoner of war camp. 'There was no sign of any other member of the crew,' Eric recalls. 'I quickly took stock of my situation. I was injured about the head, with my ears having sustained quite severe cuts, and I had a very painful right hand, but did not realise I had broken it until later … The urge for survival is strong in all of us, and this came to my aid, in forcing me to take what action I could to avoid capture.'

Eric could not remain at the site of the crash, as he knew the Germans would soon be on the scene looking for survivors. Besides, the ammunition in the burning Lancaster was beginning to explode, and bullets whizzed past Eric where he sat. He hid his parachute – with difficulty because of his broken hand – and set off alone into the night. All aircrew were instructed in basic evasion techniques and were issued with local currency, a small saw, a compass, a silk map and a survival kit containing food for two to seven days. They also carried a phrase card, which listed useful phrases in French, Dutch, Spanish and German. Phrases included: 'Can you hide me?', 'Where are the nearest British/American troops?' and 'Are the enemy nearby?' In German, they somewhat ominously included 'Heil Hitler'.[13]

Some downed airmen managed to escape thanks to the courage and selflessness of volunteers who hid and helped them. Eric Grisdale was one such fortunate airman. His parachute had deposited him in occupied Holland, and he was found by a group of Dutchmen who took him to a farmhouse. There, he was reunited with the bomb aimer from his crew, 'Pop'. 'The farmer and his wife shared all they had with us, and I am sure that if the truth were known, gave us more than they had themselves,' Eric says. 'On the way to the farmhouse, Pop and his guide had passed over a crossroad where a young helper had been strung up on a tree, riddled with bullets, and left as a warning to other Dutch helpers. It did not help Pop's morale to see this terrible sight, but it made us realise how incredibly brave the Dutch people were, and the risks they were taking in helping us.' Over the next few months, Eric and Pop were helped by a succession of kind volunteers who hid them from the Germans. Eventually, they made it into Belgium and arrived at the front line, where they could see the American forces. Two American rangers on reconnaissance escorted them to a British command post, and they were brought home.

Many airmen were not so lucky, and almost 10,000 aircrew from Bomber Command became prisoners of war. If they were captured by the Germans, they were first taken to Dulag Luft, a transit camp near Frankfurt, to be interrogated for any useful information they might possess. Ron Pain remembers the food at the camp: 'What little food appeared was almost uneatable – thin soup and bitter tasting black bread twice a day and a cup of yellow liquid which was said to be tea but bore no relation to it.'[14] After a few days of initial interrogations, prisoners were transported from Dulag Luft to a permanent camp. Life in these camps was notoriously difficult, and the airmen had no idea how long they would be there – or if they would ever leave.

After his Lancaster crashed in a fireball during the Augsburg Raid in 1942, John Sherwood was presumed dead by the RAF. He was found alive, however, and spent six weeks in a German hospital, his face severely burned. Eventually, he found himself at the Stalag Luft III prisoner of war camp, where he witnessed preparations by inmates for the famous 'Great Escape' of 24 March 1944, in which seventy-six airmen escaped. John wrote a letter to an RAF friend from the camp:

> Dear Hind – Just a line to let you and the boys know that I am OK, but not a little 'browned off'. I got away with a burnt face followed by Scarlet Fever. I have no news of the rest of the crew and fear the worst. However, it is good to think

> that we had done our jobs well. I hear that we are all 'heroes' at home. All the best to all, Flap.[15]

In the final months of the war, the Nazis scrambled to hide the extent of the atrocities they had committed and marched prisoners out of the camps and further away from the advancing Allies. John endured one such march, where prisoners who could not keep up were shot.

Alan Yates was also captured and became a prisoner of war after his aircraft was shot down en route to Düsseldorf. Alan had joined the RAF five days after his eighteenth birthday, to escape the boredom of his job as a trainee accountant with the municipal electricity department. 'I wanted to fly and have a few adventures,' he wrote. 'I couldn't have timed it better and ended up with more adventures than I cared to list.'[16] Kept at Stalag VIII-B in Lamsdorf, Upper Silesia (now Poland), Alan joined prisoners from Britain and the Commonwealth, the Soviet Union, Poland and various other occupied European countries. In January 1945, Alan, like John Sherwood, was forced to take part in a 'death march' westward. Many of the men forced on the march were in poor physical health because of years of malnutrition and overwork in captivity, and they were ill-equipped for the freezing cold, snowy weather. Alan writes:

> Some groups of prisoners were joined by German civilians who were also fleeing from the Russians. Some Russians who tried to escape or could not go on were shot by guards. Our small group, myself, some chaps captured at Dunkirk, I think they were East Kents, some Paras taken at Arnhem and six Russians were rounded up after sleeping in a barn by some front-line German soldiers... They all wore camouflage smocks, helmets and were armed with machine pistols and a wide range of other serious weapons. They immediately dragged out the Russians, lined them up against the barn wall and shot them. They then turned to us. I had been learning German in the camp just for

> something to do and could tell what they were saying. They wanted to shoot us too. I wasn't too happy about this and managed to convince them that my RAF wings, along with the Paras wings were in fact 'angels' wings' and that we were Medical Orderlies. Whether they believed me or not they accepted it and told us all to avoid the Russians at all costs and to keep moving west.

With so little food, the prisoners were forced to scavenge to stay alive. They were reduced to eating rotten vegetables and rats – anything they could find – and some men were at half of their pre-war bodyweight by the end of the conflict.

Due to extreme cold, disease, a near-starvation diet and exhaustion, hundreds of prisoners died during the marches. The lines of prisoners were also sometimes mistaken by Allied air forces as retreating columns of German troops, which put them in danger of being bombed or shot at by their own people. Many of the prisoners who survived had marched over 500 miles, and some over 1,000 by the time they were liberated.

Alan arrived in Freising, just north of Munich, where he was taken care of by some nuns and German medics in a castle. Being in Germany was still dangerous, and the USAAF bombed the town and the castle while Alan was there – he helped to dig out some nuns who were trapped beneath rubble after the raid. Alan was the senior combatant rank among the group of prisoners in the castle, and a German panzer major decided to surrender to him rather than have any more of his troops killed:

> So close to the end, he had totally given up. They had run out of fuel and tanks a long time ago! He then gave me his handgun (a Mauser), his Nazi Party Badge, his Iron Cross, and a bottle of Schnapps! General Patton liberated the town in a Jeep along with the rest of his army – I had never heard of him but he had a white helmet with stars on so I thought he

> might be quite important – and gave me 200 cigarettes for handing over Freising.[17]

Private Lawrence Leishman of the Royal Berkshire Regiment had been at Anzio when his battalion was overrun, and was one of a small number of men who managed to hold on for four days as the German Army pushed toward their position. They put up a good fight, but ultimately Lawrence became one of a handful who were captured. When he was taken into German custody, he found bullet holes in his battle dress trousers, webbing, jacket and across the top of his helmet from the battle. In the chaos that followed, a letter was sent to his family:

> I regret to have to inform you that a report has been received from the War Office to the effect that Private Lawrence Leishman of the Royal Berkshire Regiment was posted as missing on the 8 Feb 1944 in the Central Mediterranean Theatre of War. The report that he is missing does not necessarily mean that he has been killed, as he may be a prisoner of war or temporarily separated from his regiment. Official reports that men are prisoners of war take some time to reach this country and if he has been captured by the enemy it is probable that unofficial news will reach you first. In that case I am to ask you to forward any postcard or letter received at once to this Office, and it will be returned to you as soon as possible. Should any further information be received it will be at once communicated to you.[18]

The day Lawrence was captured, his son was born. His family had no choice but to wait, agonizing over what might have happened to him, taking care of his tiny new baby in his absence. Later in March they were informed that he was 'in German hands', and there was hope. A letter arrived in May: 'Dear mum, don't worry, I am safe and sound. Will write again in a few days' time. Give my love to all at home. From your loving son, Laurie.'[19] Like John Sherwood and Alan Yates, Lawrence was forced to march across Germany. As the Allies moved across Europe, liberating it piece by piece, the POWs who were lucky enough to have survived their internment at the hands of the Germans were finally freed. Now came the huge task of getting them all home.

Operation Exodus

Between 3 April and 31 May 1945, Lancasters joined a mission called 'Operation Exodus', tasked with repatriating prisoners from Europe. There were over 350,000 ex-POWs to get home, and many of them were in very bad physical condition. After time in Nazi camps, some of them having spent years interned, they were exhausted, and many were ill, injured and emaciated. They had waited a long time for basic necessities such as food and medicine, and they needed to be brought home as quickly as possible so they could receive the care they so badly needed.

Some of them, it was decided, would be repatriated by air, and the Lancaster was an obvious choice for the operation due to its size, range and adaptability. When modified, each aircraft could carry twenty to twenty-four people. POWs had been assembled at specially designated airfields – Lübeck in Germany, for example, Brussels in Belgium, and Juvincourt in France.

RAF personnel worked hard to make Operation Exodus as smooth as possible. An RAF observer watched the ex-prisoners waiting for their turn:

> The enthusiasm for the task which aircrews displayed is understandable to anyone who has seen a crowd of ex-POWs on a German airfield waiting for a plane to take them to England. They stand in patient groups, but inwardly they are sick with excitement. You realise, when you talk to them,

> that in their hearts they have built up a picture of home that, as the months of separation have grown, has got more and more beautiful and noble and unreal. When the aircraft are sighted, the men throw off all pretence of patience. They pick up their kit, start to move forward – until the officer in charge tells them to take it easy. But now their faces are wreathed in smiles, and they grow voluble – but keeping one ear cocked for their name in the roll call of passengers.[20]

Charles Bray watched Operation Exodus from Juvincourt airfield in France. 'All the might of the greatest destructive force in history has been concentrated on this mission of mercy,' he wrote.

> Lancasters with the reinforced bomb bay to carry the 20,000lb bomb are flying in and out of the airfield full of ex-prisoners instead of high explosives. They come in batches of forty-five at a time. In an hour and a half they are off again, each carrying twenty-four soldiers who have spent anything from nine months to five years in prison camps. It is one of the most impressive sights I have ever seen. And the crews cannot conceal their joy. They mother their human cargo as a hen mothers her chicks.[21]

Air Chief Marshal Sir Arthur Tedder took a personal interest in the operation, spending a lot of time out on the airfield talking to the soldiers and problem-solving when there were logistical hiccups. His wife, Lady Tedder, organized canteens to keep refreshments flowing. Bray noticed there were airborne troops waiting to be repatriated and that they were 'taking a professional interest in the intricacies of the heavy Lancaster bomber'.[22]

For the aircrew flying the Lancasters for Operation Exodus, it was a shock to see the state some of the prisoners were in. Geoff Michael joined the RAAF in Perth in 1942 and completed thirty-two wartime missions with 149 Squadron from RAF Methwold. Of Operation

Exodus, he says: 'It was a moving experience for us. I can still see the thin starved faces of those men reflecting both relief and disbelief that they were actually being taken home.'[23] Geoff's Methwold colleague Jock Bunten also remembers seeing the prisoners: 'Some were in a terrible state. I remember that we were told to leave our parachutes behind because they couldn't be provided for all the returning men.'[24] As they boarded the Lancasters, the men would see messages of goodwill written on the sides of the aircraft by ground crews back in England, with drawings of large, foaming jugs of beer.

Al Lovett watched as a column of twenty-four ex-POWs arrived and filed into his Lancaster. The aircrews got to talk to some of the men they were transporting and heard all sorts of stories. Al was approached by twenty-one-year-old Flight Sergeant Nicholas Stephen Alkemade, who asked if he might sit in the rear turret of the Lancaster for the trip home – it was the position he had occupied when his own Lancaster had been shot down.

> I told him the rear turret was our rear gunner's domain and he would have to ask his permission. He then proceeded to tell me that, on the 24 March 1944, he jumped out of the rear turret of his Lancaster at the height of 18,000ft without a parachute. His own parachute had been burnt due to it being stowed in the fuselage. The flames had driven him out of the turret and he preferred to jump than to be burnt to death. He had fallen down the slope of a mountain covered with a dense forest, the tops of the trees reducing his speed of fall, eventually landing in a snowdrift. He was found by a German patrol and taken to a hospital with a broken ankle. The German doctor who had attended him gave him a document to verify his remarkable escape which he produced. As I could not read German I regarded his story with a certain amount of disbelief. He wanted to sit in the rear turret to recover his nerve. Our rear gunner gave him permission and he appeared to be alright.[25]

Al and his crew were responsible for loading the men onto the aircraft and positioning them carefully so the weight distribution was safe. 'We proceeded to fit them with Mae Wests [life jackets] and issued them with one blanket each, a box of high carbohydrate sweets and a piece of soft flannel (4x2 pull through material) to use as ear plugs,' he says. 'The ex-POWs were dressed in a motley collection of uniforms, such as RAF trousers with khaki tunics etc. On arriving at reception centres in France they had been issued with clean but used clothing until they could be fitted out with correct uniforms on return to England.'

Alan Yates was dressed in such a way when he flew back to England on VE day aboard a Lancaster. That evening, he was refused entry to the officers' mess at RAF Wittering, as he was 'improperly dressed'.

> I was wearing British Army battledress trousers, a dirty blue (Australian Air Force) roll neck sweater knitted by my cousin Marge, a RAF battledress blouse with RAF wings, a long German Army greatcoat and Russian fur hat taken from a dead Russian in Gleiwitz. On my feet I had a pair of wooden clogs ... I was not 'best pleased'; but eventually a nurse took me back into the hospital (I weighed about 7 stone and was suffering from malnutrition and dysentery) and gave me a bottle of beer.[26]

For Lawrence Leishman, eventually his march as a prisoner came to an end and he was liberated by the Americans. He was moved to a holding barracks in Brussels, where huts were lined with bunkbeds and hundreds of ex-prisoners waited desperately to finally go home. The prisoners who had been there the longest were loaded onto the Lancasters first, and the others had to wait their turn. After so much time spent incarcerated or marching on inadequate and sometimes near-starvation diet rations, they were all very hungry. Lawrence and two of his friends were walking down a street, killing time while they waited for their turn to leave. They came across a bakery and stood for a moment to look in the window. There was a great big cream cake – the likes of which they could only have dreamed about for months and months. Pooling their money, they decided to buy it, intending to eat it together when they returned to the camp. When they got back, however, they discovered it was their turn to board a Lancaster and head home, so not wanting to waste the lovely cake, they quickly devoured it.

Lancasters were not built for comfort – but that did not matter to the men they would transport. To the tens of thousands of ex-prisoners like Alan and Lawrence, the Lancaster was a symbol of hope and survival – of happiness after hell. It was the means of getting back to their loved ones and the homes they had missed for so long. For Lawrence, the Lancaster would bring him to his young child, who he had not yet had the chance to meet. They boarded the plane, beside themselves with excitement.

On board, there wasn't much space and things were a bit tight. Lawrence started to feel a little warm and loosened his jacket. The sun was coming through the turret and the fuselage was heating up. Rather than taking them straight to England, the crew decided to give the prisoners a tour of the Ruhr and flew left, right, up and down – to soldiers not used to flying, it felt a little like riding a roller coaster. The mid-upper gunner was rotating in his turret – going round and round, and the heat persisted. Not a fan of flying at the best of times, Lawrence noticed that the man opposite him was going green. In fact, it was only the aircrew who were not. Someone at the end of the aircraft was sick and fielded a look of disgust from the gunner. His stomach having shrunk in captivity, and the cake threatening to expel itself from Lawrence at any moment in the hot, cramped fuselage, he stopped watching the rotating gunner and tried to kneel down. He didn't make it, and was sick in very close proximity to the gunner. 'I'm sorry mate,' he said apologetically. 'Everyone does it,' the mid-upper gunner sighed. 'But you could have missed my boots.' Lawrence arrived in England on 14 May 1945, and finally held his child.

When they arrived at airfields in England, the men were greeted with bands playing, and WAAF volunteers served them tea and cakes. It was reported that at one airfield the men consumed 15,000 cups of tea and half a ton of cake.[27] The men were taken to airfields in England, usually in the south, and from there they would be taken to a receiving centre. They were given food and medical attention, and could have a bath, a shave and a haircut. They were issued kit, clothing and a Red Cross bag containing a safety razor, shaving brush, soap, toothbrush and bars of vitamin-enriched chocolate, and the Women's Voluntary Services helped them to sew their badges onto their newly issued uniform. They were also given cigarettes, a railway warrant home and a little bit of cash.

Once they were safely back in Britain, the ex-prisoners had a lot of adapting to do. There were opportunities to attend resettlement courses to bring them up to date with what had happened in the war and in the country since they had been captured, as well as advice on getting civilian jobs. For many of these men, the road back to 'normal' would be a long and difficult one – not least in their minds.

At the height of Operation Exodus, repatriation aircraft were arriving from Europe in Britain at a rate of sixteen aircraft per hour, and over 1,000 men were brought home each day. Almost 75,000 ex-prisoners were brought home in total. For these men and their families, and for anyone watching, the Lancaster became a sign of relief and of hope and brought an end to so much suffering.

The Post-War Life of Lancasters

At RAF Methwold, radar mechanic John Johnson and his colleagues knew that the end of the war was imminent. Just before the aircrews left on their final operation – another food drop for Operation Manna – the word went out 'under the table' to the ground crews to stand by and be ready for the squadron's return, as they had a surprise planned to thank them for their hard work and support.

'So I stood in front of the radar section, near the perimeter track, waiting,' John says.

> Gradually the sound of Lancasters could be heard. Not one, but many. Off to the right I could see Lancasters low down and in tight formation. It was a sight that would have made any Flying Fortress squadron jealous. They came low directly over the field and it seemed that their wings were interlocked into one large carpet of aircraft. They circled the field once and then each aircraft peeled off the formation like fighters and came in to land one after the other. One aircraft would be well down the runway when another one would already be touching down. Flying control, that little chequered hut at the end of the runway, went wild. Red Very flares were being fired one after the other, arcing over the landing aircraft. But the Lancasters kept on coming. After all, were they going to put the whole of the squadron's aircrew, many of them officers, on court-martial charges? It was an exhibition of flying that I shall never forget and they left me, and I'm sure the other flight line crew standing around, with a thank-you that would last a lifetime.[28]

Wal Cryer describes how he felt when his thirty-fifth operation – his final one – was over:

> Our thirty-fifth operation was over, and I felt like shouting and screaming but only six other fellows would hear, and they probably wanted to shout and scream too. So I decided to shoot up our station. When given permission to land I made what would appear to be a normal approach except I did not lower the flaps nor undercarriage. We were probably about 50 or 75 metres off the deck when the duty officer realised that there were no wheels down. Immediately all sorts of red lights started flashing and I

> could hear him coming through the intercom shouting, 'Go round again, go round again.' From that height I gave it full throttle and four lovely big Merlin engines sprang into life with a roar. I hope it woke everyone. It was just 1 a.m.[29]

On 8 May 1945, the news came that every person on every bomber station in the country had been waiting and hoping for. 'The announcement was heard over the loudspeaker system all over the base,' says radar mechanic John Johnson.

> It was Winston Churchill, telling us that the war with Germany had come to an end. Everyone went wild for a good twenty-four hours. Naturally there was a victory dance and celebration, the radar section supplying the 'window', the metalised strips normally dropped over Germany for jamming German radar, so that trimmings could be made to decorate the ceiling and walls. Those who had served several years in the military could now look forward to demobilization and a return to civilian life.

As the Commander-in-Chief of Bomber Command, Arthur Harris had taken an ill-equipped, struggling force and turned it into an offensive weapon to be reckoned with. The introduction of new aircraft – in particular the Avro Lancaster – and technology, training and tactics under his command helped to build Bomber Command into a formidable force, which was deployed strategically to take the fight to the enemy.

Harris was a leader who had the respect of those who served under him, despite his abruptness and bluntness. He was very vocal about his belief that the bombing of German cities was necessary in order to bring the war to an end and reduce the number of Allied lives lost in the process. This strategy became controversial toward the end of the conflict, and after the war Harris became the focus of much of the criticism that was levelled at Bomber Command. The strategic bombing of German cities was, however, not initiated by Harris – it was a decision taken by the British War Cabinet before Harris had even assumed his role as Commander-in-Chief. The British bombing campaign was carried out by Harris and his command on the orders of Allied government and military leaders. As a result of it, Germany was forced to pour resources and personnel into defence against aerial attack, meaning these crucial resources were removed from the war on the ground. In this sense, Bomber Command had done what Harris set out to do: shorten the war and bring it to a close, saving Allied lives that might have been lost if the conflict continued.

Following Operation Exodus and the cessation of hostilities, various tasks were found for the Lancasters and their crews. A number took part in an aerial mapping mission, with the aim of photographing most of Europe up to the Russian demarcation lines so maps – some of which had proven inaccurate during the war – could be updated. Clare Kemp remembers that some of the Lancasters at RAF Methwold had equipment like H2S removed so that they could accommodate large cameras. 'The squadron then carried out a programme of aerial mapping,' Clare says, with flights detached to Norway and France.[30] Bomb aimer Al Lovett and his crew took part in the photographic mapping: 'The area that was to be photographed at any one time by a single aircraft was 50x25 miles. The camera used was an American Fairchild that took a photograph the size of 12x12 inches from a height of 18,500ft. It required nine runs from west to east and east to west to cover the area.'[31]

Lancaster crews found themselves using their skills in new ways. Pilots, who were used to flying zigzag routes with evasive manoeuvres, were now having to fly straight and level for long periods of time. Bomb aimers like Al used their bombsights and topographical maps to ensure an accurate track was maintained, and the rear gunner was tasked with operating the camera. 'At the request of the bomb aimer he would switch the camera on and off at the beginning of each run,' Al explains. 'He also changed the film magazines when the film ran out.' Large swathes of Europe were successfully photographed, and small gaps in the coverage were filled in by reconnaissance flights conducted by Mosquitoes and their crews.

Lancaster crews also participated in 'Cook's Tours' in May and June 1945. The RAF decided that ground personnel should be given the opportunity to see first-hand how their work had contributed to the defeat of Germany, and they were invited to board Lancasters and fly at low altitudes over areas devastated by Allied bombs. It wasn't possible to take everyone who wanted to go, so personnel were asked to put their names forward to be randomly selected.

It was special for ground crew to be able to fly aboard the Lancasters they had so lovingly maintained throughout operations and to experience just a glimpse of what life had been like for the aircrew they had supported. They flew at around 500ft over areas where Bomber Command operations had taken place, with flights lasting around four to five hours. Rear gunner Jock Bunten remembers taking ground personnel on Cook's Tours. 'The WAAFs were ordered to wear trousers so that we didn't all get too excited,' he says.[32]

In June and July 1945, the RAF conducted Operation Post Mortem. During the final weeks of the war, Hitler had instructed retreating German troops to destroy any equipment they could not take with them – including technology that was part of the Luftwaffe's air defence system. In Denmark, however, the system was fully intact and in good working order at the time of the German surrender, presenting the Allies with a rare and valuable opportunity. The RAF ran a ten-day exercise to test the system, investigate how it worked, determine its strengths and weaknesses and test radio countermeasures against it, to find out how effective it was.

A section of the network in central Denmark was chosen for the exercise, and Luftwaffe radar and fighter control officers – now prisoners of war in Allied hands – were brought in to man the system. Watched closely by RAF officers and experts, they were told to work as they normally would have, as around 200 RAF bombers flew dummy raids using their radio countermeasures (jamming radar using Window, for instance) as they had during wartime operations. This series of live exercises was 'without parallel in the history of warfare'.[33] The after-action report produced provided valuable insight into the impact of Allied radio countermeasures on Luftwaffe operations. Though Germany had been working on upgrading its radar system throughout the war, Window was found to be a consistently effective means of denying accurate radar tracking data to the Luftwaffe.[34] Overall, Bomber Command's radar countermeasures were found to have made a contribution to the decline in losses it suffered.

With the war in Europe over, the Allies turned their attention to bringing the war against Japan to an end. To this end, the RAF created 'Tiger Force'. Consisting of squadrons of long-range aircraft – Lancasters and Lincolns – the force would be based in the Pacific region to support an invasion of Japan by Allied forces. The Lancasters of Tiger Force were modified for their new mission, and despite the impressive ability of the Lancaster to cover long distances, problems with range remained a concern in an area as vast as the Pacific. Various solutions were considered, including the fitting of large saddle fuel tanks, and testing was carried out by Avro on two Lancasters in India, by No. 1577 (Special Duties) Flight. The atomic bombing of Hiroshima and Nagasaki in August, however, brought an end to the Pacific War, as Japan surrendered to the Allies. The Second World War was finally over, and Tiger Force was not needed.

In 1946, the USAAF invited Bomber Command to conduct a 'Goodwill Tour' of the United States, and sixteen Lancasters from 35 Squadron took part. They flew from the East Coast to the West, stopping at various locations along the way to reception committees of military personnel and press, and parties that went on all night. Lancaster pilot Charles Owen flew Lancaster TW909 with an important passenger aboard. In September 1945, Air Chief Marshal Sir Norman Bottomley had taken over as the new Commander-in-Chief of Bomber Command, and he now accompanied Charles and his crew in a specially converted soundproof cabin on the Lancaster. TW909 landed in Gander, Newfoundland, on 21 July 1946, where the crew feasted on an 'enormous breakfast' at 3.30 a.m. Though the war had ended in August 1945, Britain was still under food rationing. 'First unrationed food since 1939,' Charles wrote in his diary, 'and we all made pigs of ourselves. The Old Man [Air Chief Marshal Bottomley] seemed to enjoy it as much as we did.'[35] A few days later the crew landed in New York, to a reception of high-ranking American military personnel and media representatives. 'Many photographs,' Charles wrote, 'and the Old Man tickled pink.' Evidently the reception was enjoyable, as Charles recorded the next day:

> Very bumpy leaving New York, with low cloud and blistering heat, not helped by the fact that we all had shocking hangovers, including the Old Man, who was distinctly rude on the intercom about the conditions. Circled over the city before leaving and admired the skyscrapers. Cloud broke up about halfway, so climbed up to ten thou and cooled down a bit. Feeling better by the time we reached Dayton, and the Old Man a little more affable.

The crew found the sun and the heat a real struggle while flying over the desert of the south-western United States. 'I was thankful for a Texas cowboy hat which I had somehow acquired the night before,' Charles wrote. They had been sent off with flight rations of chicken sandwiches, bananas, peaches and iced milk, the likes of which they could only have dreamed of for years. On 8 August, on their way home, the crew took off in particularly bad weather. 'Weather at take-off time was distinctly duff,' Charles wrote. 'In fact it stank, but once the Old Man had seen some lunatic take off in a civilian DC-4 he seemed to think the honour of the RAF was at stake, so off we had to go.' The next day the crew arrived home and were given fourteen days' leave, which they thought 'a good show'.

Because no one could know when the Second World War was going to end, the production of Lancasters had been planned into 1946. When the war ended in 1945, it was possible to cancel some orders for new Lancasters but not all of them – not without causing serious problems for the aircraft industry in Britain. Lancasters continued to serve in Britain in various capacities. In 1946, medic Jimmy Burt was posted to RAF Waddington to care for RAF and USAAF personnel, including 617 Squadron. He decided that if he was going to be treating aircrew and lecturing them about taking care of themselves, he wanted to experience what they experienced. He asked if he might accompany an aircrew on a flight, and the next day he boarded a Lancaster. 'It looked like a big aircraft,' he says. 'I stood between the pilot and the flight engineer until we got to about 5,000ft, and then I was sent down into the nose of the aircraft where the bomb aimer/front gunner would usually be.'[36] His first flight was a wonderful experience for Jimmy. 'I loved it,' he says, 'and when they asked me if I wanted to go again, I said I'd go anytime I could. I'd look for the flying boys in the mess and ask if they had any room for me to go along.' The only position in the Lancaster Jimmy never got to sit in was the rear gunner's.

As an aviation medic, the health complaint Jimmy saw the most was varicose veins. Being at Waddington in 1946, however, he also saw evidence of 'combat stress', or what would today be called post-traumatic stress disorder. 'There was one officer who had been a POW,' he says, 'and he used to walk into the mess, walk past everyone without speaking, and pull a chair over to the window. He would just sit and stare out of it.' Lancaster pilot Arthur Bishop notes how difficult it was for those who had been 'subjected to the stresses of war' to return to civilian life, and that the adjustment was traumatic. 'You can visit any ex-servicemen's club in Canada today', he wrote in 2003, 'and pick out the tortured souls who still, after sixty years, have not adjusted.'[37]

A number of bomber units continued to fly Lancasters until 1950, by which time they had largely been replaced by the Avro Lincoln. The RAF lacked aircraft with the range to operate efficiently in the Pacific, where vast distances separated Allied bases and facilities. The Air Ministry urged A. V. Roe to work on a larger version of the Lancaster, which had proven so useful in the European theatre, and the Lincoln was the result. The first production Lincolns flew with No. 57 Squadron in August 1945, and 583 Lincolns were built. The aircraft was earmarked for the Tiger Force, but with the dropping of the atomic bombs on Hiroshima and Nagasaki in Japan, the force was stood down. Arriving on the scene just a little too late to serve in the Second World War, the Lincoln had a short post-war career as the mainstay of Bomber Command in the early years of the Cold War. The coming of the jet age highlighted the inadequacies of the Lincoln, however, and though it was used briefly in Malaya and Kenya in the early 1950s, it could not measure up to the jet V-Bombers, which superseded it from 1955. Avro Lancasters continued to be used in RAF aerial reconnaissance until they were replaced with more modern, superior aircraft – the Lancasters of 82 Squadron, for instance, were replaced by English Electric Canberras in 1953.

Where Bomber Command was phasing the Lancaster out, Coastal Command was phasing them in. During the war, Coastal Command had relied on American-owned aircraft such as the Liberator, but under the conditions of the Lend–Lease agreement these aircraft had to be returned to the US after the war. This left the command in desperate need of long-range, land-based maritime patrol aircraft, and the Lancaster was brought in to fulfil this role. With some modifications, the Lancaster became the main aircraft used by Coastal Command, serving in the roles of both aerial reconnaissance and air-sea rescue.

The Lancaster had served first and foremost as a war machine in the hands of the RAF, but it had also been added to the civilian register. When the war ended, a sudden peacetime lack of civilian transport became apparent, and several types of warplanes were considered for conversion for passenger use. The Avro Lancastrian, for example, was a Lancaster bomber converted to an airliner for nine to twelve passengers. The armour plating and gun turrets of the Lancaster were removed, and extra fuel tanks could be placed where the bomb bay would normally be. State-owned airline the British Overseas Airways Corporation took delivery of a number of Lancastrians, which it used on its long-range routes – between Britain and Australia, for instance – until September 1950. The Lancastrian was also used to transport mail and cargo and participated in the Berlin Airlift. British aeronautical engineers also made use of the Lancaster, using it as a test bed for the development of new engines, and the aircraft was used as both a tanker and a receiving aircraft in air-to-air refuelling experiments carried out by Flight Refuelling Limited.

Other countries also made use of the Lancaster in the post-war period. It was used with varying purpose by the militaries of Argentina, Egypt, France and Sweden, and the Soviet Union used two. Canadian-built Lancasters returned home to Canada and continued to fly in various capacities, including air-sea rescue, for two decades before being withdrawn from service. Canadian manufacturer Victory Aircraft also produced a version of the Lancastrian, for use in civilian transportation on long-haul routes.

The last Lancaster built was TW910, delivered to the RAF by Armstrong Whitworth on 2 February 1946. It served with 207 and 115 Squadrons until being struck off charge in March 1950. On 10 February 1956, the RAF announced that the Lancaster would be officially withdrawn from service, and five days later, it was.

CHAPTER NINE

LIFE, LOVE AND LOSS

Life

ALAN GOODALE WAS A YOUNG CHILD when the war broke out, living in Lincolnshire. With so many air bases in the county there was a huge influx of RAF personnel, which Alan remembers had quite an impact on the local area and community. The hotels, pubs and dance halls were jam-packed, and dancing was the main source of entertainment. 'The buses were packed because so many airmen were coming and going to and from the bases,' Alan says.[1] 'The cinemas were packed, and there was a queue to get in for 200 yards.'

Bomber crews could relax in between sorties, and aircrew were given a seven-day leave every six weeks. Many used these opportunities to visit their wives, girlfriends, families and friends. Navigator Peter Carpenter speaks about making friends with others in the RAF:

> We maintained 'hybrid' loyalties. We were busy keeping up our long-term relationships – in my own case with fellow navigators – and starting to forge new relationships and friendships with the crew. As we progressed through to

> HCU/LFS/Squadron crew loyalties took over and remained with us until the end of the tour.
>
> If you could make friends fairly easily social life in the service tended to take care of itself. Reasonable conversational skills were needed, and this helped to pass the time of day and overcame boredom during inevitable long hours of waiting for whatever. Discussions could be about anything – home, after the war, technical matters, the rights and wrongs in our lives ... We used the mess (it was warm) for having a drink, playing snooker or one of the many card games. Sometimes as a crew we were forced out to the local village pubs because officers could not use the sergeants' mess, and vice versa. At HCU Sandtoft, first time round, then Lindholme, we were into visiting pubs with 'singing' bars and local 'discovery' nights.[2]

Peter and his crewmates often spent their leisure time in Scunthorpe, visiting the pubs there. If they missed the buses and trains back to base, a local woman put them up – her daughter was married to a pilot from New Zealand and she had a genuine soft spot for her adopted Elsham aircrew. '"Put up" means nesting overnight,' Peter clarifies. 'A few to a bed – plus an early morning call and breakfast – all in time to catch the first train back.' Peter praises the citizens of Scunthorpe, 'who were very kind to aircrew and tolerant of our sometimes wild habits – over all the years I have always thought of them kindly'.

At RAF Methwold, bomb aimer Al Lovett and his crew also found comfort in the kindness of locals. The airmen often found themselves in the village pub and had to take jam jars with them to have their beer served because of a shortage of glasses. When Methwold began to fly heavy bombers like the Lancaster, it was necessary to lengthen the runway toward the village, and it wasn't uncommon for an aircraft to end its journey in someone's garden. 'We used to go out at 2 a.m.,' Al explains, 'clattering and banging, loading up, and the gunners would fire into pits to practise.' None of the villagers grumbled. They accepted the noise, and one of them told Al: 'We used to lie in bed and count you back.'[3]

Sometimes operations were cancelled at very short notice. 'I have vivid memories of the odd night when ops were scrubbed too late to catch the transport down to Scunthorpe,' says Jack Spark, a wireless operator who accompanied Peter Carpenter.

> 'Doc' Henderson would get the 'Blood Wagon' out and perhaps twenty of us would pile in and in due course would end up at the Oswald. This was fine, going over to Scunthorpe – but coming back, all with inflated bladders, we had to stop at least a couple of times to obtain the necessary relief. It's just as well no one had a camera in those days. Twenty airmen and one MO [medical officer] standing in line abreast, all aiming in the same direction ... talk about precision aim![4]

It wasn't just the adults in areas around bomber stations that were deeply affected by the presence of a large number of RAF personnel and their aircraft. As a young boy, Alan Goodale liked to watch the Lancasters taking off at RAF Scampton. He would crouch in a ditch very close to the runway with his friends. 'We'd get ourselves into the ditch, right at the end of the runway, looking right down it. When the Lanc was taking off in that direction, it would come straight over our heads,' he says.[5] The runway had a hump in it, which sometimes obscured the Lancasters from view. 'We couldn't see them at the far end, but we could hear them,' he says. The Lancasters would taxi around the perimeter, and then, 'with an enormous roar, you would see it heading straight for you on take-off. Pretty heavy – pretty scary, but thrilling.'

By 1944, Lincolnshire was saturated with bomber bases, many of them home to numerous Lancasters. 'In the early evening there would be the constant hum of aircraft engines with perhaps a thousand Merlins running as Lancaster bombers waited their turn to take off,' Alan remembers. Sometimes Alan's school bus would have to stop and wait when taking children to school in the mornings. There was an Avro facility near to RAF Waddington, and Lancasters in need of repairs would be towed there by a tractor, rolled around half a mile down the main road. Alan would try to get the front seat on the bus if he could, for a better view of the planes. 'There were so many Lancasters,' Alan says. 'I remember sitting and looking at the sky, wondering if there would ever not be any Lancs in it.'

Madge Allen was also a child during the war, living in the quiet Norfolk village of Methwold. When the RAF arrived, it didn't stay quiet for long. 'With an airfield sat right on the edge of the village, the comings and goings of military personnel and the aerial activity of countless aircraft, the war brought enormous changes to people's lives in Methwold,' Chris Stone of the Methwold History Group writes.[6] 'The village grew as many airmen brought their wives and families to the comparative safety of East Anglia. This brought prosperity to Methwold as not many houses were without rooms rented to service families. It also brought increased trade to the local pubs and shops, of which Methwold had a great number.'

Madge remembers airmen cycling to the farm where she lived to play cards together. 'My mother had a strict rule about not gambling,' she says, 'but provided them with a jar of farthings which were collected up at the end of a session … One of my most vivid memories of the war was sitting on a farm gate close to the airfield watching the planes take off and return. I used to spend hours doing that!'

Like their parents, children were exposed to the horrors of war through close proximity to bomber stations. Alan Goodale recalls a Lancaster crashing into a row of semi-detached houses, one of which was his home. 'Several neighbouring properties, including my own … had roof damage, chimney stacks demolished and masonry thrown down chimneys or into gardens.' On hitting the ground, the Lancaster 'slid a considerable distance, breaking off the tail and stopping only 100 yards short of high voltage cables'. Amazingly, nobody was seriously hurt.

Similarly, Ken Bancroft witnessed a crash. Standing on the steps of his father's workshop, he watched as a Lancaster circled over the town of Glossop in Derbyshire, straightened and headed towards the east. Ken knew this to be the direction of the peaks, which in that area rose to 2,000ft. He could do nothing but watch as the bomber struck the top of one of the peaks, hidden as it was in the darkness, and burst into a ball of flame. He immediately ran to the police station to tell them what he had seen, but they didn't believe him. Eventually someone was sent to check the area to see if Ken was telling the truth and the crash site was discovered. None of the crew had survived.[7]

The night that Lancaster EE118 – a Pathfinders aircraft – crashed in the Norfolk village of Wimbotsham, twelve-year-old Derek Neale's father ran into his room to check that he and his brothers were all right. Derek heard his father say to his mother: 'I think a plane has just come down near us.' Mr and Mrs Neale went outside with their torches and were horrified to find the wreckage of an aircraft in their back garden. Mr Neale ran to the telephone box on the village green to report the crash. Meanwhile, rescuers heard someone shouting. They ran toward the voice and came across Arthur Orchard, the rear gunner, lying on the ground with a large branch across his legs. Two young men prepared to lift the branch, but Arthur begged them not to, fearing his legs were broken and it might be best to wait for medical help. All six of the crew apart from Arthur were dead, and the RAF removed them during the night. The sole survivor of the crash, Arthur was taken to hospital. The next morning, Derek Neale was due to go potato picking, but it was cancelled. He was able to get past the RAF guard on duty and sneak into the crash site. The middle section of the fuselage was upside down and bent over the fence of his garden, and he found the lid of an Elsan toilet underneath. A huge Lancaster wheel was embedded in the shed and there was aircraft debris all over the garden.[8]

As the number of Lancasters being produced and ferried to bomber stations for operational use increased, so did demand for the facilities needed to operate them. Runways, in particular, had to be constructed. The building works for new runways and air stations required a vast number of people. Drawing on the expertise of architects, quantity surveyors, land agents and civil, mechanical and electrical engineers, the Air Ministry Directorate General of Works organized the building of the airfields and was responsible for their design, construction and maintenance.

The airfields were built by public works contractors, which used civilian labour. One such labourer was Herbert Ozanne, who had been evacuated to England from Guernsey before the German occupation. As the number of heavy bombers available to the RAF increased with production, airfields needed to be modified in order to be able to host them. In 1943, RAF Methwold was making preparations for the arrival of its new four-engined heavies, and three concrete runways between 1,500 and 2,000 yards in length needed to be built.

A civil engineer working for a construction company, Herbert was tasked with working on the construction of the runways. Working day and night to get the concrete down and the runways finished, Herbert and his colleagues endured Luftwaffe bombing raids, running to safety in the air-raid shelters at the sides of the runways when the siren sounded. A vast amount of labour was needed for the work, and it had to be completed as fast as possible. Herbert worked with men from Ireland, Poland and the United States, and sometimes they worked so fast they turned the diggers over.[9] Such a large workforce needed to be housed and fed. Ann Akrigg, a teenager when the concrete runways were laid at RAF Methwold, served with other local girls in a canteen for the workers:

> The canteen was in a big hangar at the end of Old Feltwell Road. The men had lodgings there too. Every morning I'd bike to work and collect my friend Joyce Giles from Cross Hill on the way. She would sit on the saddle while I stood and pedalled away. I mostly worked in the bread room making sandwiches. We needed a lot with all those mouths to feed. Dinner was often mash and some kind of roast meat. We never heated the meat, just ran the hot gravy over it! Pudding was mostly boiled rice and jam.[10]

Many of the people working on the construction of the airfields stayed with local people. Ann's family cottage became home to engineers and architects. 'I remember the blueprints for the airfield runways being spread all over our large table and there being lots of discussions about what needed to be done,' she says. The airfields were protected by searchlights. 'I remember that there was a searchlight further up the road from us towards Northwold,' Ann says. 'It really lit up the sky!'

By 1945, the combined length of the runways in Britain was said to have been around 9,000 miles long, and the island-country was like 'one vast aircraft carrier anchored off the north-west coast of Europe'.[11]

Laughter

Aircrew lived lives that were a strange mixture of unimaginable terror, danger, complete normality – and even fun. One minute they might be clinging desperately to their seats as the pilot performed an evasive corkscrew manoeuvre over a blazing inferno in an attempt to keep them from being shot out of the sky. The next they could be playing cards with friends in a pub or a practical joke on a colleague. There was no apparent rhyme or reason as to who did and did not come home from operations, and the weight of death and loss lingered in the air every day and every night.

Even in the darkest of times, however, friendships thrived and a lot of laughter was heard on bomber stations around the country. The RAF provided leisure facilities and activities, ranging from sports and dances to parties and variety shows. Bomber Command personnel visited pubs, cafés and cinemas off-station and made friends in the local community. Pilot Hugo Trotter says: 'We had a lot of fun … We didn't really take anything too seriously.'[12] Hugo and his friends played games in the evenings and made indoor fireworks out of bullets. Many airmen found that making jokes and having a laugh made life easier for them. 'In the evenings, if you were on, you'd go out on bicycles and play a game,' Hugo says. 'You didn't try to knock people off, as such, but it was a "last man standing" situation. I remember one of them saying, "Oh well, he'll get through a tour."'

Canadian Lancaster pilot Bob Purves kept his flight commander, John Gee, on his toes with practical jokes and a larger-than-life character:

> The story I was told was that Bob Purves had flown a Lancaster with a large consignment of whisky on board for some US Army Air Force base and had exchanged the Scotch for a load of Coca-Cola, complete with refrigerated cabinet. This he had loaded into the Lancaster's bomb bay and flown with it back to Wickenby. He had decided off his own bat that the mess needed a good supply of Coca-Cola![13]

Part of a 'sprog' crew paying their first visit to 'the Oswald', a local pub, Jack Spark remembers being on the receiving end of a ritual practical joke:

> We had only been there five minutes when a complete crew of hardened veterans came over and welcomed us to the Squadron. As they leaned over and shook hands with one hand – they cut off the ends of our ties with scissors held in the other hand! We were handed our tie ends and had to sit the rest of the evening with just a collar and a knot! Needless to say, this only happened to us once! We had the pleasure of doing the same thing to another crew at a later date![14]

Wireless operator Bruce Rawling's friend, navigator Tom Curson, had a motorbike on which he would travel to London to see his fiancée:

> I remember one night we decided to go to a dance in a village a few miles away. We decided Tom could take a couple on his motorcycle and he could tow the rest of us on our bikes.

> There was much laughter and merriment among the local villagers when we turned up and landed in a sprawling heap on the grass in the centre of the village square. Aircrews were treated with great kindness and forbearance by the people, especially those in East Anglia where so many of the big bomber dromes were located. I suspect they saw many of our youthful pranks as just letting off a bit of steam which indeed they were.[15]

A rear gunner for 149 Squadron, Jock Bunten, based at RAF Methwold, speaks of the balance of finding ways to have fun and coping with the seriousness of his job:

> Life on the base was great for a nineteen-year-old and there were marvellous parties. We liked to drink in the Chequers but had to move quickly if we were drinking late and the police inspector called! I remember one night when we heard him coming and had to throw my friend Bert Bays over the wall at the back of the pub to avoid being caught! We did sometimes get into trouble for doing silly things. I remember we were fined 19 shillings each ... for turning signs around and pinching a few gates! There was a much more serious side though, I remember returning from one mission with eighty-nine holes in our aircraft one of which was only 3 inches away from me.[16]

Celebrating birthdays and Christmases away from home could be hard for young men and women, and friends substituted for family. On flight engineer Eric Blanchard's twenty-first birthday, he received a home-made sponge cake from his mother. 'We sat underneath our Lancaster,' he says. 'Somebody produced a penknife, and we all had a little bit of cake.'[17]

Camaraderie was an incredibly important part of life for personnel on bomber stations, and many speak of it as a vital part of being able to cope in such difficult times. Tom Quinlan remembers realizing how close he was with his friends at RAF Elsham Wolds: 'Owing to a mistake in aircraft letters, the wrong aircraft was reported missing. It was then great, when we turned up a day late, to see the tears of joy on the faces of our ground crew – an occasion that made us all realise just how close we were.'[18]

WAAF Clare Kemp's most cherished memory of her time at RAF Methwold was 'one of close friendship and a bond' with her fellow airwomen and airmen. 'It was a comradeship similar to that experienced between friends and neighbours in the early part of the war when I lived in London during the Blitz.'[19] Clare formed very close friendships with her fellow WAAF, and the hut they shared became a haven. 'A bed, a shelf and hooks apiece with a stove in the middle of the hut … no lockers, no chairs, no carpets … but still home to us and many a laugh we had too, in spite of the rats scurrying over the metal roof and earwigs in our beds.'

In the winter, conditions in the hut could be challenging, but Clare and her friends coped. 'We pulled the beds around the stove to keep warm and have a natter but again I can remember that there were times when there was no fuel for the stove and I found that snow had blown in through the window onto my bed … Then there was the mud after the rain to contend with.'

Conditions in Nissen huts were tricky for the men too. 'It was a terrible job trying to keep those Nissen huts warm during the winter,' Ron Pain writes. 'I seem to recall that some of the toilet doors went missing.'[20] Al Lovett shared his hut with rabbits and a cat, which had kittens. 'I kept my motorbike fastened to my bed so nobody would pinch it,' he says. 'There was a shortage of carburettors, and they would just disappear if you weren't careful.'[21]

At Christmas in 1944, a group of men from RAF Methwold cut down a Christmas tree in nearby Brandon Forest and brought it back for the WAAF to decorate. They used strips of Window and various other shiny odds and ends they found lying around. 'That Christmas there were many good parcels from Australia and New Zealand which the recipients shared with us,' Clare recalls.

Love

Inevitably, where RAF and WAAF personnel served in close proximity, relationships formed. 'How I felt sorry for those gallant RAF officers from Feltwell camp who would cycle back from Lakenheath with WAAF passengers on the crossbar,' Clare Kemp says. 'It must have been quite a push for them but also the start of many a friendship or romance.'

People fell in love in all sorts of ways. When, in April 1943, Lancaster pilot Stevie Stevens called up the control tower for permission to land, he was surprised to hear a woman's voice reply. This was unusual, so after landing safely he went to Flying Control to investigate, only to find a crowd of equally curious officers looking for the woman who had cleared them for landing. The woman turned out to be a glamourous WAAF R/T operator, but as she was surrounded by pilots Stevie didn't fancy his chances and crept away. When he was posted to Scampton some time later, he heard the same voice over the radio:

> Her voice was instantly recognisable ... I was thrilled once again by those deep blue eyes and blonde hair, and this time, I did manage to ask her out. It took some courage to make the approach ... but operational aircraft captains are not so easily deflected from their target![22]

The WAAF in question was Maureen Miller. Maureen didn't consider herself the 'marrying kind', but Stevie won her heart, and the two fell for one another. 'It was the person himself that attracted me,' Maureen muses. 'The brave man who was doing a wonderful job going into battle every night.' One night when the two were walking near the airfield, Stevie said to Maureen, 'If I survive to the end of this year, we'll get married.' And get married they did.[23]

One day, flight engineer Bill Rudd's romance with his WAAF sweetheart caused something of an inconvenience on his Lancaster.

'He waved to this WAAF every time he took off,' Bill's crewmate, wireless operator Arthur Atkinson, says. 'Then one time he was waving to her, stretching his head round to wave to her and his intercom plug came out as we were tearing down the runway to take off, so when [pilot] Bob Acott said, "full power", nothing happened.'[24] Bill recovered himself just in time, and the fully loaded bomber just about took off.

With the very high rate of loss on Bomber Command stations, romance often led to heartbreak. WAAF and airmen might spend their off-duty hours visiting the cinema or a nearby café. 'The aircrew that we went to the flicks with one night would be missing the following night after a raid, in the bad times,' Clare Kemp says.[25] WAAF Aline 'Betty' Wakefield was engaged to an Australian airman named Derby, and when he was shot down and killed she struggled to cope with his loss. The pages covering the period of his death and its aftermath were torn out of her diary. 'Very miserable and tired,' Betty wrote a little while later, on the day Derby would have turned twenty-five.[26] Peggy Wallace served in the Auxiliary Territorial Service, the women's branch of the British Army, working on an anti-aircraft battery. She lost two boyfriends in Bomber Command, and her sister Maisie, a WAAF based at RAF Methwold, lost her fiancé, a pilot from New Zealand. 'In those days you just had to live for every minute,' Peggy says, 'because you didn't know what tomorrow would bring.'[27]

Loss

During the Second World War, 55,573 of Bomber Command's 125,000 aircrew were killed. A further 8,403 were wounded in action, and 9,838 became prisoners of war. Bomb aimer Al Lovett and friends were just one crew of many to feel the sting of loss. Despite being almost 6ft tall, Sergeant Ronald Edgar Tootell served as the rear gunner with his crew on their Lancaster at RAF Methwold. One night on an operation against the Hohenbudberg oil and coking plant, an ME109G Luftwaffe night fighter appeared on the starboard side of the Lancaster, firing a long burst of bullets before the pilot could perform an evasive corkscrew manoeuvre. Shortly after, either the same ME109G or another – the crew weren't sure – homed in on the Lancaster for a second attack. This time Al manned the front gun turret and the mid-upper gunner fired his guns as the pilot threw the aircraft into a series of violent corkscrews. The mid-upper gunner struck the fighter, and it was seen falling away in flames.

Once the Lancaster was level again, the pilot called all the aircrew on the intercom to check they were all right. The only one who didn't answer was Ron, in the rear turret. Damage to the Lancaster had caused cold air to stream into the fuselage, and the wireless operator was forced to abandon an attempt to check on Ron because a valve had frozen in his portable oxygen bottle. Al connected to a portable oxygen bottle and made his way down the fuselage. 'The noise of the slipstream and the cold was intense,' he says. 'It was very dark and the use of a torch was not advisable. Everything had to be done by feel. The only light was coming from the glare of the searchlights through the holes in the fuselage. Reaching the turret the doors had to be forced fully open.'[28] Al shook Ron's shoulder, but received no response. Pressing Ron's head forward, Al attempted to pull him free from the turret, but Ron's fingers were still clasping the triggers of his guns. They fired, and the pilot assumed the aircraft was once again under attack. He took evasive action, while Al did his best to release the guns from Ron's hands. With the help of the mid-upper gunner, Al removed Ron from the turret, and the two carried him up the fuselage.

Ron had sustained a leg wound, which they bandaged with the mid-upper gunner's scarf, and a head wound. 'When the barrel of a chrome-plated torch was placed close to his mouth there was no trace of condensation or any sign of breathing,' Al explains, 'and we assumed that he might be dead. He was, nevertheless, given an injection of morphine, his oxygen mask replaced, and made as comfortable as possible.' Al and the mid-upper gunner were kneeling either side of Ron when the Lancaster suddenly stalled. 'The nose dropped and we went into a dive,' Al says.

> The aircraft continued to drop earthwards eventually going over the vertical despite the efforts of the pilot to pull out of the dive. Possibly due to the damage sustained to the tail, the aircraft would not respond. The pilot called to the navigator for assistance and with their combined strength, they managed to pull the control column back and gradually the nose of the aircraft started to rise. From our original altitude of 18,000ft we had fallen over 13,000ft and we eventually resumed level flight at about 5,000ft above sea level. The ground around the area where the incident occurred was hilly and in some places the height was about 200ft. After returning to base we estimated our airspeed must have reached at least 400mph at the end of our dive. The pilot and navigator had placed their feet on the instrument panel to gain leverage when pulling back on the control column and several of the instruments had been badly damaged. This did not make our return journey any easier. After gradually climbing back to a safe altitude we set course for home, badly shaken and very cold.

When they arrived back at the base, the pilot requested an emergency landing and notified Flying Control that Ron was seriously injured. When they landed an ambulance was waiting, and an RAF medical officer climbed on board. 'I told him that I thought the rear gunner had died,' Al says. 'After examining him he said that he would not have been surprised, due to the nature of his wounds, but with the use of his stethoscope he could detect a faint sign of life.' Ron was taken to the station sick quarters and was found to have a gunshot wound to his right thigh. It had missed his femur and exited through the top of his leg, having passed through the thick padding of his flight suit.

The bullet went through his oxygen mask and into his head. He had lost a lot of blood, and the station lacked the facilities to deal with injuries of such severity. The medical officer requested air transport to take Ron to the neurology unit at RAF Benson in Oxfordshire, and although all the pilots who were in the office had been on operations that night and were exhausted, they all volunteered to fly Ron.

At around 11 a.m., just as he was being lifted into the aircraft, Ron passed away. 'Our crew did not fly again for about two weeks,' Al says. 'The wireless operator had to receive treatment for badly frostbitten fingers and remained in the station sick quarters for four days, afterwards needing treatment for quite a while.' Despite their efforts to save him, the crew had lost their rear gunner, and it hit hard. They attended his funeral a short while after his death. Al goes on:

> The day before the funeral we departed the airfield with the coffin [and] an escort of airmen and proceeded to Brandon railway station. When the train arrived the RAF vehicle carrying the coffin backed to the raised platform and the coffin was lifted out. It was draped with the Squadron flag and wreaths from the officers' mess, sergeants' mess, ground staff and airwomen. The armed escort fired three volleys over the coffin, it was then carried across the platform into a guard's van and secured to two trestles already fastened to the floor. The railway staff had done an excellent job. A compartment on the train had been reserved for crew.[29]

The crew were invited to meet Ron's wife, Olive, who was in the Auxiliary Territorial Service, as well as his family and their friends. When the coffin was driven by the undertakers to the church, the crew accompanied their fallen gunner on his final journey, lining up either side of the cortège and slow marching to the end of the road. Neighbours gathered outside their homes to pay their respects, and Ron was buried in the cemetery shortly afterwards. The six remaining crew members were granted seven days' leave on return to Methwold.

Pathfinder pilot Charles Owen lost a colleague in an extremely traumatic way. On 28 January 1944, Charles had to remove the headless body of Flight Sergeant Laurie from the rear turret of a bomber. Laurie had been decapitated by anti-aircraft fire over Kiel. Some airmen killed in Bomber Command did not lose their lives to enemy fire, but in collisions with friendly aircraft. Flying in a stream meant that if a Lancaster were to move much in any direction, it could collide with another bomber. Extreme evasive action might cause deadly crashes, and so could the aircraft lurching upwards as the bombs were released.

Leslie Temple lost his best friend, Jack Whitely, when two aircraft collided. Leslie and Jack had gone through radio school together, and they remained close until Jack's death. They would visit each other's family homes during their leave, and when he died, Jack's family wrote to Leslie. 'They fished him out of the sea. And this is the sort of life you had in the air force,' says Leslie. 'You made friends but you didn't know what was going to happen on your next trip.'[30]

Crashes could also occur when bombers that were damaged and badly shot up were trying to limp home from operations and just couldn't make it. Bad weather could be lethal, particularly fog and mist rising up from the ground. Richard Walker was on the train back to Lindholme in Lincolnshire when he opened the *Daily Herald* and saw the news of a Lancaster that had crashed into a hillside in Derbyshire. It was Lancaster PA411, and his own crew were aboard. He'd heard it had happened but hoped there had been some mistake. There were no survivors.

His eyes ran over the crew list again and again. There was no mistake. The names were those of his friends. Richard wasn't on the flight because he had been on his honeymoon. He had been married the previous week and all the crew had attended the wedding. Immediately afterwards, they had made their way back to Lindholme to continue with their training. Richard was asked to identify the bodies of his crew. A watch, still on the wrist of the rear gunner, revealed the time of the crash to be ten seconds before midnight.

Immediately when they had heard the dull bang of the crash, John Bagshaw had rushed to the site of the wreck with his four sons, aged twelve to twenty-one. The first object they came across was the tail unit and rear turret of the Lancaster, still intact. A short distance from it lay the rear gunner. Though Mr Bagshaw wiped his mouth and tried to help him, he passed away a short while later.[31]

Airmen often turned to one another when coping with loss – it was only in each other that they could find people who understood what they were going through. John Gee's entire crew was lost in a minelaying operation, along with his commanding officer, Francis Powley. 'I was so distraught at losing Francis Powley with my crew and one of my Flight Lieutenants with his that I did not know where to turn,' he wrote.[32] 'I felt I did not want to speak to anyone. Despite having been airborne himself on this hazardous operation for some seven hours, Bob Purves came to my room in the small hours and did his best to console me. He knew how I felt and stayed with me until it was time to report to the flight offices.' John appreciated Bob's compassion tremendously. Airmen who returned when their friends did not were acutely aware of how lucky they were. Sam Thompson served as a gunner and flew fifty operations in Lancasters and Halifaxes. He remembers 'two or three' close encounters with fighters over Germany. 'We were lucky to get home after other poor souls were shot down,' he says.[33]

Then, as now, people coped with death in various different ways. When Bernice Sherwood was told that her husband, John 'Flap' Sherwood, had been killed in the Augsburg raid, she flatly refused to believe it. Sherwood's Lancaster has been hit by flak and caught fire, plummeting to the ground and exploding into pieces upon impact. Witnesses were sure no one could have survived. When the story was relayed to Bernice she did not break down in tears but said, 'I would know if he was dead, and I think he's OK.'[34] Happily, she was right, and against all odds John had survived. He was catapulted clear of the blast, still fastened into his pilot's seat, and was the sole survivor, found unconscious.

Mid-upper gunner John Hughes was not so lucky and died on

the return journey from a raid on Hamburg. John's mother was 'utterly distraught', and her family said her 'hair seemingly went white overnight'.[35] John's younger brother lost a surrogate parent and protector in John, who had used his leave during RAF training to visit him when he was homesick as an evacuee. He had to grow up very quickly, almost overnight, and took on all the responsibility for his father's business and his parents' welfare. After the war when John's brother came to do his national service, he was keen to join the RAF but knew that seeing him in the uniform would devastate his mother, so he chose the army instead.

On a visit home, a young airman from RAF Elsham Wolds scribbled a poem onto a piece of paper torn out from a school writing pad. The visit turned out to be his last, and when he failed to return from an operation his father found the poem, entitled 'Great Coats'.

Hurriedly, carelessly, flung onto pegs,
In the hall where the noise from the mess filters through
Of the jokes of the crews over bacon and eggs
With no hint of the dangerous task they must do,
Like faithful old hounds with an eye to the door
The coats hang there quietly awaiting their men;
And twice must the airfield resound to the roar
Of engines, before they are wanted again.
The sound of the last planes has died from the air
And the mess is alive once more to the din
Of cold, hungry youngsters, yet warmly aware
Of another job done that is helping to win.
There is no lack of laughs, but a tiredness must creep
Into eyes that have gazed on a City enflamed
So they eat and are off to their billets to sleep
But two or three coats hang there mutely –
Unclaimed.[36]

AFTERWORD: AN UNFINISHED STORY

A Complicated Legacy

The Lancaster story did not end when the aircraft was withdrawn from service, and its legacy is multifaceted, reaching across time. The Lancaster and those who flew in and worked with it were undeniably instrumental in the Allies securing victory in 1945, and the aircraft is an important icon of British aeronautical engineering and aviation. It is, however, an aircraft with a complicated legacy.

There is little doubt that the damage done by the strategic bombing campaign to Germany's war production and economy shortened the war. Using aircraft to drop bombs so fewer soldiers were sent into battle on the ground meant a lot of Allied lives were saved that might otherwise have been lost. The campaign is controversial, however, in that so many lives were lost as a result of it. It is estimated that the combination of Bomber Command's operations against Germany and those carried out by the US Eighth Air Force caused the deaths of around 600,000 German people – mostly civilians. In addition, in the course of the Second World War, 55,573 airmen lost their lives in the service of Bomber Command.

Whether or not these losses can be justified remains a subject of debate, but they should be viewed in the historical and global contexts in which the bomber war played out. In the heat of the second global and total conflict in the first half of the twentieth century, the morality of the bombing campaign was not what preoccupied Allied planners. It certainly wasn't something that Bomber Command's airmen and personnel had time to consider, and they carried out the orders they were given by their politicians, as they were bound to do. Their aim, on a daily basis, was simply to survive and to do what they were tasked with as part of a wider Allied plan to defeat an enemy that had little regard for morality and left death and destruction in its wake. War is ugly, and it is far from simple.

'The Lancaster is so many things to so many people,' says RAF pilot and flying instructor Seb Davey – bomber leader and pilot of PA474, one of the last two flying Lancasters in the world. First and foremost, it continued, for decades and into the present, to have a deep and profound effect on those who flew in and worked with her during the war in which she was born. Some of those people found it difficult to talk about their war in Bomber Command, but it stayed with them.

Oliver Owen's father Charles, a wartime Lancaster pilot, sobbed continuously as he watched the troops returning home when the Falklands War ended. 'His war was over,' Oliver says, 'but it obviously never really left him.'[1] Some former aircrew visited their old airfields later in their lives and attended events dedicating memorials to Bomber Command personnel. Australian wireless operator Tony Adams served at RAF Methwold in Norfolk from 1944–45, completing a tour of thirty-six operations on Stirlings and Lancasters. He visited Methwold in 1975. 'It was a funny old war,' he mused when Chris Stone interviewed him for the Methwold History Group's archive. 'For several hours it would be horrible with flak being thrown at you and aircraft going down in flames and then you would return to a little village in the quiet English countryside, and on some occasions within hours be enjoying a few drinks in a local pub or a dance or film in Methwold village hall or another nearby village.' On one occasion, Chris accompanied Tony to the old airfield, where two hangars still stand. Tony, who lost good friends during the war, looked out at the church and the village with tears in his eyes and said quietly, 'That's what I remember.'

Chris and the Methwold History Group work hard to preserve the history of what Tony and his friends experienced. 'It's about keeping their memory alive,' Chris says.[2] For Hugh Gascoyne, who had also served in Norfolk, the sound of the Lancaster would never leave him: 'I will never forget those big Norfolk skies and the sight and sound of those Lancaster bombers. One of the two remaining Lancasters still flying flew over my home recently and before I saw the aircraft I knew what it was from the unmistakable sound of those Merlin engines.'[3]

Some former Lancaster crewmen were moved to write poems when they returned later in life to the airfields they had flown from in the war. Walt Scott, a wireless operator and gunner with 630 Squadron, wrote 'Old Airfield' about his time on Lancasters at RAF East Kirkby:

I lie here still beside the hill,
Abandoned long to nature's will.
My buildings down, my people gone,
My only sounds the wild bird songs.
But my mighty birds will rise no more,
No more I hear the Merlins roar.
And never now my bosom feels,
The pounding of their giant wheels.
From the ageless hills their voices cast,
Thunderous echoes from the past.
And still in lonely reverie,
Their great dark wings swing down to me.
Laughter, sorrow, hope and pain,
I shall never know these things again.
Emotions that I came to know,
Of strange young men so long ago ...
I shall remember them.[4]

P. G. Russell, an ex-airframe fitter with 149 Squadron at RAF Methwold in Norfolk, spent night after night watching aircrews climb aboard their Lancasters and take off into the darkness. When he visited Methwold in September 1988, he wrote 'Return to Methwold':

The windblown tin, the rusting door
Strives to shelter last year's straw.
Twas once the home of awesome bird
Whose crackling song, now seldom heard
Would soar aloft in darkened flight
As weary men toiled through the night.

The tannoy's silent message calls
From swinging wires on crumbling walls
Rubble now where once the fires
Of eager youths, plucked from their shires,
Burned so brightly ... now they're gone,
Life snuffed out ere it began.

So long ago but Oh! So clear
The memory stays and sheds a tear
For those who died in yesteryear
For those who died in yesteryear.[5]

Some aircrew wanted the memory of their wartime service to remain with them until the very end. Lancaster pilot Thomas Tobin requested that when he passed away, his ashes be spread over Scampton. His daughter, Jane Eblen, ensured that his wish was carried out when he died in 1991.[6]

Past and Present

The legacy of the Lancaster has been passed on to the generations that followed, and this aircraft is woven as an important symbol into our personal and collective memory of that conflict. 'What the Lancaster was and what it has come to symbolise are different,' says Bomber Command historian and International Bomber Command Centre digital archivist Dr Dan Ellin.[7] 'The Lancaster was an efficient war machine expressly created to deliver a large and deadly cargo of bombs and incendiaries to targets in mainland Europe. Now, the Lancaster is a symbol of remembrance for the aircrew who died in the war and for the passing of their generation. Whenever I see or hear a Lancaster, I think of the veterans I have met and interviewed for the IBCC Digital Archive.' Ultimately, the Lancaster story might begin by being about an aircraft, but right at its centre are people. 'It's not just about military life,' Nicky van der Drift, CEO of the IBCC says. 'It's about being a human.'[8] It is also about the link between past and present – connection across time between those who lived and worked through the war and those who are here today because of them.

Losses archivist and volunteer Dave Gilbert and his team at the IBCC have spent more than a decade building a database containing the details of the 58,438 Bomber Command personnel who died during the command's existence. 'It's not just a list of deaths – it's a list of young men and women whose age we now know, the names of their parents, the towns they were from. You know what they gave up.' This project means a great deal to Dave and his team – especially when they are able to help someone find out what happened to a family member all those years ago. 'You can't help but be on that aircraft with them,' Dave says. 'And it's almost a bereavement process. It changes you.'[9]

Like Dave, IBCC volunteer Tony Hibberd has spent many hours preserving Bomber Command history – specifically, building a database of memorials. 'It gets under your skin,' he says. 'It's a duty that you owe.' Tony has driven all over the country and visited over 1,000 memorials so far. These range from the national memorial to Bomber Command in London to small, local ones, like the plaque recently added to the base of the village sign in Wimbotsham in remembrance of the crew of Lancaster EE118, who lost their lives when their aircraft crashed in the village in September 1943.[10] Efforts to dedicate a memorial plaque in the village of Wimbotsham to the crew of EE118 were led by local researcher Carolyn Seymour, who carried out detailed and meticulous research to get to the bottom of what had happened.

Though it is aircraft they are charged with maintaining and flying, it is people who are at the centre of the Battle of Britain Memorial Flight too – including a dedicated team of maintenance engineers who help to keep Lancaster PA474 in good working order. Carl Walker is one of them. 'With their logbooks open,' he says, 'you get a feel for what they did – their age, what they did at the time. The Lancaster symbolises them.'[11] Engineer Deb Williams agrees: 'When you get on the aircraft, it's awkward to climb over the main spar with normal clothes on – it would have been *very* difficult to do it in full flying gear. It makes you appreciate what they did – the conditions they flew in.' Dave Wilcox volunteered to work with the team keeping PA474 flying. 'It's a living thing,' he says. 'Sometimes you need to be ready to put extra heart in – she can play you up.' Dave also dwells on the lives of the people who flew and worked with the Lancaster in the war – particularly the aircrews. 'It was deeply personal,' he says. 'You and your six mates.'

The BBMF believes strongly that it is important to make the Lancaster available to Bomber Command veterans, and Mark Arnold has enjoyed being able to meet and spend time with them. 'We had a rear gunner in his nineties visit,' he explains, 'and he wanted to get inside the turret, but he was in a wheelchair. I turned around and he was in the turret – he was eighteen years old again.'[12]

An Unfinished Story

Just as the Lancaster affected and influenced lives during the Second World War, it continued to do so for decades after the conclusion of the conflict, and still does today. As a child, the course of Trevor Woodgate's life was affected by a personal association with the Lancaster – specifically LM650. 'My father would tell me of the time he saw a Lancaster crash near my home village of Robertsbridge when he was a young lad,' he says.[13] As an apprentice studying with British Aerospace at Kingston-upon-Thames, Trevor was tasked with an aviation-related project, and he made a study of LM650. Once the project was completed and Trevor shared it with his colleagues, the decision was made, with permission from the Ministry of Defence, to carry out an excavation at the crash site and pieces of the Lancaster were recovered.

Years later, Trevor is working with the Aircraft Restoration Company at Duxford, where maintenance works are sometimes carried out toward keeping PA474 flying – including the recent manufacture of new tailplanes. 'I was able to play a small part in this work', Trevor says, 'by providing original tailplane components and controls from Lancaster LM650, untouched since 1944 for the team to view.'

More than just an inanimate object made of metal, the Lancaster is a link between those who are still here, and those who are gone. Rear gunner Bob Howes' granddaughter, Sharne Cracknell, remembers fondly the way that her grandfather would talk about his time working with Lancasters in the war. 'He talked about it a lot,' she says. 'He loved being up in the plane – he loved the Lancaster.'[14] Sadly, Sharne's grandfather is now gone, but he passed his love of the Lancaster on to her:

> I've always loved the Lancaster because it meant so much to my grandad. The sight, the sound and even the smell when I've been lucky enough to go inside a Lancaster, instantly makes me feel connected to him. Growing up there were always pictures and models of it everywhere in my grandparents' house and despite the war being one of the most challenging periods of his life, it was also one of the happiest. The Lancaster captured his heart and because of that, she will always be part of mine.

Bob's family still have the belt Bob was wearing when a bullet struck him in the rear turret. Sharne and her husband Jonny, co-author of Lancaster pilot Stevie Stevens' biography, have dedicated a lot of time to preserving the memory of Bomber Command veterans, some of whom they came to be good friends with. 'I've been inspired enormously by this incredible generation throughout my life,' Jonny says.[15] His experiences taking veterans to events, supporting them, listening to them, capturing their recollections and writing about them are an important part of capturing and preserving the lives and legacies of Bomber Command personnel. Jonny sees the Lancaster as an important reminder of what must not be forgotten. 'The Lancaster is a modern-day symbol – flying in remembrance of all the men and women who served in Bomber Command. Each and every time I see and hear her fly, I can't help but think of the many brave men who flew in Bomber Command, those I was privileged to meet and know, and those who never came home.'

Warren Stace's connection to the Lancaster is through his great-grandfather, Lawrence Leishman, who was brought home on a Lanc during Operation Exodus. 'It finally brought my grandad home safely and allowed him the chance to carry on with his life and create people that I love deeply,' Warren says.[16] When Oliver Owen thinks about his father, he thinks of a 'young man, fresh-faced and at the controls of a Lancaster. He is a hero and he is going to bring his boys home.'[17]

So many people have a connection with the Lancaster, and wherever one is it is the centre of attention. Historian Dan Snow flew aboard Lancaster PA474 with the Battle of Britain Memorial Flight (BBMF). The flight took Dan and the crew from Lincolnshire to the Derbyshire dams used by the Dambusters in their training for the bombing of those in the Ruhr Valley. Along the way the BBMF carried out flypasts. 'The effect on people on the ground was amazing,' Dan says.[18] Some locations were pre-scheduled into the flight plan, but it was the reactions of people in places that hadn't been forewarned that the Lanc would fly over that really demonstrated how special this aircraft still is to us. 'People stopped cars, kids left school by the windows – it was like squashing a grape, they flooded out of windows, doors and fire exits. People dropped everything to see it. We flew past Chatsworth and the hills were lined with people.' The Lancaster flew low over the Derbyshire dams, just as its sisters would have with 617 Squadron's pilots at the controls.

A total of 7,377 Lancasters would be built over the years in which the aircraft was manufactured. 'It did what it was supposed to do,' IWM Duxford's Liam Shaw says.[19] 'It flew as high and as fast as possible, carrying the heaviest payload of any aircraft in the European theatre – the most versatile bomber we had.' Indeed, the Lancaster was a roaring success, and as Arthur Harris wrote: 'This emergency design turned out to be without exception the finest bomber of the war.'[20] Bomber Command aircrews agreed. 'The Lancaster proved a dream of an aeroplane,' wireless operator Bruce Rawling muses.[21]

> They had plenty of power and a good Lanc could maintain height on one engine at 4,000ft and so the loss of one engine was no great worry. They were also very manoeuvrable and could be thrown all over the sky in the most violent manner. They weren't quite as comfortable as the Stirling being built for action and speed but we were more interested in performance than comfort.

The Lancaster dropped 608,612 tons of high explosives on primary targets – almost two thirds of the total tonnage dropped by Bomber Command from March 1943 to May 1945 – plus 51,513,106 incendiaries. It also dropped 6,684 tons of food to the starving and desperate in Holland, and repatriated 74,178 liberated prisoners of war. Some 3,349 Lancasters were lost on operations. The Lancaster was a weapon of war – it took lives, and it cost them. It was also a vehicle of hope and of freedom, of saving lives and of bringing lost men home. There are seventeen surviving Lancasters around the world today, four of which are in the UK. R5858, or S-for-Sugar, resides at the RAF Museum in Hendon, huge and imposing in her hangar, a main attraction for visitors from all over the world. KB889 has her own corner in the air space hangar at Imperial War Museum Duxford, and visitors regularly climb aboard to hear the history of the Lancaster and get just the tiniest of inklings as to what it might have been like to be inside one in the war. NX611 – 'Just Jane,' as she is known – thunders around the airfield at the Lincolnshire Aviation

Heritage Centre in Britain, taxiing those who want to get an even deeper sense of what life was like aboard Lancasters. Restoration work is ongoing to try to get Just Jane airborne again. And PA474 – one of two airworthy Lancasters in the world – stops people in their tracks as she glides through the sky around the country.

Early in the process of writing this book, I visited all four of the Lancasters in Britain. I walked around S-for-Sugar and sat inside KB889 while the resident experts at the RAF Museum and IWM Duxford imparted their knowledge and deep understanding of who these aircraft are and what they mean. I taxied on Just Jane and closed my eyes so I could imagine the terror that must have been induced as each engine started and the aircraft began to vibrate. And I stood beside 15,000 other people and watched PA474 roll into view, a living memorial and link to the past. Very recently, I visited the Lancaster at Duxford again, with 101-year-old Jimmy Burt and his family. Jimmy and I climbed into the Lancaster, and I listened to him reminisce – he knows the old girl well, and it is like seeing two old friends reunited. I took a moment to think about the many wonderful people I have met and read about in the process of writing this book. The Lancaster has become quite a different thing to me – because of them. They are the Lancaster, and the Lancaster is them. This is her story, and it is theirs.

ACKNOWLEDGEMENTS

One of the best things about writing this book was being afforded opportunities to meet so many wonderful people – people without whom this book simply would not exist. Before I started writing, I decided I needed to get to know the Lancaster as an aircraft, inside and out. I am grateful to the dedicated folks who care for and preserve the history of the four Lancasters left in the UK and who were kind enough to introduce me to them – to Liam Shaw and Sam Lee at IWM Duxford, to David Green at the RAF Museum, Hendon, to the team at Lincolnshire Aviation Heritage Centre and to the BBMF team. I am also immensely grateful to the wonderful team at the Avro Heritage Museum, Woodford – in particular Roger, Steve, Tony, James and Eric – for their help with research and with understanding the Lancaster as an aircraft. I am, as always, indebted to the many archivists, librarians, museum staff and volunteers who took time out of their busy days to assist with my research queries. These fantastic people of the Imperial War Museum, the RAF Museum, the National Archives, the International Bomber Command Centre and the Royal Air Force Memorial Flight Club, to name but a few, shared their often encyclopaedic knowledge of the past with me, and the book has benefited greatly from their input.

Then there are the families of those whose stories fill this book – people who have been kind enough to allow me, and who have trusted me, to tell those stories – a responsibility I have not taken lightly. To Jonny and Sharne Cracknell, Christine Knights, Alex Trotter, Sally Haggis, David Murray, Shaun Hullis, Peter Carpenter, Dave, Anne and Elain Coventry, Barry Wiseman, David Sneddon, John Sandbach, Mark Reeder, Angus Matheson, Mark Orchard, Oliver Owen, Warren and Patrick Stace, Roger Yates, Trevor Woodgate, John Warburton,

Thomas Hughes and all those who allowed me this privilege – thank you. I am also grateful to those who shared their own research with me – in particular, Chris Stone and the Methwold History Group, and Carolyn Seymour. Their meticulous and committed work has been so important in preserving the memory of the people in this book. I am deeply grateful to James Jefferies, whose lifelong interest in and encyclopaedic knowledge of Bomber Command was extremely valuable in writing this book, and whose support as a colleague and friend is always appreciated. I was most grateful to be able to spend some time with the team at the IBCC – including CEO Nicky van der Drift, digital archivist Dr Dan Ellin, losses archivist Dave Gilbert and memorials archivist Tony Hibberd. Writing about Bomber Command leaves a mark on any author who attempts it, and meeting kindred spirits helps with both the process of writing and the processing of what you have written.

I was determined to explore not just the history of the Lancaster but also its legacy. I am grateful to those who were able to speak into this with their own insight – including current BBMF Lancaster pilot Seb Davies, who very kindly wrote the foreword to this book, and historian Dan Snow, who recounted his flight in PA474 to me. Huge thanks also to the BBMF ground crew personnel I spoke with: Carl Walker, Deb Williams, Dave Wilcox and Mark Arnold – their insight has been extremely valuable. Thanks also to those who have facilitated interviews – in particular to Jack McBride at the Aircraft Restoration Company and to Jason Kilcoyne and the Aces High Gallery.

Interviews with Lancaster veterans have been, by far, my favourite part of this experience. From stories about watching the Dambusters take off as a child from Alan Goodale, to hearing about what it was like to fly in Lancasters just after the war from Jimmy Burt, I have enjoyed hearing first-hand accounts immensely. It was not until I began the research for this book that I discovered that my great uncle, Donald Knight, was a Lanc pilot in the Second World War. Sadly, Donald is no longer with us, but I have been able to imagine a little of what he might have experienced through speaking with Lancaster pilot Hugo Trotter, wireless operator Roy Briggs and bomb aimer Al Lovett, all of whom graciously answered my many questions and helped me to even begin to understand what it must have been like to fly on Lancasters during the Second World War. I cannot thank them enough and feel extremely privileged to have been able to meet and know them.

Of course, none of this would have been possible without the constant support of my family. My husband, Isaac, my parents, Peter and Mandy, and my grandparents, Susan and Brian, have, as always, been the source of the encouragement every writer needs to persist when the going gets tough. I am, and forever will be, very grateful to them.

The first Bomber Command veteran I ever met was Lancaster pilot Flying Officer Hugo Trotter DFC. My husband and I spent a wonderful afternoon with Hugo, looking through thick photo albums of his days as a young man in the RAF and listening intently as he told us his stories with a twinkle in his eyes. We were very sad to hear of Hugo's passing just before this book was finished. Though he may not be able to read it, it contains the spirit of Hugo and all those like him, who displayed incredible courage and commitment and who persisted through the horrors and difficulties of total war in the hopes of better things to come. It is to them that the greatest thanks of all are owed.

PICTURE CREDITS

The publishers would like to thank the following sources for their kind permission to reproduce the pictures in this book.

Plate photographs in order of appearance:

1. BAe Systems via Avro Heritage Museum, 2. International Bomber Command Digital Archive at the University of Lincoln, 3-6. BAe Systems via Avro Heritage Museum, 7. © Imperial War Museum (IWM MH 7951), 8. International Bomber Command Digital Archive at the University of Lincoln, 9. Photograph courtesy of Alex Trotter, 10. © Imperial War Museum (IWM CH 8183), 11. Authors collection, 12. Photograph courtesy of the Carpenter family, 13. © Imperial War Museum (IWM CH 9923), 14. Photograph courtesy of Oliver Owen, 15. Photograph courtesy of Barry Wiseman, 16. Photograph courtesy of the Howe family, 17. The RAF Memorial Club, 18. Photograph courtesy of Al Lovett, 19. Photograph courtesy of Shaun Hullis, 20. © Imperial War Museum (IWM C 4973), 21. Photography courtesy of Angus Matheson, 22. International Bomber Command Digital Archive at the University of Lincoln, 23. BAe Systems via Avro Heritage Museum, 24. SSPL/Getty Images, 25. Photograph supplied by Jonny Cracknell and used with permission from the Stevens family, 26. International Bomber Command Digital Archive at the University of Lincoln, 27. DGB Images/Alamy Stock Photo, 28. Photograph courtesy of Roy Briggs, 29-30. Photograph courtesy of Chris Stone, of Methwold History Group, 31. International Bomber Command Digital Archive at the University of Lincoln, 32. Photograph supplied by Warren and Patrick Stace and used with permission from the Leishman family, 33. Photograph courtesy of Alex Trotter, 34. International Bomber Command Digital Archive at the University of Lincoln

Special thank you to the Archive Team at the Avro Heritage Museum, Woodford, Stockport, SK7 1AG

Every effort has been made to acknowledge correctly and contact the source and/or copyright holder of each picture and the publisher apologises for any unintentional errors or omissions, which will be corrected in future editions of this book.

BIBLIOGRAPHY

Archives and Museums

Air Transport Auxiliary Museum and Archive at Maidenhead Heritage Centre
ATA Museum
Australian War Memorial Archive
Avro Heritage Museum, Woodford
BAE Systems Heritage
Battle of Britain Memorial Flight, Royal Air Force
BBC People's War Archive
Bomber Command Museum of Canada, Nanton, Alberta
Fleet Air Arm Officers' Association
IBCC Digital Archive
Imperial War Museum
International Bomber Command Centre
International Churchill Society
Jewish Virtual Library
Lincolnshire Aviation Heritage Centre
Methwold History Group, 149 Squadron, Archive
National Archives at Kew
RAF Elsham Wolds Association
Royal Air Force Museum
University of Lincoln Repository
https://www.memorialflightclub.com

Books

Air Ministry, *Bomber Command* (HMSO, 1941)

Ashworth, Chris, *RAF Bomber Command, 1936–1968* (Patrick Stephens Ltd, 1995)

Baughan, Joan, *The Inimitable Joan: The War Years* (Square One Publications, 1996)

Beck, Pip, *Keeping Watch* (Goodall Publications Ltd, 1989)

Becker, Captain Dave, *Yellow Wings: The Story of the Joint Air Training Scheme in World War 2* (The SAAF Museum, 1989)

Bennett, Air Vice-Marshal D.C.T., *Pathfinder* (Goodall Publications Ltd, 1988)

Bishop, Murray Winston and Arthur Adelbert Bishop, *The Bishop Brothers of New Minas in World War Two* (personal memoir produced and printed by the brothers, supplied by Arthur's daughter, Sally Haggis)

Bishop, Patrick, *Bomber Boys: Fighting Back 1940–1945* (Harper Press, 2007)

Bishop, Patrick, *Target Tirpitz: X-Craft, Agents and Dambusters* (Harper Press, 2012)

Bishop, Patrick, *Wings* (Atlantic Books, 2012)

Cahill, William, 'The Unseen Fight: USAAF radio counter-measure operations in Europe, 1943 to 1945', *Journal of Aeronautical History* Paper 2020/06

Chadwick, Roy, BBC Broadcast, Monday 8 June 1942, Manchester, 8.30 p.m.

Cracknell, Jonny, and Adrian Stevens, *Tomorrow May Never Come: The Remarkable Life Story of 'Stevie' Stevens* (Wing Leader Ltd, 2021).

Currie DFC, Jack, *The Augsburg Raid* (Goodall Publications Ltd, 1987)

Deighton, Len, *Bomber* (Cape, 1970)

Dunnell, Ben, *Duxford Air Shows 50: 50 Years of Duxford Air Shows* (IWM, 2023).

Fahie, Michael, *A Harvest of Memories: The Life of Pauline Gower MBE* (1995)

Franks, Norman, *Fighter Command's Air War 1941: RAF Circus Operations and Fighter Sweeps Against the Luftwaffe* (Pen & Sword Aviation, 2016)

Frayn Turner, John, *The WAAF at War* (Barnsley: Pen & Sword Aviation, 2011)

Grisdale, Eric, *One of Many* (pamphlet written by Eric Grisdale and printed by Gwasg Pantycelyn, Caernarfon)

Hall, Grace, *We Also Were There* (Merlin Books Ltd, 1985)

Hamilton-Paterson, James, *Empire of the Clouds* (Faber & Faber, 2018)

Harris, Marshal of the RAF Sir Arthur, *Bomber Offensive* (Pen & Sword Military Classics, 2005, originally published in 1947)

Harvey DFC, Doug, *Boys, Bombs, and Brussels Sprouts* (McClelland & Stewart, 1981)

Hastings, Max, *Bomber Command* (Pan Books, 1999)

Holland, James, *Big Week* (Transworld Digital, 2018)

Holland, James, *Dam Busters* (Black Cat, 2014)

Holland, James, *The Second World War* (Michael Joseph, 2023)

Holmes, Harry, *Avro Lancaster: The Definitive Record* (Airlife England, 1997)

Iredale, Will, *The Pathfinders* (Penguin, 2021)

Jones, R. V., *Most Secret War* (Penguin Books, 1978)

Lepine, Mike, *The Avro Lancaster: WWII's Most Successful Heavy Bomber* (Sona Books, 2022)

Lettice Curtis: Her Autobiography (Red Kite, 2004)

Lindqvist, Sven, *A History of Bombing* (Granta Books, 2001)

McKinstry, Leo, *Lancaster* (John Murray, 2010)

Middlebrook, Martin, *The Berlin Raids: The Bomber Battle Winter, 1943–44* (Pen & Sword, 2010)

Nichol, John and Tony Rennell, *Tail-End Charlies* (Penguin, 2005)

Nichol, John, *Lancaster* (Simon & Schuster, 2021)

Overy, Richard, *Bomber Command 1939–45* (HarperCollins Publishers, 1997)

Overy, Richard, *The Bombing War: Europe 1939–1945* (Penguin, 2014)

Overy, Richard, *Why the Allies Won* (Jonathan Cape, 1995)

Price, Alfred, *Instruments of Darkness: The History of Electronic Warfare, 1939–1945* (Greenhill Books, 2005)

Price, David, *The Crew* (Apollo, 2021)

Terrain, John, *The Right of the Line: The Royal Air Force in the European War, 1939–1945* (Hodder & Stoughton, 1985)

Webster, Charles and Noble Frankland, *The Strategic Air Offensive Against Germany, 1939–1945*, 4 vols. (HMSO, 1961; reprinted Naval & Military Press, 2006)

Wilson, Kevin, *Bomber Boys* (W&N, 2006)

Zamoyski, Adam, *The Forgotten Few: The Polish Air Force in World War II* (Pen & Sword Aviation, 2022)

ENDNOTES

Epigraph

1 Extracted verses from poems by Audrey Grealy of North Thoresby and Walter Scott, ex. 630 Squadron, Lincolnshire's Lancaster Association, Supporting the Battle of Britain Memorial Flight (Spring 1993, No. 19), p. 14.

Introduction

1 Stevie Stevens, quoted in Jonny Cracknell and Adrian Stevens, *Tomorrow May Never Come: The Remarkable Life Story of 'Stevie' Stevens* (Bridgwater: Wing Leader Ltd, 2021), p. 87.
2 Ben Dunnell, *Duxford Air Shows 50: 50 Years of Duxford Air Shows* (London: IWM, 2023), p. 9.
3 'Libya 1911: How Italian pilot began the air war era', BBC News, 10 May 2011.
4 'Zeppelin Raids', The National Archives, education resource.
5 Edgar Jones, 'Air Raid Casualties in the First World War', History of Government Blog, 19 January 2015.
6 Fleet Air Arm Officers' Association.
7 'Jan Smuts, the Formation of the RAF, and Air Policing', International Bomber Command Centre Blog (IBCC), 1 April 2018.
8 'Report by General Smuts on Air Organisation and the Direction of Aerial Operations, August 1917', RAF Museum, object No. B404.

Chapter One: Inception of a Legend

1 Air Ministry Specification No. P. 13/36 Medium Bomber, 5 September 1936, Appendix B, National Archives, AIR 9/77.
2 Roy Chadwick, BBC Broadcast, Monday 8 June 1942.
3 'Roy Chadwick: Avro's Great Designer, 1893–1947', Biography of Roy Chadwick by his daughter, Margaret Dove (2006).
4 Harry Holmes, *Avro Lancaster: The Definitive Record* (Airlife England, 1997), p. 9.
5 Stevie Stevens, quoted in Cracknell and Stevens, p. 77.
6 Bomber Command Museum of Canada.
7 Holmes, p. 9.
8 Ibid., p. 9.
9 Ibid., p. 11.
10 Ibid., p. 14.
11 Statistics from the Avro Heritage Museum. The National Archives currency converter calculates £58,974.00 in 1940 as £2,320,414.59 in today's money.
12 RAF Museum Hendon and Bomber Command Museum of Canada, Nanton, Alberta.
13 Avro Heritage Museum.
14 'Lancaster Bomber crews reunite at WW2 plane factory', BBC News, 4 September 2019.
15 Audrey Callaghan, BBC People's War Archive, Article ID A3283742, contributed on 16 November 2004.
16 'Rosie the Riveter', *Manchester Evening News*, 7 February 2017.

17 Pauline Gower in Michael Fahie, *A Harvest of Memories: The Life of Pauline Gower MBE* (GMS Enterprises, 1995), p. 170.
18 RAF Museum.
19 ATA Museum.
20 *Lettice Curtis: Her Autobiography* (Walton-on-Thames: Red Kite, 2004), p. 106.
21 RAF Museum.
22 M. Wilberforce, Log Book 2, Air Transport Auxiliary Museum and Archive at Maidenhead Heritage Centre.
23 BAE Systems.
24 'Lettice Curtis: Second World War Pilot', *Independent*, 11 August 2014.
25 Pip Beck, *Keeping Watch* (London: Goodall Publications Ltd, 1989), p. 44.
26 Ibid., p. 44.
27 Jack Currie DFC, *The Augsburg Raid* (London: Goodall Publications Ltd, 1987), p. 23.
28 Interview with F/O Hugo Trotter DFC, 12 Squadron, 1 Group, Bomber Command, Sunday 29 October 2023.
29 Air Cdre Graham Pitchfork, 'Airborne Sea-Mining Operations in World War Two', *Royal Air Force Historical Society Journal*, vol. 45 (2009), pp. 142–3.
30 'Churchill's Greatest Triumph: Bomber Command', International Churchill Society, 17 September 2019.
31 Directive No. 22, Air Ministry to Air Marshal Baldwin, 14 February 1942 in C. Webster & N. Frankland, *The Strategic Air Offensive Against Germany* (London: HMSO, 1961), vol. iv, Appendix 8.
32 Marshal of the RAF Sir Arthur Harris, *Bomber Offensive* (London: Pen & Sword Military Classics, 2005, originally published in 1947), p. 15.
33 Ibid., p. 31.
34 Ibid., pp. 51–2.
35 Ibid., p. 73.
36 AHB/II/117/1 (C), pp. 134–5, as quoted by John Terrain, *The Right of the Line: The Royal Air Force In the European War, 1939–1945* (London: Hodder & Stoughton, 1985), p. 470.

Chapter Two: Bomber Command People

1 Interview with Al Lovett at his home, 21 January 2024.
2 Stevie Stevens, quoted in Cracknell and Stevens, p. 23.
3 Ibid.
4 Harry Parkins, oral history interview, IBCC, Identifier: AParkinsH150605.
5 Flight Sergeant Peter Raeburn Jenkinson, DFM, Life Story, 153 Squadron newsletters, provided to author by Philip Heath.
6 'Service History of Benny Goodman', IBCC, Identifier: BGoodmanLSGoodmanLSv1
7 'A message of welcome from the Secretary of State for Air (Archibald Sinclair)', 4 July 1942, in binder compiled by Al Lovett, Methwold History Group Archive.
8 Murray Winston Bishop and Arthur Adelbert Bishop, *The Bishop Brothers of New Minas in World War Two* (personal memoir produced and printed by the brothers, supplied by Arthur's daughter, Sally Haggis).
9 Ibid., p. 17.
10 Ibid., p. 68.
11 Australian War Memorial, Article XV Squadrons.
12 Bomber Command Museum of Canada.
13 Australian Government, Defence: Remembering WWII Bomber Command Aviators, 12 May 2021.

14 'RAAF Losses in Bomber Command: Understanding the Numbers', Lachlan Grant, Australian War Memorial: 15 July 2020.
15 Adam Zamoyski, *The Forgotten Few: The Polish Air Force in World War II* (Yorkshire: Pen & Sword Aviation, 2022), p. 125.
16 Ibid., p. 126.
17 Ibid., p. 137.
18 Ibid., p. 137.
19 Ibid., p. 146.
20 Air Ministry Confidential Order, 'Pilots of the Caribbean', RAF Museum.
21 Sonia Thompson, 'West Indians in Britain During the Second World War', Imperial War Museum catalogue no. CH11677.
22 Information on Flying Officer John David Murray, P. Eng., from communications with his grandson David Murray.
23 LAC Kenneth Ball, exercise book for No. 80 Entry Mk XIV Bombsight Course, October 1944. In the possession of Kenneth's great-nephew, Shaun Hullis, kindly provided to the author.
24 Correspondence between the author and John Warburton.
25 Hugh Gascoyne, personal testimony, Methwold History Group Archive.
26 'An "Erk" – the "Tommy" of the RAF', Air Ministry Photograph, IWM catalogue number CH 7994.
27 John Johnson, personal testimony, Methwold History Group Archive.
28 Hugh Gascoyne, personal testimony, Methwold History Group Archive.
29 Ron Pain, written testimony, personal papers of Peter Carpenter's papers, kindly lent to the author by Peter Carpenter.
30 Anecdotes from RAF Elsham Wolds Association, Issue 50. Personal papers of Peter Carpenter.
31 Clare Kemp, personal testimony, Methwold History Group Archive.
32 Doug Harvey DFC, *Boys, Bombs, and Brussels Sprouts* (McClelland & Stewart, 1981).
33 Bomber Command's main report, 'The War in the Ether', October 1945, as quoted in R. V. Jones, *Most Secret War* (London: Penguin Books, 1978), p. 471.
34 Joan Baughan, *The Inimitable Joan: The War Years* (Worcestershire: Square One Publications, 1996), p. 66.
35 John Frayn Turner, *The WAAF at War* (Barnsley: Pen & Sword Aviation, 2011), p. 51.
36 Grace Hall, *We Also Were There* (Devon: Merlin Books Ltd, 1985), p. 19.

Chapter Three: Aircrew

1 Interview with Roy Briggs, Sunday 19 November 2023. W. G. Grace was an English amateur cricketer who was important in the development of the sport. He is considered to be one of the greatest cricketers of all time.
2 Harry Parkins, oral history interview, IBCC, Identifier: AParkinsH150605.
3 Interview with F/O Hugo Trotter DFC, 12 Squadron, 1 Group, Bomber Command, Sunday 29 October 2023.
4 Correspondence with Dave, Anne and Elaine Coventry and Barry Wiseman.
5 'Don Miller, Rear Gunner, Waddington', IBCC, 'Veterans' Stories', written by Jon, Don's nephew.
6 Flight Engineer's Duties, extract from A.M.O. A.538/1943, Methwold History Group Archive.
7 'Robert Jay, Flight Engineer, No. 75 (New Zealand) Squadron', IBCC, 'Veterans' Stories', written by Vic Jay, Robert's son.
8 Flight Engineer's Notes, A. V. Roe & Co. Ltd.

9 Ibid.
10 Mike Lepine, *The Avro Lancaster: WWII's Most Successful Heavy Bomber* (Sona Books, 2022), p. 32.
11 Personal papers of Peter Carpenter.
12 Ibid.
13 Binder compiled by Al Lovett, Methwold History Group Archive.
14 Recommendations for the Distinguished Flying Medal, 9 March 1945, Squadron Leader E. R. Riches, Commanding No. 103 Squadron, RAF, The National Archives, AIR 2/9083.
15 Recommendations for the Distinguished Flying Medal, 19 March 1945, Air Commodore F. R. D. Swain, Commanding No. 13 Base, RAF & 14 March 1945, Wing Commander D.F. Macdonald, Commanding RAF Station Elsham Wolds, The National Archives, AIR 2/9083.
16 Binder compiled by Al Lovett, Methwold History Group Archive.
17 Correspondence with David Sneddon.
18 DFM Citation for Keith Sneddon, Australian War Memorial, RCDIG1068957.
19 Binder compiled by Al Lovett, Methwold History Group Archive.
20 Bomber Command Museum of Canada, *General Hints for Air Gunners (Condensed)* – from a gunnery course manualized at No. 2 Bombing and Gunnery School, Mossbank, Saskatchewan, donated by D. A. Eglison, Coquitlam, British Columbia.
21 Interview with Roy Briggs, Sunday 19 November 2023.
22 Sam Brookes, 'Airborne Cigar: A Young Wireless Operator's Story – and a Lifelong Loss', 6 November 2003, BBC People's War Archive, Article ID: A1981442.
23 Interview with Roy Briggs, Sunday 19 November 2023.
24 'Air Borne Cigar', IBCC, Identifier: PThompsonKG15010046, PThompsonKG15010047.
25 Sam Brookes, BBC People's War Archive.
26 J. A. Davies, *A Leap in the Dark* (London, 1994), p. 22. As quoted in Martin Sugarman, 'World War II: Jewish RAF Special Operators in Radio Counter Measures with 101 Squadron (September 1943–May 1945)', Jewish Virtual Library.
27 Ibid.
28 Andrew Sadler, 'Interview with Leslie Temple,' IBCC Digital Archive, accessed 3 January 2024, available at: https://ibccdigitalarchive.lincoln.ac.uk/omeka/collections/document/1289
29 Sam Brookes, BBC People's War Archive.
30 John Johnson, Methwold History Group Archive.
31 Tony Adams, Methwold History Group Archive.
32 Owen Arthur Jones, personal testimony, Methwold History Group.
33 Harry Parkins, oral history interview, IBCC, Identifier: AParkinsH150605.
34 'Service History of Benny Goodman,' IBCC, Identifier: BGoodmanLSGoodmanLSv1
35 Interview with Roy Briggs, Sunday 19 November 2023.
36 Stevie Stevens, quoted in Jonny Cracknell and Adrian Stevens, p. 80.
37 Harry Parkins, oral history interview, IBCC, Identifier: AParkinsH150605.
38 Stevie Stevens, quoted in Jonny Cracknell and Adrian Stevens, p. 80.
39 Ibid., p. 87.

Chapter Four: On Ops

1 Bruce Rawling, 149 Squadron, Methwold, 1944–45, 'The Exploits of a Team of Amateur Airmen as Seen Through the Eyes of their Frightened Wireless Operator', Methwold History Group Archive.
2 Wal Cryer, personal testimony, Methwold History Group Archive.

3 Bob Cox, binder compiled by Al Lovett Binders, Methwold History Group Archive.
4 Lucy Jane Lillie, IWM catalogue no. CH 7198.
5 Barbara Watkinson Bulleyment, Misc. Anecdotes from RAF Elsham Wolds Association, Issue 50, personal papers of Peter Carpenter.
6 Misc. Anecdotes from RAF Elsham Wolds Association, Issue 50, personal papers of Peter Carpenter.
7 Author's own family records.
8 Al and Audrey Lovett, Owen Jones, Arthur Gray, 'Methwold', 1996, Methwold History Group Archive.
9 Bruce Rawling, Methwold History Group Archive.
10 Currie, p. 43.
11 Finlay McRae: Last letter home written by Finlay to his parents, sent by the RAF in December 1944. Kindly provided to the author by Finlay's family.
12 Flying Officer Colin Kelvin Flockhart. Australian War Memorial, Accession Number P04048.001.
13 Stevie Stevens' prayer, quoted in Jonny Cracknell and Adrian Stevens, p. 247.
14 Donald Knight is the author's great-uncle. Correspondence with his granddaughter, Josie.
15 Interview with Al Lovett at his home, 21 January 2024.
16 Bruce Rawling, Methwold History Group Archive.
17 Wal Cryer, Methwold History Group Archive.
18 Bruce Rawling, Methwold History Group Archive.
19 Jack Currie DFC, *The Augsburg Raid* (Goodall Publications Ltd, 1987), p. 48.
20 Clare Kemp, Methwold History Group Archive.
21 Interview with Al Lovett at his home, 21 January 2024.
22 Eric Grisdale, *One of Many*, pamphlet written by Eric Grisdale and printed by Gwasg Pantycelyn, Caernarfon.
23 Misc. Anecdotes from RAF Elsham Wolds Association, Issue 50, personal papers of Peter Carpenter.
24 Stevie Stevens, quoted in Jonny Cracknell and Adrian Stevens, p. 89.
25 Al Lovett, Methwold History Group Archive.
26 Arthur Atkinson, oral history interview, IBCC, Identifier: AAtkinsonA150623.
27 The Raid Where Everything Went Wrong: P/O Gordon Cleminson (NZ), 75 Squadron, March 1945, correspondence with John Sandbach, Gordon's nephew.
28 Murray Winston Bishop and Arthur Adelbert Bishop, *The Bishop Brothers of New Minas in World War Two*, p. 61.
29 Quoted in Jonny Cracknell and Adrian Stevens, p. 214.
30 Ibid., p. 220.
31 RAF Mildenhall Take Off and Landing Procedure (Feb 6th, 1945), Landing Procedure, Methwold History Group Archive.
32 Interview with F/O Hugo Trotter DFC, 12 Squadron, 1 Group, Bomber Command, Sunday 29 October 2023.
33 Written by Peter Carpenter's son, Peter, and kindly lent to the author.
34 Arthur Wolstenholme, personal papers of Peter Carpenter.
35 Binder compiled by Al Lovett, Methwold History Group Archive.
36 John Johnson, Methwold History Group Archive.
37 Doug Harvey DFC, *Boys, Bombs, and Brussels Sprouts* (McClelland & Stewart, 1981).
38 Misc. Anecdotes from RAF Elsham Wolds Association, Issue 50, personal papers of Peter Carpenter.
39 Harvey, *Boys, Bombs, and Brussels Sprouts*.
40 John Johnson, Methwold History Group Archive.

41 Ibid.
42 Correspondence with John Warburton.
43 Harvey, *Boys, Bombs, and Brussels Sprouts*.
44 'Service History of Benny Goodman,' IBCC, Identifier: BGoodmanLSGoodmanLSv1.
45 Air Vice Marshal Blucke, June 1945, binder compiled by Al Lovett, Methwold History Group Archive.
46 Tony Adams, Methwold History Group Archive.
47 Bruce Rawling, Methwold History Group Archive.

Chapter Five: The Lancaster Goes to War

1 Rod Rodley, as quoted in Richard Overy, *Bomber Command 1939–45* (London: HarperCollins Publishers, 1997), pp. 82–3.
2 Rod Rodley, as quoted in Overy, pp. 82–3.
3 Flight Lieutenant Patrick Dorehill, 'Augsburg Raid's 70th Anniversary Marked By Veteran', BBC News, 18 April 2012.
4 'The Augsburg Raid', No 44 (Rhodesia) Squadron Association Newsletter, 02/21, September 2021.
5 Flight Lieutenant Patrick Dorehill, 'Augsburg Raid's 70th Anniversary Marked By Veteran', BBC News, 18 April 2012.
6 Rod Rodley, as quoted in Overy, pp. 82–3.
7 Ibid.
8 Avro Heritage Museum.
9 Roy Chadwick, BBC Broadcast, 1942.
10 AHB/II/117/1(C), p. 186, as quoted in Terrain, p. 472.
11 C. Webster and N. Frankland, *The Strategic Air Offensive Against Germany 1939–45*, HMSO, 1961 (official history), pp. 143–4, as quoted in Terrain, p. 474.
12 Ibid.
13 Overy, p. 101.
14 Air Vice-Marshal D. C. T. Bennett CB CBE DSO, *Pathfinder* (Goodall Publications Ltd, 1988), p. 133.
15 Webster and Frankland, official history, p. 432, as quoted in Terrain, p. 501.
16 Harris, pp. 129–30.
17 Bennett, pp. 134–5.
18 Will Iredale, *The Pathfinders* (London: Penguin, 2021), pp. xx–xxi.
19 Victory Message to the Path Finder Force, from Air Vice Marshal D.C.T. Bennett, VE Day, 1945, quoted in Bennett, p. 222.
20 Friends of RAF Skellingthorpe, Home of No. 50 and No. 61 Squadrons, History of No. 61 Squadron.
21 'Royal Air Force 1939–1945: Coastal Command', IWM Catalogue no. HU 91243.
22 Immediately after the practice operation Gillon wrote down her impressions in a memoir she later called 'Dress Rehearsal'. This was published for the first time in Richard Morris, *Guy Gibson* (London: Viking, 1944), pp. 160–62.

Chapter Six: From the Dams to Berlin

1 Stevie Stevens, quoted in Jonny Cracknell and Adrian Stevens, p. 91.
2 Interview with Roy Briggs, Sunday 19 November 2023.
3 Bruce Rawling, Methwold History Group Archive.
4 Finlay McRae: Diary, kindly provided to the author by Finlay's family.

5 Norman Edward Wilkins, interview with IBCC, Identifier: AWilkinsNE170922, PWilkinsNE1704.
6 Personal papers of Peter Carpenter.
7 'Service History of Benny Goodman,' IBCC, Identifier: BGoodmanLSGoodmanLSv1.
8 Interview with Bob's family, Sharne and Jonny Cracknell, and Bob's daughter Christine, 20 January 2024.
9 Bruce Rawling, Methwold History Group Archive.
10 Tony Adams, Methwold History Group Archive.
11 Arthur Atkinson, oral history interview, IBCC, Identifier: AAtkinsonA150623.
12 Interview with F/O Hugo Trotter DFC, 12 Squadron, 1 Group, Bomber Command, 29 October 2023.
13 John Johnson, Methwold History Group Archive.
14 'A Pilot's Story – One Hell of a Bombing Run', Flying Officer Roy Yule DFC, IBCC, 'Veterans' Stories'.
15 'Operation Gomorrah: Firestorm created "Germany's Nagasaki"', BBC News, 2 August 2018.
16 Ibid.
17 Ibid.
18 Sgt Arthur Orchard, handwritten notes passed to Carolyn Seymour by Mark Orchard (Arthur's nephew), 28 September 2023, Wimbotsham, Norfolk.
19 Interview with Mary Knight, the author's grandmother, in 2017.
20 Actuality recording of RAF bombing raid over Berlin, Germany, 4 September 1943. Recorded in Lancaster "F" Freddy of 207 Squadron RAF. Narrated by Wynford Vaughan Thomas of the BBC. Australian War Memorial, Accession no. SOO199.
21 Harris to Winston Churchill, 3 November 1943, in Charles Webster and Noble Frankland, *The Strategic Air Offensive Against Germany, 1939–1945*, 4 vols (London: HMSO, 1961; reprinted Naval & Military Press, 2006), II 9.
22 Charles Owen, operational diary with extracts from 97 Squadron's ORB. Correspondence with Oliver Owen.
23 Ibid.
24 Correspondence with Finlay McCrae's family.
25 Flight Sergeant David Wilson Inglis, Rear Gunner, No. 1 Group, 166 Squadron Bomber Command, IBCC, 'Veterans' Stories'.

Chapter Seven: Overlord to Dresden

1 Correspondence with Oliver Owen.
2 S/LDR Kenneth George Bickers DFC, IBCC, 'Veterans' Stories'.
3 Charles Owen, operational diary with extracts from 97 Squadron's ORB. Correspondence with Oliver Owen.
4 Bruce Rawling, Methwold History Group Archive.
5 Correspondence with the family of Finlay McRae.
6 Leslie Temple, quoted in Martin Sugarman, 'World War II: Jewish RAF Special Operators in Radio Counter Measures with 101 Squadron (September 1943–May1945)', Jewish Virtual Library.
7 Bruce Giles DFC, Methwold History Group Archive.
8 Charles Owen, operational diary with extracts from 97 Squadron's ORB. Correspondence with Oliver Owen.
9 Hurricane I and II, Webster & Frankland, vol. iv, Appendix 8, Directive 42, pp. 174–6, as quoted in Overy, p. 133.
10 'Target the Tirpitz', Gary Haines, Archivist, 6 November 2019, RAF Museum.

11 D. C. T. Bennett, *Pathfinder* (London: Frederick Muller Ltd, 1958), p. 221.
12 Arthur Bishop, p. 62.
13 'Fog Disposal', RAF Museum, https://www.rafmuseum.org.uk/research/archive-exhibitions/worth-a-thousand-words-air-diagrams/fog-dispersal/
14 Ron Pain, written testimony, personal papers of Peter Carpenter.
15 James Holland, *The Second World War* (Michael Joseph, 2023), p. 182.

Chapter Eight: Food and Freedom

1 153 Squadron papers lent to author by Philip Heath.
2 Interview with Roy Briggs, Sunday 19 November 2023.
3 Norman Edward Wilkins, interview with IBCC, Identifier: AWilkinsNE170922, PWilkinsNE1704.
4 Binder compiled by Al Lovett, Methwold History Group Archive.
5 Hans Onderwater on Operation Manna, IBCC, Identifier: AOnderwaterJG170727
6 Ibid.
7 Ibid.
8 Norman Edward Wilkins, interview with IBCC, Identifier: AWilkinsNE170922, PWilkinsNE1704.
9 Ron Pain, written testimony, personal papers of Peter Carpenter.
10 Eric Grisdale, *One of Many*, pamphlet written by Eric Grisdale and printed by Gwasg Pantycelyn, Caernarfon.
11 Author's correspondence with Ian Davies.
12 Grisdale, *One of Many*.
13 Personal papers of Peter Carpenter.
14 Ron Pain, letter to Arthur Wolstenholme dated 14 November 1993. Personal papers of Peter Carpenter.
15 'WWII bomber pilot cheated death in fireball explosion and witnessed The Great Escape', Wales Online, 29 October 2021.
16 Originally handwritten by Alan Yates, transcribed by his son, Roger Yates. Kindly lent to author by Roger.
17 Ibid.
18 Personal papers pertaining to Lawrence, kindly lent to the author by his family.
19 Ibid.
20 Binder compiled by Al Lovett, Methwold History Group Archive.
21 Newspaper clipping of story by Charles Bray, 'Our bombers are busy on their biggest mission'. Juvincourt airfield, France. Binder compiled by Al Lovett, Methwold History Group Archive.
22 Ibid.
23 Geoff Michael, Methwold History Group Archive.
24 Jock Bunten, Methwold History Group Archive.
25 Binder compiled by Al Lovett, Methwold History Group Archive.
26 Originally handwritten by Alan Yates, transcribed by his son, Roger Yates. Kindly lent to author by Roger.
27 Binder compiled by Al Lovett, Methwold History Group Archive.
28 John Johnson, Methwold History Group Archive.
29 Wal Cryer, Methwold History Group Archive.
30 Clare Kemp, Methwold History Group Archive.
31 Binder compiled by Al Lovett, Methwold History Group Archive.
32 Jock Bunten, Methwold History Group Archive.

33 Alfred Price, *Instruments of Darkness: The History of Electronic Warfare, 1939–1945* (London: Greenhill Books, 2005), p. 253.
34 William Cahill, 'The Unseen Fight: USAAF radio counter-measure operations in Europe, 1943 to 1945', *Journal of Aeronautical History*, Paper 2020/06, p. 238.
35 Charles Owen's diary, and correspondence with Oliver Owen.
36 Interview with Jimmy Burt, 28 January 2024.
37 Bishop, pp. 68–9.

Chapter Nine: Life, Love and Loss

1 Telephone conversation with Alan Goodale, 17 November 2024.
2 Written by Peter to Arthur Wolstenholme, 6 March 1993, personal papers of Peter Carpenter.
3 Interview with Al Lovett, 21 January 2024.
4 Misc. Anecdotes from RAF Elsham Wolds Association, Issue 50, personal papers of Peter Carpenter.
5 Telephone conversation with Alan Goodale, 17 November 2024.
6 *RAF Methwold, 1938–1958*, booklet produced by Methwold History Group, 2010.
7 Lincolnshire's Lancaster Association, Supporting the Battle of Britain Memorial Flight (Spring 1993, No. 19), p. 26.
8 'Derek Neale: Memories of the Night of 29 September 1943, Lancaster EE118', kindly lent to the author by Carolyn Seymour.
9 Herbert Ozanne, Methwold History Group Archive.
10 Ann Akrigg, Methwold History Group Archive.
11 Paul Francis, Richard Flagg and Graham Crisp, 'Nine Thousand Miles of Concrete: A Review of Second World War Temporary Airfields in England', Historic England Report Number 75/2016, published 18 October 2017.
12 Interview with F/O Hugo Trotter DFC, 12 Squadron, 1 Group, Bomber Command, Sunday 29 October 2023.
13 Squadron Leader John W. Gee, *Wingspan: The Recollections of a Bomber Pilot* (SPA Ltd, 1988), in 153 Squadron papers, lent to the author by Philip Heath.
14 Misc. Anecdotes from RAF Elsham Wolds Association, Issue 50, personal papers of Peter Carpenter.
15 Bruce Rawling, Methwold History Group Archive.
16 Jock Bunten, Methwold History Group Archive.
17 Imperial War Museum, Eric Blanchard, Oral History, Catalogue no. 21580. As quoted in Cracknell and Stevens, p. 80.
18 Misc Anecdotes from RAF Elsham Wolds Association, Issue 50, personal papers of Peter Carpenter.
19 Clare Kemp, Methwold History Group Archive.
20 Ron Pain, letter to Arthur Wolstenholme dated 14 November 1993, personal papers of Peter Carpenter.
21 Interview with Al Lovett, 21 January 2024.
22 Stevie Stevens, quoted in Jonny Cracknell and Adrian Stevens, p. 218.
23 Stevie Stevens and Maureen Miller, quoted in Jonny Cracknell and Adrian Stevens, p. 220–21.
24 Arthur Atkinson, oral history interview, IBCC, Identifier: AAtkinsonA150623.
25 Clare Kemp, Methwold History Group Archive.
26 Aline Elizabeth 'Betty' Wakefield, personal diary kindly lent to the author by Betty's family.
27 Peggy Wallace, ATS, posted to Royal Artillery to work on an anti-aircraft battery, Methwold History Group Archive.

28 Binder compiled by Al Lovett, Methwold History Group Archive.
29 Ibid.
30 Leslie Temple, quoted in Martin Sugarman, 'World War II: Jewish RAF Special Operators in Radio Counter Measures with 101 Squadron (September 1943–May 1945)', Jewish Virtual Library.
31 Lincolnshire's Lancaster Association, Supporting the Battle of Britain Memorial Flight (Spring 1993, No. 19).
32 John W. Gee, 1988.
33 'Lancaster Bomber crews reunite at WW2 plane factory', BBC News, 4 September 2019.
34 'WWII bomber pilot cheated death in fireball explosion and witnessed The Great Escape', Wales Online, 29 October 2021.
35 Correspondence with Thomas Hughes. John was Thomas's great-uncle.
36 Misc. Anecdotes from RAF Elsham Wolds Association, Issue 50, personal papers of Peter Carpenter.

Afterword: An Unfinished Story

1 Oliver Owen, 'My Father the Hero', *Guardian*, 30 November 2008.
2 Interview with Chris Stone of the Methwold History Group, 3 November 2023.
3 Hugh Gascoyne, Methwold History Group Archive.
4 Walter Scott, 'Six poems', IBCC Digital Archive.
5 *RAF Methwold, 1938–1958*, booklet produced by Methwold History Group, 2010.
6 Flying Officer Thomas Patrick Tobin, Pilot, IBCC, 'Veterans' Stories'.
7 Dr Dan Ellin, correspondence with author.
8 Interview with Nicky van der Drift, 17 January 2024.
9 Interview with Dave Gilbert, 17 January 2024.
10 Interview with Tony Hibberd, 17 January 2024.
11 BBMF Ground Crew Interviews, Aircraft Restoration Company, IWM Duxford, 23 August 2023.
12 Ibid., interview with Mark Arnold.
13 Correspondence with Trevor Woodgate.
14 Interview with Sharne Cracknell, 20 January 2024.
15 Correspondence with Jonny Cracknell.
16 Correspondence with Warren Stace.
17 Oliver Owen, 'My Father the Hero', *Guardian*, 30 November 2008.
18 Telephone interview with Dan Snow, 5 December 2023.
19 The first thing I did when I knew I was going to write this book was to contact Liam Shaw at Duxford. Liam kindly showed me around the Lancaster there, and explained some of the history of the aircraft.
20 '80th Anniversary of the Avro Lancaster's First Flight', Avro Heritage Museum, Woodford, 9 January 2021.
21 Bruce Rawling, Methwold History Group Archive.

INDEX